Couples, sex and power

THE POLITICS OF DESIRE

Couples, sex and power

THE POLITICS OF DESIRE

Sally Dallos
and
Rudi Dallos

OPEN UNIVERSITY PRESS
Buckingham · Philadelphia

Open University Press
Celtic Court
22 Ballmoor
Buckingham
MK18 1XW

and
1900 Frost Road, Suite 101
Bristol, PA 19007, USA

First Published 1997

A catalogue record of this book is available from the British Library

ISBN   0 335 192394 (hb)   0 335 19238 6 (pb)

Library of Congress Cataloging-in-Publication Data
Dallos, Sally, 1951–
    Couples, sex, and power :   the politics of desire / Sally
Dallos and Rudi Dallos.
        p.   cm.
    Includes bibliographical references and index.
    ISBN 0–335–19239–4 (hb). — ISBN 0–335–19238–6 (pbk.)
    1. Sex in marriage—Psychological aspects.   2. Couples—
Sexual behavior—Psychological aspects.   3. Power (Social
sciences)   4. Equality.   5. Sex role.   6. Marital
psyohotherapy.   I. Dallos, Rudi, 1948–   .   II. Title.
HQ734.F695   1997
306.7—dc21   97–12124
                                                            CIP

Typeset by Graphicraft Typesetters Ltd, Hong Kong
Printed in Great Britain by Biddles Ltd,
Guildford and King's Lynn

Contents

Acknowledgements

We wish to thank Roger Sapsford for his invaluable advice, guidance and encouragement with this project, and all the couples and individuals who shared intimate details of their relationships with us.

Introduction

LYSISTRATA:
> I will have nothing to do with my husband or my lover
> Though he come to me in pitiable condition,
> I will stay in the house untouchable,
> In my thinnest saffron frock,
> And make him long for me,
> And if he constrains me,
> I will be cold as ice and never move . . .
>
> Aristophanes, *Lysistrata*, 421 BC

In the play *Lysistrata*, by Aristophanes, the women of Athens, with heavy hearts and much reluctance, took up the strategy of sexual withdrawal in order to persuade the men to cease their bloody fighting and war-making. Nothing else had been effective in influencing the men, and as a final desperate measure the women decided to deny their husbands their conjugal 'rights'. As a consequence the women experienced much taunting and criticism, not only from the men but also from other women; they were branded as unnatural, cruel, failing in their duties as wives, even as sexually deviant or pathological. Much bawdy and graphically detailed fun is made of the men's 'suffering' and 'distress' at their deprivation. In this book sexual problems and their relationship to power will be one of the central themes. But unlike Aristophanes' story we will be arguing that this withdrawal is rarely a deliberate strategy, rather it is a desperate reaction which is often associated with misery and negative consequences, especially for the women.

It is now several decades since feminist theorists first stated that 'the personal is political' and Millett defined 'political' as 'power structured relationships, arrangements whereby one group of persons is controlled by another' (Millett 1977). However, there have been very few detailed studies of how exactly gender inequality may affect intimate heterosexual relationships, especially how it may affect sexuality in the relationship. The intention of this book is to contribute some evidence based on our therapeutic work with heterosexual couples suffering from relationship and sexual difficulties, and on research with non-clinical couples. The main focus in the research and the book is an exploration of the effects of gender inequality on the nature of sexuality in intimate relationships. This research, in combination with our clinical experience, both builds on and challenges assumptions about the problems faced by couples. The book offers some new theoretical orientations to guide therapeutic analysis and formulations, and also some specific ideas and techniques, especially in the final chapter, 'Implications for therapy with couples'.

It is only relatively recently that psychologists have started to study intimate relationships in detail. Previously the studies that were available had explored a narrow range of factors, such as first impressions between strangers in laboratory situations. The study of the day-to-day flow of intimate relationships and the nature of sexuality and power differences has, however, still received little attention. Sexuality has mostly been studied in the context of therapy but this has largely employed psychodynamic or learning theory approaches, which focus on the history of individual emotional or learning experiences. Interactional therapies, such as family therapy approaches based on systems theory, have focused on the dynamics of relationships, communicational processes, and patterns and cycles of escalations, but these have had less to say about the function of sexuality in such dynamics. Overall most of these frameworks have tended to ignore the wider societal contexts, such as structural inequalities between men and women and the pervasive ideologies which set out expectations, prohibitions and assumptions about sexuality, especially ideas about 'natural' differences between men and women.

Of course feminist approaches have now become influential in some areas of theory and therapy. The striking examples here are the major inroads to theoretical understanding and therapy in the areas of child sexual abuse – for example, Gordon (1989) and Parton (1997) – and domestic violence (Goldner 1991). However, the feminist spotlight has yet to be directed fully onto the area of sexual difficulties in relationships. As we will suggest later, this failure to perceive that gender inequality may be a major contributory factor in relationship difficulties can result in ineffective and inappropriate solutions to the couple's problems and to our wider understanding of sexual intimacy in relationships.

To illustrate some of the core issues that this book will cover we start with an example from our clinical work.

> Jill and Paul were both in their early forties, had been married for 20 years and had two daughters aged 13 and 15. Jill worked as a secretary. Paul was a university graduate and worked as a professional engineer in local government. The main problem they presented was that Jill was no longer interested in sexual intimacy with Paul and said

that she now saw him as 'like a brother'. Their relationship embodied a common cycle whereby Paul would try to initiate sexual intimacy, Jill would respond with reluctance and would usually 'engage' in sex in a cold and passive manner, making it obvious to Paul that she neither enjoyed nor found it in any way satisfying. She revealed in therapy that in fact she had never experienced an orgasm when making love to Paul.

Like us as you read this brief extract you probably contemplated various explanations for the problem. Maybe Jill no longer found Paul sexually attractive? Maybe neither of them had much previous sexual experience and possibly Paul's 'technique' was not conducive to Jill's sexual satisfaction? Jill's 'upbringing' may have been sexually repressive, leading to her having sexual problems later? Had she been sexually abused? One or both of them were suffering from deep unmet emotional needs stemming from their childhoods? Were they unconsciously locked in a perverse and compelling interactional cycle or 'game'?

Jill and Paul were similarly struggling to find explanations for their difficulty: they would fluctuate from 'blaming' themselves to blaming the other; fluctuate from one explanation to another during the session or from one session to another. One of the most dominant of their explanations was that the cause of the problems was largely due to Jill's repressed 'upbringing' resulting in her having become 'prudish'. Jill partly accepted that it was mainly 'her fault' but criticized Paul for his 'sulky' and childish behaviour. At times they both also considered that the problems may have been connected to the fact that neither of them had much previous experience and that in particular Paul's sexual technique was inadequate. They also voiced the idea that 'times had changed' and that attitudes were more permissive now – for example, towards masturbation – and this might have helped Jill to learn what was satisfying for her and could have helped her to express her needs. However, she did not wish to engage in this since she still felt it was 'inappropriate'. Most interestingly, Jill declared that she was willing to tolerate the 'quickie', passive sex mainly to keep the peace, while Paul wanted their sex to be mutually enjoyable and blamed Jill for not being willing to try to achieve this. Underlying this was a view that something was wrong, perhaps at an unconscious level, and that this was largely unresolvable.

Pursuing these and other hypotheses had produced very little in the way of positive change in their relationship. Our initial failure to help them to generate significant change made us wonder whether we were doing something wrong as therapists. Did we lack the necessary skills? Were we overlooking some important aspect of their relationship or experience? Were we blinkered by our own perceptions and emotional needs? Or were we taking sides?

However, this sexual interactional cycle of male 'demand' and female 'reluctance' is extremely common. Jokes regarding women's 'bedtime headaches' abound. Generally the cycle is seen as almost inevitable, based on the differences between the genders in sexual/biological terms. Recent sociobiological theories stress that fundamental biological differences underpin 'inevitable' differences between men and women and their sexuality. Dawkins, in his book *The Selfish Gene* (1978), for instance, can be seen to add support to popular notions that men, because of their 'biology', will be active in the pursuit of sexuality, 'inseminate and move on'; and women, because of their 'biology', will be more concerned with a 'secure relationship'. This belief is extremely common, yet is also empirically unproven and, it could be argued, highly dubious as the main explanation for this sexual interactional cycle. Many couples, social scientists, psychologists and therapists at least in part believe that there are such fundamental biological differences. However, there is considerable evidence of sexual diversity, not least in relation to homosexuality and differences within genders, which suggests that it is such biological beliefs or discourses which serve to shape sexual behaviour rather than any simple biological differences.

For Jill and Paul, there were obviously idiosyncratic features to their problems: 'upbringing', their individual experiences of life, the history of their relationship and so on were obviously contributing factors. However, at the same time there were striking inequalities between them in their relationship. Jill was financially dependent on Paul; early on in their relationship she stated that she had also been more emotionally dependent on him than he had been on her and he had acted as if he did not really need her, going off with friends instead of spending time with her. Paul always had more freedom than she did; he was more highly educated; went away to university early on in their relationship and had apparently been far more confident than her. The power she currently had stemmed from that ensuing from her role as a mother, power through the children and the 'fact' that Paul was now more interested in sex than she was, that he ostensibly found her more attractive than she found him and that he needed her sexually more than she needed him. Although her sexuality had not been such a powerful influence early on, she had engaged in an affair wherein she had 'discovered' that she could enjoy sex, but with someone other than Paul. This had seriously challenged their previous explanations that it was 'her fault' (her upbringing and 'prudishness'). Subsequently Paul had now become very depressed, felt that it was his 'technique' that was at fault, felt rejected by Jill and, whilst Jill had initially been more emotionally dependent on Paul than vice versa, to some extent the 'tables had turned'; now he appeared to be more emotionally dependent upon her than she was on him.

The focus of this book will be to explore how both structural and ideological factors in combination affect relationships, and how an analysis of these can offer directions for therapeutic work with couples and families.

Patriarchal structures (for example, financial inequality) and patriarchal beliefs or discourse (for example, the belief that men 'need sex' more than women) are both intimately interrelated in their effects on intimate hetero-sexual relationships. This has led us to a view that problematic sexual inter-actional cycles, as Paul and Jill's above, are associated with women's relative powerlessness, especially their financial dependence on their partners. When women are not financially dependent and the distribution of power is more equal, and felt to be so, the characteristic cycle of male demand/female reluctance may be far less likely to occur. This implies that an analysis in terms of economic and material factors as suggested by a Marxist-feminist perspective is necessary and highly relevant: namely that structural inequality in the form of financial power is a central contributory factor. At the same time we will explore what might be termed 'invisible' power: for instance, the evidence from our research and clinical studies that men do generally tend to have more self-confidence and freedom than women, which in turn is related to both structural and discursive/ideological power, and also related to whether women are sexually 'reluctant'.

We will also explore how some of the dominant explanations of sexuality and problems can be seen to be based in patriarchal discourses or beliefs which shape the explanations for difficulties and attempted solutions, includ-ing not only those of couples but also therapists and researchers thinking about these issues. It is worth noting that such influence is pervasive and virtually inescapable; for instance, there is a proliferation of advice on sexual matters in magazines, books, television and the radio. It is hard to ignore the barrage of information about sex; how to do it, how to make it more satisfying, how often is normal, what to do about it and so on. This advice, as we will consider in detail later, contains many unsupported assumptions about the nature of sexuality. As Foucault (1979) has pointed out we have seen the construction of a so-called science and technology of sex, including ways of analysing, classifying, labelling and measuring sexual activity. There has also been an apparent move towards 'liberalism', a rejection, for instance, of economic determinism and Marxism, yet a questioning of gender relations and greater tolerance of homosexual relationships. However, this apparent encouragement of diversity, of postmodernism, of a rejection of a so-called 'simplistic' materialist view of power, whilst arguably helpful and inform-ative in many ways, has in itself contributed to a distortion of the 'real' inequalities in relationships between men and women. In effect this repres-ents an example of the production of a 'false consciousness'; sexuality has come to be seen as a matter of individual sexual orientation, of personal choice. If we take all the prevailing advice on board we can 'sort out' our own relationships ourselves and, rather like a 'user's manual', we can apply the advice to 'improve' our sex lives. This also leads to the view that couples can and should be able to 'sort things out', including their sexual problems, for themselves and that they are inadequate in some way if they cannot, despite, for example, the evidence of high divorce rates, which testify to the obvious difficulty of this task. By colluding with the false notion that all could be sorted out by the partners, we were perhaps inadvertently supporting a false and oppressive view which covered over issues of power and inequality.

OUTLINE AND STRUCTURE OF THE BOOK

This book is based on research and clinical work with heterosexual couples (Foreman and Dallos 1992; Foreman 1996). The main body of the empirical work discussed in the book is drawn from a recently completed PhD study by Foreman (1996). The research study was based on three interrelated studies.

1 *Survey of couples* A questionnaire which explored sexual behaviour, sources of power and ways of exerting influence was especially developed for the study (see Appendix 1). Twenty couples took part in this part of the study.
2 *Interviews* A sample of eighteen people from a broad range of backgrounds was used. Experience of relationships, occupation and education were interviewed in-depth regarding power and sexuality in their current, or most recent relationship. The focus of the interviews in particular was on the beliefs held regarding sexuality, power and ways of exerting influence in the relationship. (Some biographical details of the participants are given in Appendix 2 along with details of the interview guide).

In addition this research included material from both authors' clinical work and investigations.

3 *Clinical case studies* The PhD study included material from the authors' clinical work. Specifically the cases described here feature work with ten couples who were attending a clinic (within the National Health Service Clinical Psychology Service) with a focus on marital and sexual problems. This work consisted of clinical sessions (at two-week intervals) with the couples and was videotaped. Apart from observation of the couple's dynamics the recording allowed verbatim transcripts to be made of the sessions. Also, the clinical work offered an opportunity to test ideas and hypotheses about the nature of power and sexuality through observing the couple over an extended period of time, and noting the effects of various clinical interventions.

Flowing through the book are ideas and observations drawn from the authors' cumulative clinical experience and research with couples and families over a period of 15 years (Dallos 1991, 1997; Foreman and Dallos 1992).

The clinical implications of our work are indicated at various points in the body of the book but they are drawn together specifically in Chapter 7, where three detailed case studies are described, and in Chapter 8, 'Implications for therapy with couples', which draws out some of the implications for analysis and clinical formulations, and also suggests some specific clinical techniques for work with couples. Though it is important to suggest some specific clinical techniques and strategies, we also believe that the book as a whole offers some new ways of viewing sexual difficulties. This can dramatically and helpfully alter how relational, and specifically sexual, problems are seen and inevitably changes the nature of the therapeutic encounter, more fundamentally than perhaps proposed new 'techniques' of doing therapy.

The following is a brief overview of each chapter indicating the progression of ideas through the book.

Chapter 1   This chapter offers an analysis of the concept of power and how power may function in intimate relationships. A central distinction will be drawn between structural and ideological power: the former, it is suggested, can be seen in terms of tangible and material sources of power, such as money, physical strength, accommodation, possessions and access to work and training. The latter is more intangible and functions by shaping people's thinking, for example about how relationships 'should' be, the role of men and women in relationships and what are seen as 'natural' differences between men and women. Both, it is argued, shape and constrain people's freedom – their choices of action. It is argued that the combination of a lack of structural and of ideological sources of power tilts unequal heterosexual relationships towards the possibility that sex becomes one of the few resources for many women with which some influence can be exerted.

Chapter 2   Four psychological theories which have been influential in informing clinical work and theoretical models are outlined: psychodynamic, learning theory, cognitive/constructional and systemic. It is suggested that these have not only shaped the thinking of 'professionals' but have also permeated the thinking of ordinary people. Specifically, they can be seen to represent essentially individualistic, or at best relational (systemic theories), explanations which feature in partners' accounts of their relationships and problems. As such they come to shape their thinking and most importantly to direct attention away from an analysis of power not only at the relational level but in terms of possible societally structured inequalities between men and women.

This chapter forges connections to Chapter 8, in which some clinical implications are outlined.

Chapter 3   This chapter takes up and develops an analysis of structural issues by outlining ways that power can be considered in terms of a profile of resources or power bases that partners possess and by which they may attempt to influence each other. A taxonomy of different resources developed from the PhD research is offered. It is suggested that partners possess different profiles of power bases and these constrain and guide the ways that they can exert influence on each other. In turn the value of the power bases as methods of exerting influence is related to partners' beliefs reflected in their statements about their relative importance. It is also suggested that this analysis of power bases can be usefully applied in clinical work to help couples to reflect on their relationship and clarify the contribution of inequalities of power.

Chapter 4   The discussion of power bases is developed to consider how the different profiles of power possessed by each partner lead them to employ different strategies of influence. A taxonomy is offered of the main categories of influence employed within relationships. The body of the chapter summarizes the findings from Foreman (1996) and compares two groups of couples; the first where the women are financially dependent and the second where the women are financially independent. The findings reveal that woman who are financially dependent are significantly more likely to withdraw from engaging in sexual intimacy. The findings are employed to discuss the prevalent sexual cycle of male demand/female avoidance and to relate this to financial and other structural inequalities. It is suggested that such an analysis helps both clinicians and couples in distress to gain more productive understandings of their experiences and destructive interactional patterns.

Chapter 5   Chapters 3 and 4 signal the importance of taking partners' beliefs into account, for example which power bases are commonly regarded as most influential. This is developed in Chapter 5 to discuss how these beliefs in turn can be seen to be related to wider societally shared ideologies or discourses about power and relationships. A prominent proposition developed is that due to the effect of patriarchy the dominant ideas about power, sexuality and relationships have been developed, promoted by and seen to serve the interest of men. These not only construct particular views but serve to subjugate alternative discourses. In particular the prevalent concept of male–female relationships as being based on different but equal resources is examined. It is argued that this, along with individualistic discourses, distorts and denies the real inequalities of structural power between men and women, especially in relationships where the women are financially dependent. The discussion is illustrated by extracts from material relating to people's perceptions of power from the interview study (Foreman 1996).

Chapter 6   Here an analysis of discourse is continued but with the central emphasis now moving to sexuality. Four influential discourses are outlined: the male sexual drive or biological discourse, the have/hold or relationships discourse, the permissive discourse and feminist discourse. Extracts are employed from the interview study to illustrate how these discourses appear in people's accounts and how they shape their ideas about sexuality. These discourses are seen to serve to encourage the likelihood of the male demand/female avoidance cycle. Evidence from the interviews suggests that feminist discourses which emphasize equality of power as an important component are relatively marginalized or subjugated. The chapter ends by considering how one of the most pernicious processes of subjugation of alternative discourses is to pathologize, that is, to label sexual problems as signs of 'mental illness' or 'neurosis'.

Chapter 7   This chapter is focused on three detailed case studies of couples who were attending for therapy with sexual problems as a central symptom. The women in the three couples vary in the extent of their financial dependence, from extremely dependent to independent. This clinical work offers an integrated view of the couples over time and how structural and ideological factors are woven into their relational dynamics. It is argued that financial dependence, and more specifically abuse of power by the men, is linked not only to the development of sexual problems but to these being pathologized. The ability of the women to resist this labelling is seen to be related to their dependency. The validation and increased freedom offered through work is particularly helpful in enabling resistance. This chapter also starts to draw together the theoretical discussion to indicate its therapeutic applications.

Chapter 8   This concluding chapter draws together the twin analysis of structural and ideological power and in particular builds on the analysis of the clinical cases in Chapter 7 to develop a range of implications for therapeutic work with couples. The chapter draws out some broad indications, such as the need for therapists to be aware of, and sensitive to, issues of power and specifically to reflect on their potential role in colluding with the pathologizing of couples, especially the women. It is also argued that psychological perspectives (discussed in Chapter 2) – individualistic and even interpersonal – are likely to pathologize one or other partner, or the relationship, and miss the contribution of the oppressive and pathologizing nature of prevalent discourses and structures of inequality. A range of clinical implications is then described including some suggestions for therapeutic orientations as well as specific activities, techniques, interventions and exercises.

1

Perspectives on power

Power is an extremely widely used concept and therefore has accumulated many layers of meanings. Our interest in this book is to consider the nature of power in relationships. Looking at various forms of relationships can start our thinking about the nature of power. For example, parents have power over their children, in terms of providing food; shelter; rights to guide their activities, including discipline, praise and punishment; and skills and knowledge that they can hand on to them. Employers have power over their employees: control of how much they are paid; ability to order their activities; and ability to take their jobs away. We can see that power is intimately related to freedom or choice of action, thought and feeling. More specifically what starts to become evident when we look at various forms of relationships is that power appears to have two distinct, though inter-related aspects: on the one hand, power is about tangible, objective factors such as protection, money, physical strength, shelter, food and so on. These factors constrain in a very real way the choices that are available, what people are able to do or not to do. For example, how much pocket money a child or a financially dependent partner is allowed to have determines where they can go, what they can eat, what clothes or goods they can buy, what activities they can engage in inside or outside the home. On the other hand, power can also be seen as more intangible, for example in terms of the nature of the relationship, what roles people are expected to play, or what kinds of needs, such as love, affection and protection are encouraged. This form of power operates by shaping and constraining how people feel and think and thereby constraining the choices they perceive to be possible, rather than directly controlling their avenues of action.

The distinction we are drawing out corresponds broadly to the widely employed distinction between structural and ideological power. The first can be seen as the power of domination – the power to be able to get someone to do something we want, or to prevent them from doing other things. In its most basic form we can see this in the ability that the phys-ically stronger partner has to dominate the other by the threat of, or use of actual, physical force, or by the withdrawal of money and so on. The second can be seen in terms of the power of beliefs, construings, understandings which shape how we think about ourselves and relationships; for example, the different roles, duties and expectations that men and women are guided into in any given society. As we will see these can operate in subtle ways by shaping what aspects of relationships are seen as natural, inevitable and not worthy of comment. Yet it can be just these unarticulated, even unconscious beliefs which are most influential. These ideological aspects of power need to be seen as the broad backcloth to any relationship. For example, the ideologies of family life, that children need both parents, that women should be maternal bear down on single-parent mothers just as heavily as they do on women who are married (R. Sapsford, personal communication 1996).

This distinction between structural and ideological power will form one of the major conceptual axes in this book. The two aspects of power, however, are intimately interrelated. Many aspects of structural power, such as who has more money in the relationship, are partly determined by cultural ideas about the role of men and women, who should be the breadwinner/provider as opposed to the homemaker/dependent. The ability to get the other partner to do, or not do, something is determined by both these aspects, though the balance may vary. Similarly, Weber (1947) defines *power* as 'the probability that one actor will be able to realize his own objectives even against opposition from others with whom he is in a social relationship'. Weber's definition highlights the important issue of conflict in relationships. At the point where two people are in disagreement the issue of power, who has more of it and the ability to make the other comply, becomes central. One of our central concerns will be with the study of power processes – *how* people influence each other; by what means does an actor 'realize his or her own objectives' and what form does the 'opposition' take'; for example, by what processes is power exerted: control, coercion, persuasion, oppression, exploitation of another and what forms of resistance are evident.

Power in relationships, however, also involves intentions and aims, plans, strategies on each partner's part. This idea is also apparent in Weber's definition of power in terms of the extent to which partners 'realize their own objectives'. In effect this requires a consideration of the objectives of each partner and the extent to which each of them actually realizes these. If one realizes their objectives more than the other then we might conclude within this definition that one has more power than the other. This might also mean that one partner is able to use more effective means or strategies than the other, that one is more able, by whatever means, to influence the other than vice versa. However, power may operate even when there is no apparent conflict, when things appear to be proceeding smoothly. Also, it suggests that we are in some sense aware of our objectives though it may be that for much of the time we are not aware of these until some conflict of interests arises and we become aware of what our unconscious or semi-conscious objectives were. Frequently in relationships power emerges as an issue at the point of changes, for example due to the birth of children, illness, gaining or losing a job and so on. At these moments the structural aspects of power and the hitherto taken-for-granted beliefs and expectations may surface and be contested.

What factors allow one to have more probability of realizing his/her own objectives than the other, or what factors allow them both to have an equal probability of realizing their own objectives? These factors may be personal, interpersonal or societally based. An example of 'personal factors' might be that one is generally better at 'persuading' others, better at putting forward their own opinions, more articulate and able to hold to their own position (Scanzoni 1979b). An example of interpersonal factors might be that one partner values the relationship more and therefore may be more likely to 'give in' or concede in order to ensure that the relationship is not threatened or more likely to end (Safilios-Rothschild 1970). In this example 'giving in' might mean that the other does not realize their own objectives, get their needs and goals satisfied to the same extent as the partner. Other needs and goals are subsumed by the need to keep the relationship going. Psychoanalytic theory suggests that such a 'need' to preserve the relationship could be personal, e.g. if the individual believes that they need to be in a relationship, need to be attached and would not be happy on their own. Alternatively, the 'need' may also be societally and structurally induced; for instance, women are often unable to support themselves financially and are dependent on others in order to get even their basic needs met; they might therefore 'give in' in order to get their financial or shelter needs met. In effect they are coerced and constrained by the societal structure into a position whereby some of their needs will not be met in order to get their financial needs met. The 'probability' of either realizing their own objectives, then, can also be related to societal structures.

Similarly, the strategies that either partner may use to 'influence' the other may be linked to the bases of the power of each; interpersonally, if one values the relationship more than the other then the latter can influence the former by threats to end the relationship; the former cannot use the same threat so effectively. Again, the constraints and controls of societal structures, especially financial bases of power will allow the financially independent partner to use this to influence the other, perhaps by threatening to end the relationship or withdraw financial support. Emerson (1981) suggests that 'power resides implicitly in the other's dependency'; this dependency may be personal, interpersonal or societally induced. Unequal dependency may mean that strategies available to one partner are not available to the other. One definition of inequality might be a situation wherein one individual or group is more dependent on the other than vice versa; this dependency could include various needs or goals, attachment, affection, sex, money, accommodation and so on. There could be a situation or relationship whereby one partner is dependent in some ways and the other dependent in others; similarly they might use different strategies but these will be equally effective in terms of influencing each other. This raises the question of whether some forms of dependence are more significant than others; for instance whether financial dependence as opposed to emotional dependence proffers more influence. A related question is whether some strategies are more influential in the relationship than are others. Empirical studies on relationships, conflict and negotiation have approached this question by asking 'who wins the argument' or 'who makes the decisions' and presuming that the one who 'wins' must be the one who has the most effective strategies or is the least dependent.

In an unequal relationship one individual or group can influence another individual or group more than vice versa. Their influence on each other is unequal, one is more able to shape, alter, maintain behaviours, thoughts, feelings in the other than vice versa. If the relationship is unequal in terms of influence it is possible for one partner to *dominate* the other, that is, they can influence what the other thinks, feels, and their behaviour more than vice versa. They could also *oppress* the other, for instance constrain their behaviour, limit their options and choices and prevent them from expressing their thoughts, opinions, feelings, their own subjective experience. Oppression may be similar to the concept of *control* as used in a general sense to mean control of thoughts and feelings as well as behaviour. They could also *exploit* the other by influencing them to act, think or feel in ways which are more to the advantage of the dominant partner than themselves.

In an egalitarian relationship both partners should theoretically be able to influence each other to the same extent, neither partner having overall dominance in the relationship. Both could attempt to control or even exploit the other, restrict each other's actions, offer similar threats and try to change the other's thoughts, opinions or feelings. One question that arises is whether any relationship can ever be completely egalitarian, even if societally related power bases were equal; for example, if they both had the same degree of financial power, would there inevitably be differences in personal or interpersonal factors? Further, what factors if any are the most fundamental in relation to equality or inequality? For instance, is financial equality the main factor that makes a relationship equal or unequal, or do personal factors matter more than financial equality in relationships?

To summarize, a question that we may be tempted to ask is whether structural factors such as financial inequality are more or less influential than ideological factors, such as the constructs, beliefs, expectations that partners have. In reality these two strands may be intertwined. For example, for a woman in a financially dependent relationship her lack of economic resources physically constrains her choices in terms of being able to leave, find another home, have enough to eat and so on. At the same time, ideology – such as children needing two parents, the damaging effects of separation on the children, a sense of failure as a woman that she has not managed the relationship well enough – may also serve to constrain her perceived choices. Arguably though, the structural factors are not negotiable in the same way as ideological ones – we cannot simply think our way out of them. Some therapies have perhaps been guilty of making this mistake, assuming that talking about the problems can overcome these structural factors. A vivid example here was that due to the emergence of available refuges for battered women many more women 'chose' to leave oppressive and violent relationships because this option was physically possible. Talking about their situation alone would not have allowed this choice. Alternatively, it can also be the case that a sense of powerlessness can lead people to feeling that they have even fewer choices than they actually do have.

RESOURCES AND POWER BASES: STRUCTURAL POWER

Blood and Wolfe (1961) define resources as any property of a person or group which can be made available to others as instrumental to the satisfaction of their needs or the attainment of their goals and Emerson (1981) suggests that 'power resides implicitly in the other's dependency'. Much of what individuals want can only be gained through, or from, relationships with other members of society. Individuals or groups have to negotiate somehow with others to get what they want. They have to use what they themselves have when they are negotiating. These 'things' that people want and have can be described as resources; resources may be tangible or intangible (Scanzoni 1979a, 1979b). Tangible resources may include 'concrete' resources such as money or material objects, expertise in certain areas, legal rights over others, physical strength and so on. Intangible resources may include love, affection, approval, validation and so on.

The resources of each individual (or group) may be exchanged for the resources of another individual (or group). The resources that each has to use in negotiation may also be described as power bases (Raven *et al.* 1985; Williams and Watson 1988). Money, for instance, is a resource that can be used in negotiation with others for access to other resources; having money is a power base because it can be used to get other resources. Inequality exists when one individual (or group) has more of a particular resource than the other. If A has more money than B then financial inequality exists between the two. If A has a resource that B needs or wants or perceives themself to need or want and cannot or believes they cannot get this resource from another source (i.e. B is dependent on A for this resource) then A will potentially have more power relative to B than B has in relation to A. What A does with this power in the relationship with B may vary; it could be used to exploit, control, abuse, oppress, subordinate, have conditions attached to it, or it may be quite freely given to B in order to improve B's life. Those who are in a less dependent position, i.e. those who have the resource(s) that the other wants or needs are potentially in a dominant position relative to the other. In general men tend to hold more tangible resources than women.

IDEOLOGY AND DISCOURSE

Ideology has been defined as a set of ideas, assumptions and images by which people make sense of society. These ideas are shared or held in common and serve in some ways to legitimatise relations of power in society (Abbott and Sapsford 1988; McLennan 1991). It is argued that ideology may function not only to construct ideas which shape our thinking but also to disguise or obscure, for example the fact that there is a conflict of interests between the more powerful and the less powerful.

> Inequitable relationships are most effectively masked by the ideologies that obscure the existence of inequality and mask the continuous and pervasive conflict of interests between the groups concerned. By ideology we mean a socially produced construction of ideas and explanations, a set of procedures and practices which both account for and organize the social system.
>
> (Penfold and Walker 1986: 10)

Ideas, assumptions, images, explanations, goals and objectives, then, are both socially constructed and tend to be constructed by the more powerful groups. Alternative constructions may be ignored, dismissed, and in some cases not even thought of. Bachrach and Baratz (1962) support this idea of ideology as obscuring as well as shaping ideas. They comment that power can operate to prevent some issues being raised; alternate viewpoints, explanations, preferences may be 'blocked' from reaching the point of being discussed. It may thus appear that there is no conflict.

One of the main problems in studying power is the idea of 'realizing one's own objectives'. This is a problem in that it could be argued that many people do not have a clear idea about their own objectives and needs. Furthermore this is compounded by the predominant ideologies of the society at a particular time in history which tends to add a massive degree of confusion and indeed illusion regarding individuals' needs and goals. Apparent objectives and goals may themselves be socially constructed. According to a Marxist or feminist perspective most if not all societies contain fundamental inequalities between various groups; gender, class, race and so on. Dominance of one group rather than another according to these perspectives is based primarily on the holding of economic power. The holding of economic power allows for these more dominant groups in turn to ensure that other aspects of society are organized to serve their own interests, objectives, goals rather than those of the less powerful groups, their own interests including the maintenance of their dominant positions. This implies that there is a conflict of interests between the more and the less powerful groups.

Ideology and power can be seen as inextricably interlinked. This view is emphasized further in the concept of discourse:

> A discourse is a group of statements which provide a language for talking about – i.e. a way of representing – a particular kind of knowledge about a topic. When statements about a topic are made within a particular discourse, the discourse makes it possible to construct the topic in a certain way. It also limits the other ways in which the topic can be constructed.

> (Hall 1992: 291)

Discourses are not simply a set of explicit beliefs shared in society but perhaps most importantly they contain implicit or largely unconscious assumptions. It is often these apparently 'natural' and unquestioned aspects which are more powerful. An example that will run through much of this book is the biological discourse that men need sex more than women. This contains a sort of plumbing metaphor that pressure will build up inside them if it is not released and they will 'explode'. More sinister and implicit aspects of this discourse may be that women who therefore 'provoke' men sexually by dressing in an overtly sexual way 'deserve whatever they get', for example being raped. A complementary discourse is that women in contrast seek relationships to be emotionally close, committed, in love, and that sex is secondary. However, this also implies that women who do not act like this are deviant, 'sluts', 'slags' or even pathological – 'nymphomaniacs'.

In order to change social structures, organizations, systems of beliefs and regimes of power and inequality, there has to be a clearly articulated and understood alternative to that which already exists, yet it is just this that ideology and discourse and an unequal social structure make very difficult. For example, demands for women's right to vote were delayed and obstructed in part by eliciting existing dominant discourses as a counter-argument to prevent them gaining this right. Arguments against this right were, for example, that they were congenitally over-emotional and incapable of rational thought needed for participation in political decision-making. Similarly women were discouraged from entering higher education because their brains were weak and likely to become fevered (Abbott and Wallace 1991). Though such arguments may seem ridiculous now women had both to generate alternative discourses as to why they should be given this right, and also articulate it and attempt to get it understood and accepted by others. They also, of course, had initially to become even aware that they wanted to vote, that it was not in their best interests to have no political power in the face of prevailing discourses that encouraged them to think that it was.

The less powerful may not even realize that the situation is not in their best interests; overt conflict may not even arise; they may not be aware that things could be different and attempt to change the situation.

Lukes (1984) describes how power operates to prevent the less powerful realizing that the situation is not in their best interests. He refers to this as the two-dimensional view of power and describes it as an attempt to construct a set of rules, beliefs, and values which operate for the benefit of one group against another. The values and beliefs that are constructed serve to smother possible dissension (resistance) by the subordinate group. He argues that the most insidious use of power is when it prevents conflicts arising in the first place. Power can function to shape our beliefs, perceptions and choices so that legitimate grievances are suppressed and existing roles are accepted as natural and inevitable.

To return to Weber's idea of 'realizing one's own objectives', discourse and ideology can operate to prevent the less powerful becoming aware that their objectives are different from those they are encouraged to believe in, that their objectives are being constructed by the more powerful groups in society and are not necessarily actually in their own best interests. Similarly when he refers to 'opposition' or resistance (which in turn implies a conflict of some kind) the power to oppose is restricted by the prevailing discourses and ideology which often deny that there is a conflict of interests, that there is any problem at all.

The distinction between the concepts of discourse and ideology are subtle and to some extent the terms will be used interchangeably here. However, some differences must be mentioned. Ideology has typically been used in the sense of a set of beliefs which produce knowledge that serves the interests of a particular group or class. This book is centrally concerned with such differences in interests and power between men and women. Foucault (1972), however, points out that ideology has been employed to suggest that there are some true statements about the world vs false statements and that by coming to know what is true, real or *fact* we can more clearly distinguish between truth and fabrications. Politically this has been exemplified in early Marxist and feminist positions that emphasize that *real* inequalities exist and ideologies are constructed to deny these because they serve to maintain the interests of the ruling classes of men. In contrast Foucault in his conception of discourse argues that statements about the world are rarely ever simply true or false, 'facts' can always be construed in different ways:

> Foucault's use of 'discourse', then, is an attempt to side-step what seems an unresolvable dilemma – deciding which social discourses are true or scientific, and which are false or ideological . . . values enter into all our descriptions of the social world, and therefore most of our statements, however factual, have an ideological dimension.
>
> (Hall 1992: 293)

Hall's advice here will be borne in mind but the emphasis will be on ideology with the assumption that some structural differences can be identified with some certainty. Where the term 'discourse' is used it is employed as somewhere between ideology and discourse and vice versa. It is recognized that this may be somewhat vague but one defence is that the blurring of the terms appears widespread, especially in much of the literature upon which this book will draw. A more important defence is that one reading of Foucault's use of the 'discourse' is that it becomes a rather 'soft' pluralistic concept which plays down 'real' structural inequalities, oppression and abuses of power. The combination with the term ideology, with its emphasis on a more or less deliberate misleading, or denial of 'real' inequality, is therefore seen as a reasonable working compromise for our purposes.

STRUCTURE AND IDEOLOGY

> The ideas of the ruling class are, in every age, the ruling ideas . . . the class which has the means of material production has the means of mental production, so that in consequence the ideas of those who lack the means of mental production are, in general, subject to it.
> (Marx and Engels 1970: 35)

Structural power and 'ideological' power interrelate; each reflects and maintains the other. Those who are dominant, for instance in terms of holding particular resources, are also likely to be able to ensure that their beliefs, ideas, opinions, are more influential than those who are subordinate; this in turn may justify inequality. According to Williams and Watson (1988) ideology also 'covers up' inequality between the genders by justifying it in terms of it being natural, God-given, functional or complementary. Ideology also disguises inequality by labelling reactions against oppression as 'madness' or 'mental disorder' or 'abnormal', and by encouraging those who are in a subordinate position to explain their experience as not to do with social inequalities but to do with there being 'something wrong with them'.

Dominant shared beliefs or ideologies define expectations, ideas of identity, gender and other roles in relationships, and a system of perceived rights and obligations. These beliefs may shape the practical more obvious aspects of life but also the internal dialogues we hold with ourselves which through language and other societally organized and defined symbolic systems connect us to our immediate and historical legacy of ideas and meanings. Especially in our recourse to language we are social beings, even as we reflect upon our life and pursue our thoughts. Feminist analyses have been helpful in drawing attention to how language itself contains and perpetuates a variety of assumptions, directs our attention and may perpetuate ways of thinking which support inequalities. The production of dominant systems of ideas and meanings, ideologies, is shaped and maintained according to distributions of power. As a telling example people of the lowest socio-economic groups and ethnic minorities generally have poorer physical and mental health. To put it bluntly they die younger and appear to have generally more tormented lives.

However, it has rarely been acknowledged that these differences are predominantly due to basic inequalities in our society, rather than due to 'poor health habits', 'fecklessness' and so on. The crushing effects of poverty and stress have been frequently minimized in terms which extol the virtues of personal autonomy and choice. However, such conceptualizations can be regarded as systems of knowledge or ideologies which serve to disguise or justify the privileges of the most powerful groups.

In short, the dominant classes have privileged access to a variety of means, education, the media, commerce and industry to promote systems of thought which maintain their superior opportunities and position. The foundations of this position can be seen to have derived inspiration from Marxist perspectives, in particular the proposition that dominant groups in society have the power to produce and sustain dominant beliefs or ideologies. The dominant sections of society, the ruling classes, are seen as able to disseminate and enforce by a variety of practices, beliefs which suit and maintain their positions of dominance. These ideologies may also serve to distort, as in the view that society is structured according to fundamental abilities and that the poor are in that position because they have less ability, are less intelligent or don't want to work.

Identities and gender

Ideologies and structure can be seen to shape experience in various profound ways, e.g. by virtue of men and women belonging, of being located within the wider groups comprising society (Williams and Watson 1988). A wife is a member of the family but also belongs to a wider class or group – women, workers, mothers, daughters, housewives, wives and so on. Membership of these various groups is not a neutral act but has important consequences. Various privileges and sanctions may be associated with these, e.g. access to work, finance, freedom and also an imposition of identities. More subtly, membership of these various groups confers identities which set out personal expectations, aspirations, ideas of self and how we should relate to others. For women this has typically involved an identity based on mothering, physical attractiveness, lower expectations of achievement and independence than men. More recently some of the contradictions for women have become all the more clear; for example, though encouraged to become mothers, as part of their 'natural' function, women have become increasingly stigmatized if they do so as 'single parents'.

Dichotomization

A fundamental way in which any group maintains power and dominance is through the process of dichotomization (Williams and Watson 1988). The major justification for inequality appears to be the belief that the dominant group has particular traits or abilities and that the other group(s) have different ones. This could imply either that one group is superior to the other, or that neither is superior but that they are simply different. In relation to gender, for many centuries women were perceived not only as different from but also as inferior to men; by the end of the nineteenth century they were beginning to be perceived as different but equal. In the latter women were construed as having particular traits or abilities and men as having others; the genders were construed to be essentially different but this was not to imply that one was inferior to the other. Women and men were said to be equal because women's abilities were as highly valuable as men's and because each was said to depend upon the other for each other's skills or resources.

However, the equal but different discourse has been uncovered as an ideological disguise for a continuing underlying inequality, the 'traits' that men were said to have also tended to be the most highly valued traits (Hollway 1983; Henriques *et al*. 1984). The 'traits' that women had were also used as a justification for excluding them from access to certain power bases; for instance, their presumed 'emotionality' was used to justify not giving them the vote or having access to their own property up to the late nineteenth century. Gladstone, for instance, justified not giving women the vote in the 1890s by suggesting that he was too concerned about their 'delicacy, purity [and] refinement' to condone involving them in the vulgar nature of political life (Tannahill 1980).

Positive and negative aspects of power

Foucault argues that discourses operate in both positive and negative ways. By positive he does not mean 'good' but that they operate to construct ways of thinking about the world. The positive effects of power and knowledge are to promote dominant ideas or 'truths' that people accept and that thereby come to shape their lives. The negative aspects are the processes whereby ideas are suppressed, abandoned, ignored. The acceptance of these 'truths' makes people into 'docile bodies', i.e. apparently willingly accepting these truths unquestioningly and thereby being shaped and controlled by them. Knowledge and power are seen to be inextricably intertwined and a prime aspect of this is the rise in the influence of scientific thought, medicine, technology, economic analyses and so on. These forms of knowledge make claims to 'objectivity', i.e. to be fundamentally true, for example, the idea that women are naturally 'maternal'. Access to these bases of knowledge is regulated, e.g. the selection processes for training for medicine or to gain entry into the higher levels of the political domain were confidential.

DOMINANT AND SUBJUGATED DISCOURSES

Foucault suggests that a repertoire of dominant discourses is constructed in society, and these shape our thinking and experience, how we think about ourselves, our inner conversations and how we interact with each other. These are not simply imposed from 'above' but are shaped, maintained and enacted locally in the interactions between people in various groups, relationships and families. Not all stories have equal status and in fact he argues that some are made peripheral or subjugated. Examples are discourses which are relegated as historical, no longer relevant, e.g. attempts to frame Marxist ideas as 'out of date', no longer relevant to modern society.

What Foucault's ideas point to is a view of society as containing a hierarchy of discourses with some relegated to the periphery. He suggests that our 'personal' explanations and narratives and their formation are not simply or predominantly personal. Couples do not have an infinite number of ways of viewing events; instead there is a limited array of discourses (which are internalized to form people's subjective or 'personal' narratives) which have been made available to us through our socialization or immersion in our culture. Arguably discourses are not simply absorbed wholemeal or incorporated in a straightforward manner, but translated, transformed or some elements taken up and others excluded, depending on our belief systems. We may end up with an internalization of a mixture of fragments of discourses leaving an internally inconsistent, fluctuating and ambivalent view of the world and our relationships. In short this sets limits to our thinking and serves to constrain our perceived domain of options or avenues of action. Significantly this analysis also suggests that people attempt to employ these dominant narratives to fit their experiences. Partners in an intimate relationship can be seen to have unique patterns of experiences and histories but they are likely to select a dominant narrative to embrace these.

Similarly they may explain any difficulties they may be having in terms of dominant discourses; that they do not 'get on' because of one or the other's, or both, partners' 'personality' or 'upbringing', for instance. The possibility that difficulties and their experiences are to do with an inequality of power is a peripheral or subjugated discourse. One of the main problems with this is that the 'dominant' discourses or narratives do not often quite 'fit' as an explanation for difficulties; they often do not reflect people's experiences accurately, and, at the same time, lead to inappropriate attempts to 'change' things. We attempt to fit our experiences into the narratives that are available:

> There exist a stock of culturally available discourses that are considered appropriate and relevant to the expression or representation of particular aspects of experience . . . persons experience problems which they frequently present for therapy when the narratives in which they are storying their experience, and/or in which they are having

their experience storied by others, do not significantly represent their lived experience, and that, in these circumstances, there will be significant aspects of their lived experience that contradict this dominant narrative.

(White and Epston 1990: 27–8)

These discourses or narratives shape people's aspirations and beliefs, they map out what we believe to be possible and desirable, they give us 'ready made' explanations and interpretations, they limit and constrain the possibility of alternative aspirations, explanations, interpretations. We may experience distress when our experiences do not 'fit'. Such ruptures between dominant narratives and what we are actually experiencing can lead us to 'self blame'; a view of ourselves as incompetent, abnormal or deviant.

Feminist writers have suggested that all aspects of relationships, from the daily routines to the most profound experiences, involve issues of power which are shaped by culturally shared discourses of gender (Goldner 1991; Hare-Mustin 1991). For example, 'wife battering' is often seen as deviant behaviour on the part of the man; a man who uses physical violence against his wife is positioned as being different from other men; as abnormal or pathological. Similarly women who do not leave the relationship when their husband is using violence against them may be seen as similarly 'abnormal' or 'pathological'. Work with couples where the man has used violence against his wife suggests that, rather than being deviant, these relationships may more accurately be seen as embodying *in extremis* the dominant assumptions in society about relations between the genders. The men seem to be caught in attempts to establish a culturally sanctioned view of themselves as dominant, in control and invulnerable and the women as nurturant, sensitive and responsive to, and needing others. When men find that they cannot be in control or believe that the woman is not doing what she 'should do', then they may resort to physical coercion and violence in order to make the relationship more similar to dominant discourses that dictate what the relationship between the genders should be. Similarly women may feel that they should stay in the relationship despite the violence because they have internalized dominant discourses which suggest that they should be nurturant, attempt to satisfy men's needs and that the violence is an indication of their failure to do what 'women are supposed to do'.

At the same time many women say that they do not leave violent relationships because they cannot support themselves financially and would have difficulty in finding alternative accommodation and that they would not feel safe if they left. This explanation, it could be argued, is often dismissed as not being the central reason for them staying. Material factors and material inequality are often subjugated as explanations for why women do not leave violent partners and more generally are played down as a central factor that may lead to conflict and problems in intimate relationships more generally.

RESISTANCE

Power is invested in discourse, equally, discursive practices produce, maintain and play out power relations. But power is not one-sided or monolithic, even when we can and do speak of dominance, subjugation or oppression. Power is always exercised in relation to a resistance, though a question is left about the equality of forces . . . furthermore the talk of power and resistance does not imply that resistance is necessarily equal or successful or indeed that it is fundamentally subversive . . . the concept of resistance, in the general sense . . . includes both conscious opposition and the mute automatic resistance of that which is in the process of being shaped.

(Henriques *et al.* 1984: 115)

Just as there are different kinds of powers, there are different kinds of resistances; resistance is both a way of avoiding being controlled and influenced and a way of attempting to influence as well. Dominant individuals (or groups) may be attempting to resist others gaining power for themselves, that is, they resist in order to maintain their dominance. Subordinate individuals may be attempting to challenge or change the relationship of dominance/subordination; to gain power for themselves or to prevent or mitigate the other's dominance over them. To some extent the process is the same for both; both are resisting the other, both are attempting to gain power by resisting. However, one is resisting from an already dominant position, the other is resisting from an already subordinate position; the kinds of resistances they can evoke may differ according to their already existing positions. The dominant individual (or group) having power already is more likely to be able to resist the subordinate individual (or group) than vice versa. The dominant individual may be attempting to keep the status quo through resistance; the subordinate individual may be trying to change it.

The kind of resistance attempted may depend on the kind of resource or power base that the individual has to base its resistance upon. This is obviously going to create problems for the subordinates as their subordination stems from their lack of resources; the fact that they are more dependent upon the dominants than vice versa. Ideology and beliefs may also create difficulties if the subordinate group has internalized the dominants' beliefs. According to Marxism, capitalist ideology creates a 'false consciousness' in the working classes, so that they do not even realize that they are being exploited or oppressed. Likewise, patriarchal ideology may have the same effect on women.

Henriques *et al.* (1984) suggest that resistance may be conscious or 'mute and automatic'. A fundamental question is whether individuals resist consciously, deliberately, unconsciously, overtly, covertly, directly or indirectly and indeed whether they see what they are saying, doing, feeling as a resistance or as merely a reaction to others' power. The former implies an active and the latter a passive model of resistance. There are many examples of overt, direct, conscious and organized resistance by women against their subordinate position, not least being the growth of the feminist movement and campaigns for equal pay, greater freedom of roles and careers, campaigns against domestic violence and so on. At the interpersonal level women may 'nag' or point out that things are not 'fair' in their relationship; make suggestions about how things could change or do things that will evoke change. This conscious and direct approach may be effective; however, on the other hand, it may not; and more covert and indirect resistance may emerge; banging the dishes to hint that domestic tasks are not being shared equally or 'forgetting' to do things that they did not want to do but did not feel able to object to directly. Indirect resistances may well be more likely if the individual is in a subordinate position, lacking resources or power bases of their own they may fear the consequences of direct resistance or overt communication. At the same time women may be socialized to resist in a different manner from men; gender and power may interrelate.

One of the central themes that this book will explore is that one of the most pervasive and also self-destructive forms of indirect resistance is to 'develop' a psychological 'symptom' of some kind. In particular a likely candidate will be sexual 'symptoms'. As we will discuss in detail in later chapters, given that men are seen as needing sex more than women, sex may be one of the few sources of power that a financially dependent woman possesses. A frequent scenario may be that the woman 'goes off sex' and the man continues to seek or demand it. However, this can be seen as not simply a conscious strategy on the woman's part but a reaction to a position where she lacks power. It is highly unlikely to be perceived as a resistance or as deliberate in any way; it is more likely to be perceived as a reaction than as an active strategy. Indeed ideology may be so influential that the aetiology of a 'symptom' is not perceived as related to inequality at all but to pathological factors of some form.

Arguably power is implicated as a factor in many kinds of 'pathologies', yet it is rarely seen as that; indeed an intrinsic part of some ideology or discourse is to deny that inequality exists, or to deny that it has specific effects. 'Power' may in some ways be a 'taboo' word; denied or negatively construed within some ideologies, especially perhaps in ideologies about intimate relationships. Madanes (1981) and Haley (1963, 1966) offer an explanation of the development of symptoms in terms of power variables in the relationship. They suggest that if the 'balance of power' cannot be resolved satisfactorily then a symptom may emerge that, in an indirect manner, redresses the balance. A sexual symptom therefore could be seen as a covert form of resistance. Although Madanes and Haley do not discuss it in these terms, the implication is that if one of the partners cannot resist effectively, if one is 'realizing their own objectives' more than the other, then a symptom will emerge. A symptom could be seen as a kind of 'last resort' when other attempts at influence or resistance have failed. However, as we will consider further, such sexual symptoms are not simply forms of resistance, they are a reaction to a sense of oppression, of lacking choices and are also self-punishing since the woman also loses out on pleasure and physical intimacy.

PSYCHOLOGICAL THEORIES AND POWER

All societies have a choice about how to distribute the available resources or power bases; any society could attempt to distribute them equitably or inequitably, or as Marx (1967) and Marx and Engels (1970) suggested, 'according to need'. In all societies structures of power, dependencies and domination are constructed and these are usually explained and justified by reference to 'human nature', or to the apparently practical issue of economics; the two are interlinked. Psychology has played its part in explaining and maintaining inequality. Human nature has been variously described as competitive or co-operative; self-interested or altruistic (socio-biology), malleable and determined by the environment (learning theory), driven by instinct (socio-biology, psychodynamics), capable of exercising choice and autonomy, adaptive and creative (cognitive and humanistic theories). Individuals may be seen as unique, as having different abilities, capacities, skills, needs or as fundamentally similar. These beliefs about human nature may in turn affect the ways in which resources are distributed, for instance a belief that we are essentially competitive implies that we will be motivated by inequality in the distribution of resources.

Psychological theory has also been used to counteract resistance by the less powerful by enlisting the support of 'scientific evidence', for example psychological studies which claimed to reveal 'fundamental instincts' such as mothering or women's lesser capacity for rational thought. Williams and Watson (1988) also comment that ideology disguises inequality by labelling reactions against oppression as 'madness' or 'mental disorder' or 'abnormal', and by encouraging those who are in a subordinate position to explain their negative experiences as not to do with social inequalities but to do with there 'being something wrong with them'.

Defining and measuring power

Psychological theories, however, also offer some potential clarifications, for example in attempts to define and measure power. Important to developing an understanding of power in relationships is an attempt to clarify what is involved in measuring it – some agreed procedures for what do we do in order to measure it (operationalization) so that different researchers can compare and amalgamate their findings. Attempts to 'measure' power are obviously linked with definitions of what it is. Problems in defining it also lead to problems in 'measuring' it. As suggested above, past studies have attempted to measure it by asking 'who wins' in negotiations, 'who realizes their objectives the most' or 'who makes the decisions'. Most studies of power assume a degree of overt conflict: wherein A and B know what they want, know what their own 'best interests are', and the 'realization' of their respective 'goals' is going to put them into a situation of conflict and disagreement. Operationalization therefore would seem fairly simple. Each could be asked what they want, and then we could look at who gets what they want and who does not and conclude that the one who gets what they want has more power than the one who does not. We can also look at *how* they managed to achieve this.

However, as suggested above, inequality may function in such a way that people do not have a clear idea as to what their objectives are, may not realize that the objectives that they are trying to realize may not be the kind of objectives that are actually in their best interests and there may be no overt conflict due to the impact of ideology and discourse. This potentially creates massive problems for attempts to define and measure power. Recent attempts to do so have therefore attempted to take account of the wider social context in which couples exist. For example, studies of negotiation and bargaining between men and women need to take into account a variety of learning and socialization processes that construct a set of beliefs, expectations and gender roles which shape how people will act.

The next chapter will outline four influential psychological theories and consider how these also represent forms of dominant discourses regarding relationships and power.

2

Psychological perspectives on relationships

Couples, like researchers and therapists, are trying to make sense of relationships. Furthermore, all of us are consciously or otherwise employing 'theories' in a more or less formal sense (Kelly 1955). Psychodynamic ideas in particular have pervaded the general consciousness so that we are all familiar with some of the core concepts. As Foucault (1979) suggests these scientific formulations or 'knowledges' have served to map out, shape and constrain our experience. In this chapter we will outline four influential theoretical frameworks: psychodynamic theory, learning theory, cognitive perspectives/personal construct theory narratives/accounts, and systems theory, which have guided research in the area of relationships and sexuality. These have been dominant both in research on relationships and also in guiding therapeutic work. Not all of these frameworks are employed equally by non-specialists, for example systems and personal construct theories are relatively unfamiliar in any formal sense to the 'general public'. However, even these are commonly employed in some sense, for example in the idea of vicious cycles or the view that problems in relationships are due to inappropriate perceptions and misunderstandings between partners.

Our intention here is twofold: first, to set out some of the tenets of these theories which shed light on relationships, power and sexuality; and second, to enable us in later chapters to link couples' explanations to these influential 'scientific' beliefs. In adopting this approach we are suggesting that it is more fruitful to consider not only whether or in what ways a theory is 'true' but how it serves to shape our thinking and consequently our actions. The theories can also be seen in terms of the extent to which they adopt an 'outside' perspective in which as 'experts' we make assumptions about what is happening as opposed to an 'inside' perspective which is interested in couples' own perceptions, the beliefs and explanations which guide their choices of action. Learning theory, psychodynamic theory and systems theory all make assumptions from the outside about people's actions, their motives, rewards and so on. Of the four, cognitive perspectives are most centrally fundamentally concerned with people's personal perceptions, the meanings that they develop and which guide their actions. Psychodynamic theories, though also concerned with perceptions, are more concerned about the unconscious, relatively unavailable emotional meanings that have been attached to past events. In looking at how partners may be employing these theories we are not simply suggesting that the partners would have articulated the same analysis of their own beliefs as ours. Nevertheless, we feel it is valuable to consider how their thinking has been shaped by pieces of ideas which can be seen to be derived from these dominant theoretical perspectives. In fact people's accounts often display an integration of aspects of these theories that psychologists and other theorists might tremble at attempting.

PSYCHODYNAMIC THEORY: OBJECT RELATIONS THEORY

Psychodynamic theories have perhaps had the greatest impact on the thinking of professionals and lay people. Fundamental to these theories is the idea that we are driven by biologically based instincts or needs. As infants the key amongst these basic needs are food, protection and emotional intimacy. For Freud sensuality and sexuality arose as powerful needs in the young infant and these shaped the nature of his or her relationships with adults, especially the mother.

Object relations theory

Object relations theory developed out of Freud's basic assumptions but pays special attention to the nature of the early social relationships (Klein 1946; Fairbairn 1952; Dicks 1967; Skynner 1976; Kaplan 1979; and Scharff 1982). Individuals are seen to develop through several 'stages'. Klein refers to these as 'positions'; a position is not simply a stage through which the individual passes but a specific configuration of object relations, anxieties and defences which persist through life and come into play most clearly in adult intimate relationships. For instance, if an individual's relationship with his/her early caregiver is extremely problematic s/he may learn to distrust others. Relationships where trust is important will stir up anxieties, these anxieties will then be guarded against by the same defence mechanisms that were associated with the same anxieties originally.

At birth the infant is seen to be helpless, powerless and dependent upon its parents. Frustration of needs is inevitable and the infant defends against such feelings by 'splitting off' and repressing or keeping out of conscious experience two aspects of the caregiver (usually the mother); the frustrating depriving aspect and the need-exciting aspect (Fairbairn 1952). The infant's conscious experience is therefore an idealized version of the mother – neither too frustrating nor too exciting. Extreme affects, intolerable longings, frustrations, desires, rage, are thought to be likely to resurface in adult intimate relationships (Scharff 1982). However, as these are largely unconscious, individuals will not be able to understand why they are experiencing such extreme emotions and it will be difficult for them to make sense of what is going on between them.

Scharff (1982) suggests that sexuality is not merely physical but has a symbolic component and sexual intimacy can reawaken repressed object relations for both partners. It symbolizes the struggle to hold on to the memory of the 'good', loving, giving parents and the struggle to overcome the image of the withholding parent. If the sexual relationship 'works', i.e. is satisfying this means that the inner object world feels integrated and characterized by a feeling of well-being. Successful sexual relationships promote feelings of a 'good' self, 'good other' and 'good' interrelationship, and also represent the mastery of the 'good' over the 'bad'. In contrast sexual 'failure' is seen to promote feelings that the 'bad' objects, external and/or internal, have somehow more power than the 'good' and evokes the infantile experience of feeling that the self and/or the other is 'bad'; overwhelming, in control, depriving and untrustworthy.

Choice of intimate partner

Dicks (1967) suggests that when there is a relatively 'free' choice of partner, as is common in Western cultures, partners may often be chosen for unconscious reasons, for example because they have had, in some way, similar or complementary early experiences: they might both come from families where there was difficulty in expressing emotion, affection, anger or envy. Alternatively, they may choose each other because they 'think' the other will allow them to keep their defences; will not offer any challenge or because they 'think' that the other will challenge their defences. Partners may also be chosen who seem to embody 'lost aspects' of themselves or because the other somehow reminds them of the parent unconsciously.

The choice of partners and important aspects of how people relate to others is seen to be shaped by the nature of early attachments and in particular how various emotions and anxieties are dealt with.

Transference and stages

A central concept for psychodynamic theories, especially object relations theory, is that the emotional experiences and the nature of the early attachments are transferred onto our adult relationships. Most importantly we are typically unaware that we are acting towards our partner 'as if' they were our mother (or father). As the child develops he or she may, for a variety of reasons, such as their own parents' personalities and anxieties, experience problems at a particular stage. Each stage is seen as having different implications for the style of relating and form of relationships that people 'choose' or find themselves in.

Oral stage

The earliest stage is seen to be the oral since the child's experience is focused around the intake of food, milk through his or her mouth. The oral stage issues centre around dependency since the infant discovers that he or she is dependent and vulnerable. This leads to experiencing *split* feelings of need and anxiety, fears of loss; the fear that the person on whom it is dependent will go away. In order to defend against such feelings the infant is seen to develop a range of defences such as control, whereby the other is compelled to fulfil his or her needs – a controlled object is, up to a point, an object that can be depended upon. Alternatively contempt may be employed, so that by denying the worth of the other the fear of its loss is reduced.

A couple where both partners have unresolved problems from this stage are seen to become excessively dependent and cling to each other excessively in order to deny their fear of independence and separateness. Both may make continual attempts to control each other, feel stifled and frightened of doing anything separately. Sexually neither may be able to initiate sexuality and both may wait around hoping for the other to take the initiative. Likewise, a couple may consist of two people who both deny their need for dependency and have a separate and cold relationship. Neither of them has their needs for dependence met and considerable anxiety may result if one partner becomes dependent, for example through illness. Sexuality may be problematic since neither partner can admit needing the other and may be cold and mechanical so that emotions and hence dependencies are not exposed.

Alternatively one partner may be dependent and the other independent. They are seen to be attracted to each other because each allows the other to stay defended; one does not have to face up to fears of being independent and separate, the other does not have to admit to dependency needs. The dependent partner is potentially vulnerable, powerless and open to abuse, especially if punished for dependency because of their partner's projection. This is an example of the traditional or 'dolls' house' marriage – usually where the woman is apparently dependent and the man is apparently independent. Likewise, the woman may be sexually passive and dependent upon the man to take responsibility for the sexual interaction. She may also be inorgasmic because she feels unable to express her sexual needs directly as that would be too assertive and might threaten his apparent 'strength'. He on the other hand may feel anxious, strained at having to take the responsibility, worry that he is not 'doing it properly' and resentful when she does not appear to be thinking about his needs and therefore possibly suffer from impotence or premature ejaculation.

Anal stage

The child starts to gain independence and autonomy, being able to walk away, or come when called, to control its sphincters, to obey or disobey, potentially leading to power struggles with the parents. If the parents are too strict and controlling the child may be timid, fearful, unable to take risks or stubborn and rebellious. If too permissive an attitude is taken, a self-centred uncompromising attitude may develop, or restrictions of activity may occur because they were allowed to do what they wanted to such an extent that they literally hurt themselves. Difficulties resulting from the anal stage are revealed in dynamics which are characterized by self-centredness, difficulties in compromising, lack of understanding of the other, rebelliousness towards the partner's wishes, resentful, passive stubbornness and/or fear of taking risks. Power can be gained by overt rebellion and refusing to do what the other wants. It can also be gained by passive stubbornness and by being self-centred.

Skynner (1976) describes how relationships can be characterized by endless stubborn obstructiveness, an incessant struggle for power with resistance to anyone being granted it. In relation to sexuality there may be feelings that all bodily functions are 'dirty' and 'shameful' or embarrassing. There may be fears of 'letting go', a fear of taking risks sexually, e.g. inorgasmia, impotence and premature ejaculation. There may also be fears of being a 'nymphomaniac' or rapist so that there is over-control of sexuality; even at the level of feelings of arousal or desire. Conversely there may be the avoidance of being controlled by the other, leading to attempts to control the sexual situation. Skynner (1976) suggests there may be a preoccupation with mastery and dominance, either in overt form or with emphasis on defensive aspects where the surrender of the body to the other is feared and avoided.

Phallic stage

The key feature is a focus of sexual desire for the opposite sex parent. This is seen to lead to potential rivalry and conflict with the same sex parent and potentially resulting in emotional conflicts in the child, such as castration anxieties (Scharff 1982). Resolution is seen to occur through identification, as in the boy becoming more like his father on the supposition that if he is like his father his mother will love him as well. Scharff (1982) suggests that in the positive oedipal resolution the mother becomes the object choice of the boy, the father is the feared rival; and in the negative oedipal position the father is the object choice and the mother the feared rival. A negative oedipal position can develop if the mother is a too fearful, rejecting or absent figure to be the object of desire. For girls the reverse applies.

According to Skynner (1976) the child has several needs during this phase. They need to be able to express their feelings without fears of retaliation, rejection, punishment or loss of love of either parent. The child needs to 'see' an unembarrassed sexual relationship between its parents. The child also needs to be unsuccessful in 'seducing' the opposite sex parent as this would result in fears that they have lost the love of the other parent.

In the phallic stage there may be a fear of success, related to fears of loss of one of the parents' love, which may lead to a tendency always to choose unavailable partners, e.g. often already married. Once they have succeeded in seducing them earlier fears of loss of love may resurface and the relationship abandoned only to go on to another unavailable person. There may be general problems with the opposite sex; getting too close evokes fears of retaliation. In heterosexual relationships there may be a tendency to see their partner as like the opposite sex parent, leading them to react and behave towards their partner in a similar way as they did towards this parent. They may respond in the same way that their same sex parent behaved towards their own partner. This would also be likely according to learning theory.

Power and sexuality

The issue of power is central to object relations theory. The young infant is seen to experience anxiety as the potential loss of the breast of the mother. Early development is concerned with attempting to gain some control and power over its world. In adult relationships these issues of power and control surface as partners re-enact their early anxieties and consequently attempt to control each other in various ways. Conflict, tensions and power struggles are therefore seen as inevitable in adult relationships. Such anxieties may also result in rivalry, jealousy and fears of 'losing' one's partner. Doyle (1989) suggests that sexual rivalry between men is highly prevalent and often quite overt; many men worry that they are not 'as good' at sex as other men and fear that they will lose their female partner to another man; consequently they may become very anxious about their 'performance'. They may attempt to control their female partners excessively in order to prevent them going anywhere near other men.

In addition to this basic formulation it is suggested that conflict is further fuelled by the fact that each gender is envious and jealous of the other, men are envious of women because they have the capacity to bear children, women are envious of men's penises. Indirect hostility, resentment, attempts to prove that one is better than the other, competition between the genders as to who is better, may result (Klein 1946; Kaplan 1979). 'Penis envy' is said to emerge when the girl realizes she does not have a penis and wishes that she did. A 'healthy' woman is seen to be one who has resolved this envy and assumed a passive receptive role and developed a preference for vaginal rather than clitoral orgasm. An unresolved penis envy is seen to lead to a competitive, masculine, aggressive personality. Women suffering from penis envy are also thought unconsciously to hate and wish to destroy and castrate men. Unconscious penis envy is also suggested to result in various sexual symptoms, such as vaginismus, which is seen as an avoidance of penile penetration because of fears of feeling that they wish to castrate men. It is also seen to impede the so-called 'normal' transition from the 'neurotic' enjoyment of clitoral stimulation to the 'healthy' enjoyment of vaginal penetration and orgasm. Premature ejaculation is argued to be derived from a sadistic wish to punish or deprive the woman; retarded ejaculation is suggested to be related to the fear of ejaculating inside the woman (Kaplan 1979). An alternative view would be to argue that the penis is simply symbolic of male power and women's oppression. Women do not wish literally to have a penis, but they want to have the power and privileges attached to having one; in a sense women may wish to 'castrate' men symbolically, i.e. to render them 'impotent' and less powerful.

Gender and identification: Feminist object relations theory

Within psychodynamic theory the individual is seen to develop an identity proper when s/he identifies with the same sex parent and transfers his/her 'desires' to the opposite sex parent. Both sexes are seen as developing sexual feelings for their opposite sex parent and come to resolve the rivalries and jealous feelings therefore aroused towards the other parent by identifying with them – by becoming more like his father the boy in a sense reduces his feelings of conflict. Likewise, the girl by becoming more like her mother not only reduces her conflict but also becomes a potentially more suitable partner for the desired father. Within this framework homosexuality is due to a disorder or breakdown of this identification process. Within Western societies this identification also means that boys become active and dominant and girls passive, generally and especially in relation to sexuality.

However, this analysis, it has been argued, is only partial and does not really address the question of how and why men and women appear to develop different emotional personalities. Chodorow (1978) suggests that both boys and girls are initially attached to their mothers but subsequently their experiences diverge. Girls may continue to be connected to their mothers but boys are encouraged to separate, to become different, to adopt a male as opposed to female identity. For both development is potentially problematic: girls through staying emotionally fused to their mothers may find it hard to develop a sense of themselves as individuals. Boys on the other hand start to shut down their emotions, to deny their vulnerabilities and also to lose the capacity to care emotionally for others. To stay 'too close' to their mothers, for example, runs for them the risk of being teased and branded as a 'mummy's boy'. There are relative advantages for both too: girls gain a greater capacity to relate and become attached to others. Boys develop a greater capacity for autonomy and self-confidence. Chodorow (1978) suggests that due to the almost universal division of gender roles – women responsible for childcare and men for earning outside of the home – this attachment to the mother is inevitable, as is the gender differentiation that results.

This analysis has far-reaching consequences. One of the most pessimistic implications is that men and women develop identities which make them fundamentally unsuited to each other. Conflict is bound to arise because women are seeking attachments but men are frightened of this because it reminds them of the attachment to their mothers which they have been driven to break in order to become 'real men'. In effect this illustrates the frequently observed cycle of men trying to avoid commitment and attachment and women desperately seeking it. However, rather than seeing this process as predominantly a problem within families it can be seen as related also to power and the position of women. Typically the female value of capacity for attachment and emotional connection has a low value and status compared to male characteristics of autonomy, independence and material achievements.

For adult relationships this may mean further that the kinds of anxieties associated with particular stages, for example the anal stage, are given gendered meanings for partners. For example, men's realization of their dependencies conflicts with their male role expectations, leading them to act in ambivalent ways, both expressing their needs and denying them. Likewise, women may try to be less dependent and more assertive. The combination can result in cycles of loving and hating. The pattern of the relationship may consist of rows and euphoric making up, even violence. Goldner (1991) describes how some men may simultaneously attempt to be both emotionally close and distant by, for example, coercing their partner into sexual intimacy. This avoids the risk of exposing their vulnerability but makes it more likely that they will be rejected, or that sex will be unsatisfactory, in turn fuelling anxieties, recriminations and anger. The remorse that some men subsequently show may provide a measure of the emotional closeness that the woman seeks but this may be dissipated over repetitions of this cycle. Furthermore, men often attempt reparation by sexual intimacy, which for them is safer in signifying their power but may not offer the emotional connection that women seek. Chodorow's (1978) analysis suggests that sexual problems will invariably emerge at some stage in most relationships if it is not possible for men and women to become at least a little more similar in their capacity for intimacy and how they express these needs.

Early attachments and adult relationships

Psychodynamic theory helps reveal how some of the history of each partner's emotional experience may unconsciously shape the current relationships. Many studies suggest that men are more likely to deny their dependency needs than are women and that men are generally less comfortable with talking about or expressing their more 'vulnerable' feelings than women (Hite 1981; Chodorow 1978; Doyle 1989). These differences influence all aspects of a couple's relationship. Tannen (1991) has suggested that women in conversations find it helpful to talk over their troubles and are likely to empathize with and reciprocate the other's disclosures of problems and anxieties; 'I know just what you mean'. Men in contrast are more likely to want to take a protective role and offer advice and practical solutions, rather than reciprocate by disclosing their own problems and vulnerabilities. When they do disclose, they appear to prefer that their problems are regarded as rather unique and that they are given full personal attention. Perhaps this is because for men such disclosure involves taking an emotional 'risk', of revealing their vulnerabilities. Chodorow (1978) suggests that this pattern of seeking closeness and denial of need underlies many relationships and can be seen as resulting in women turning towards others, especially their children, for emotional intimacy. This playing out of the unconscious needs in everyday conversations (or lack of them) between couples can be seen as serving also to reproduce the patterns around sexuality.

Empirical studies have offered some further confirmation of the importance of early emotional experiences by establishing clear similarities between the nature of early forms of attachment and adult relationships (Hazan and Shaver 1987; Bartholomew and Horowitz 1991). Attempts have been made to categorize the pattern of early attachments to parents into three or four types; secure, anxious, avoidant and rejecting. A similar analysis of attachment style with the most significant intimate adult sexual partner has been found to correlate closely with the pattern of early attachment. However, a problem with psychodynamic theories generally can be that they offer a rather rigid, fixed view of attachment. Many couples, however, recount that the pattern of their dependencies has changed. For example, early in their relationship Jill had felt very dependent on Paul, who had made efforts to encourage her to be more independent:

JILL	He wanted me to be independent, he was always saying why don't you do this or that. I felt I wasn't quite up to scratch . . . he's so perfect, so accomplished.
PAUL	I said you must do something you like . . . become more independent. She relies on me less now . . . loves working . . .
THERAPIST	Have your emotional dependencies shifted?
PAUL	I would say its a rejection thing . . .

| THERAPIST | Do you feel more dependent on her than she does on you? |
| PAUL | Yes, possibly . . . |

However, this work on patterns of early attachment also indicates that the effects can be explained in terms of cognitive models or expectations that we learn as children which then come to shape our subsequent relationships. Such patterns of beliefs are more openly observable and hence accessible to study and comparisons between different observers than the nebulous and speculative concepts that proliferate in early psychodynamic theories. For example, 'transference' can be seen as the application of a set of beliefs learned in one situation (childhood relationships) to another (adult relationships). Furthermore, it is suggested that emotions, anxieties, fears and so on are not separate phenomena but are based upon systems of meanings or beliefs, for example, we may fear relationships because through learning experiences in childhood we have come automatically to expect certain negative consequences to occur (Oatley 1991). Such a cognitive approach also suggests that, as in the example above, patterns can also change as couples reflect on their relationship and their material and other circumstances change.

Yet arguably these differences between men and women which fuel adult relationships are not a biological imperative but are socially and culturally determined, with considerable variations across cultures and historical periods. In fact the process of the development of gender identification does not necessarily imply these traditional active/male – passive/female divisions. It could theoretically be possible and quite appropriate for this to be the reverse as long as identification takes place. For example, a girl could become attached to and identify with a strong, active, non-emotional assertive and powerful mother.

LEARNING THEORY

The fundamental focus of learning theory approaches is that behaviour is acquired through processes of conditioning based upon rewards and punishments. In effect this implies that the histories of our experiences as children predispose us to act in certain ways in our adult relationships. This captures commonsense notions that we learn how to be in relationships and also that we expect 'fairness' – to get a 'reasonable return', to gain as much as we put in rather than simply being 'used'. Relationships are seen to develop as a result of the mixture of individual histories of learning experiences that each partner brings to a relationship and subsequently how the partners then influence each other. Each partner may have learnt to use threats, to withdraw, to cry, to be indirect, to be cooperative, passive or conciliatory and so on. They might have been punished for some behaviours and rewarded for others. Rewards and punishments may take various forms, tangible or less tangible, and partners may differ, for example one partner might have been rewarded for being compliant, the other rewarded for being assertive.

Imitation and modelling

Learning merely through experiencing rewards and punishments would be a slow and cumbersome process. Bandura (1965) suggested that much of our important social learning is through observation and imitation. He demonstrated this through a series of experiments where children observed adult 'models' engaged either in passive or aggressive behaviour towards a large life-size doll. When the children were subsequently allowed to play with this doll they were likely to imitate whichever type of behaviour they had seen, i.e. they had learnt aggressive behaviour through the mechanism of imitation. These experiments also suggested that learning may be vicarious and latent; the children tended to imitate the models depending on whether the adult appeared to be rewarded or punished for the behaviour. If the adult was punished the children were less likely to imitate him but when the context was altered so that the children knew they would be rewarded for aggressive behaviour they demonstrated that they had learnt the techniques of the adult aggression. Bandura described this as latent learning – the behaviour had been observed and learnt but its behavioural manifestation was related to other factors. This suggests that a wide range of behaviour may be learnt but not necessarily enacted; however, the knowledge that it could be enacted exists for the individuals concerned; in a way it could be that those learnt behaviours are there as a kind of 'last resort' if all else fails. Often individuals say that they will never do what their parents have done and yet in interaction they shock themselves by doing exactly the same.

Such learning may also be gender specific, such that males and females learn different kinds of behaviours. Bandura noted that children also appeared to take into account the prestige and gender of the adult they are observing. In a study exploring gender differences in imitation, of children aged from 37–69 months, it appeared that some children had made assessments about what they saw to be gender appropriate behaviour; for instance, girls saw aggressive behaviour as less legitimate than boys. Such ideas of modelling and imitation are apparent in the accounts that many couples offer for their own feelings about sexuality and relationships. In the next extract, Steven and Katrina, a young couple in their twenties, are describing their family backgrounds – Katrina had become unable to engage in sexual intimacy:

STEVEN   Dad would be very embarrassed ... whereas Mum
            appeared open, she told me the facts of life ... made it
            clear sex was a loving thing ... not just something you did
            to create children ...
KATRINA   Mum told me about periods ... nothing else ... she seemed
            embarrassed ... mother laughs at sexual things on
            television ... weird ...

Learned helplessness and locus of control

A critical question is the extent to which learning experiences can account
for the extent to which people feel in control of their lives and their own
actions. Rotter (1966) has suggested that people differ with respect to the
sense of control they feel they have over their lives – 'locus of control'.
Some people feel that they are relatively helpless, that things happen to
them irrespective of whatever they try to do, fate, luck, the power of others
– *external* locus of control. In contrast some people feel that events are a
result of their own actions, that they have the power to determine what
happens to them – *internal* locus of control. The extent to which a child
develops an internal versus an external locus of control is seen to depend
on the style of parenting. If parents respond in a way which acknowledges
the child's action and encourages the child to develop a sense of being in
control and having influence over others this encourages a sense of autonomy and internal locus of control. In contrast parents who ignore their
children or disqualify their actions are likely to produce children who feel
that whatever they do will have little effect on what happens to them. If a
child has been offered explanations as to why some of her/his requests
cannot be granted this can inculcate a sense of control and power more than
a situation whereby the child is ignored, dismissed, or simply told to 'do it'
because the parent says so. The patterns of controlling others that children
develop can therefore be related to the patterns that have been established
with their parents.

Seligman (1973) has suggested that a condition he describes as 'learned
helplessness' can develop when we are subjected to conditions of punishment with no possibility of escape. People exposed to such circumstances
are seen as 'giving up', becoming behaviourally passive and developing an
attribution that nothing they can do will make any difference. This is likely
to persist even when the situation changes so that they could influence
what is happening to them. In learning theory terms this is an example of
a generalization effect; that what is learnt in one situation becomes applied
to a variety of other situations. Though much formative learning is seen to
take place in childhood it also appears that, for example, continual violence
in an adult relationship can in a similar way to childhood abuse lead to a
passive, helpless orientation (Dobash and Dobash 1980, 1992). More generally

it has been suggested that women are more likely to develop an external locus of control than men (Brown and Harris 1978). This may be because their lives are in fact externally controlled and so they are accurately reflecting this. Also they might, partly because of this, generalize this to seeing themselves as lacking internal control in some situations where they might be able to exert some influence.

Relationships

Learnt interactional patterns

Individuals may learn interactional patterns from their parents or from other significant sources rather than simply learning individual behaviours. For instance, a child may observe that his/her parents shout at each other when they are in disagreement:

STUART   My Mum and Dad used to have rows, I used to hate it, better not to say anything. I've grown up with that, found it difficult until I started to realize how you work through these problems by talking about it ... I've got this manner of cutting off and I can distract myself and veer off and go cycling, do something else, enjoy that activity, it puts up a screen and I feel things are OK now I'm happy again ... So in our relationship I have a fear of making people fly off the handle or upsetting them, making them mad, real problem for me, between us a fear of upsetting the apple cart.

According to Bandura's perspective, whether people adopt the patterns learnt from observation of their own parents will be related to whether it is seen to work (i.e. to them being rewarded) and to gender. For example, a couple might believe that disagreements can be resolved through shouting or having a 'row' as opposed, for instance, to 'sitting down quietly with the partner and talking through their disagreements'. Problems are likely if the partners disagree on how to sort things out; one partner might think that shouting will work and the other may think that some other strategy is better. One partner may think that 'rows' are positive in that they clear the air, the other that 'rows' can lead to things being said that are very destructive. Couples may even have 'rows' about whether they should have 'rows' or not.

Relationships as exchanges of rewards and punishments

Relationships have been regarded within an economic metaphor as based on an exchange of rewards (Thibaut and Kelley 1959; Walster *et al.* 1978). The original formulations simply argued that good relationships were based on an equity of rewards, that fairness could be quantified. However, it became clear that in reality relationships were more complicated and partners' beliefs and expectations played a vital part, so that what counts as fair or positive varies from relationship to relationship. Subsequently it became clear that we develop not only patterns of behaviours but also patterns of thinking, explanations, belief about needs, power and how to influence others. Psychoanalytic theorists also pointed out that people often appear to act 'irrationally', for example staying in relationships which appeared to be less than fair, negative or even punishing for one or both partners. Suggestions such as 'masochistic' personalities were offered, i.e. that one or other partner unconsciously wished or 'needed' to be punished. In response feminist learning theorists suggested that negative behaviours – for example, threats and invalidation – may be rewarding because they allow the actor to keep a dominant position or to give them power. The partner may respond to these abusive behaviours by actually doing what the actor wants despite their own resentment and thus reinforce the behaviour.

COGNITIVE PERSPECTIVES: PERSONAL CONSTRUCT THEORY, NARRATIVES AND ACCOUNTS

Learning theory has difficulty in dealing with the complexity and sophistication of the range of potential meaning that people can give to their own and others' actions. It is not even an easy task to define what might be rewarding for any particular individual. It is necessary therefore to consider people's cognitions, their beliefs, explanations and expectations. Couples, as apparent in the earlier examples, request and offer accounts for their own and each other's actions, including justifications, attributions of responsibility and blaming. In this section we will briefly outline George Kelly's (1955) personal construct theory and link this to approaches which explore the accounts which feature in couples' conversations.

Kelly's (1955) theory centres on the metaphor of 'man the scientist'. We are all, he argued, concerned to predict or anticipate events in our lives. Like scientists we form hypotheses about other people, our relationships, ourselves and try to predict events so that we formulate plans or strategies of actions. He added that though there is arguably a reality 'out there', we can only know this in terms of our own experiences. Our constructs are seen to be organized into a hierarchical system whereby any given construct is linked to others and some are super-ordinate (*core* constructs) or more important to our decision-making than others. Included in these are our constructs of self, our identity and in particular how we wish to be seen by others – our *preferred view of self*.

Kelly suggested that our understandings are essentially in terms of constructs which are made up of contrasting concepts, such as friendly vs withdrawn, intelligent vs unimaginative (the contrasts being personal and potentially differing between people). An account or explanation can be regarded as a set of connected constructs. Kelly emphasized two further points: (1) our views, construct systems, are to some extent unique; and (2) if we accept that others may see things differently then we can concede that there are alternative constructions possible. How we see events, other people and their reasons for action, what they seem to want from us, guides how we choose to act towards them. In turn our actions have an effect on others and in turn they formulate plans of action based upon their interpretation of our actions. Watzlawick *et al.* (1967) refer to this as self-fulfilling prophecies; in effect that our constructs lead us to, at least in part, create our relationships.

Types of constructs and accounts

Our constructs and accounts are seen as covering a range of events or circumstances. To take an example, a construct 'bullying' may for one person be restricted to examples of physical coercion but to another imply a wider range of actions: verbal attacks, withdrawal of privileges and so on. Since circumstances change we need to be able to revise our beliefs and accounts but these differ in the extent to which they are capable of being modified.

Pre-emptive constructs and accounts have an all-or-nothing quality and frequently feature the adjectives 'always' and 'never'; for example, a woman may see her partner as *always* withdrawing or that he is *always* selfish and *never* kind. This functions to dismiss contradictory evidence and makes it difficult for any elaboration or development of alternative ways of seeing his actions. Similarly constructs and accounts can cluster together to form a stereotyped, fixed view of a person, for instance, seeing a partner as withdrawn may also imply that he is cold, uncaring, selfish and hostile. Alternatively constructs can be flexible or *propositional*, more like scientific hypotheses or propositions in that they imply that our way of seeing an event is a hypothesis to be tested and may be replaced by a more effective hypothesis, i.e. it encourages a range of alternatives to be contemplated; for example, that the man may be 'withdrawing', or he may be 'tired', or 'feeling sad', or 'protecting' her from his worries and so on.

Control and power

Kelly stressed that a central aspect of our constructs is to be able to predict and therefore exert some influence and control on our environment and other people. A sense of powerlessness may result when we are unable to predict what will happen, how others will act and what we can do to influence the course of events and others' actions. Our sense of control and ability to predict events increases when our constructs are 'validated'. Conversely invalidation occurs when others define our constructions as non-legitimate, meaningless, in error or stupid. A sense of power, of being in control of our lives, relates to the extent to which we can develop or elaborate our construct systems so that we can predict changing or new events. This is also related to the power of the other(s) to invalidate us. In particular how we see ourself, our 'preferred view' of ourself is seen to be central and a variety of negative feelings are seen to arise when this is invalidated. People who experience their relationships as problematic frequently talk in terms of being stifled, put down or attacked by their partner and powerful negative feelings are usually associated with this.

DOROTHY   I wish he could be more sociable, not so neurotic about people looking at him. You know if he goes into a room with a lot of people he has to sit in the corner, he can't bear anyone behind him . . .

TONY   I'm very self-conscious. She's always telling me how puny I look, I can't bear to look in the mirror, how can you not be self-conscious?

DOROTHY   I'm only telling you the truth, you tell me to say what I see and feel.

TONY   Yes, but there is no need to say it and put the boot in as well.

DOROTHY   He's the nicest man in the world, really, but he's just got so many hang-ups – well I can't say anything I suppose.

Relationships

In order to engage in relationships Kelly argued that we need to have two types of understandings, commonality and sociality.

Commonality   In order to have some understanding, and to be able to communicate and interact with each others, partners need to share or hold in common some constructs and accounts about their relationship.

Sociality   Partners also need to have some empathy or understanding of how their partner sees them, their relationship and events that occur.

Relationship difficulties are seen to result when partners fail to understand the other's way of seeing things. Events such as loss of a job, illness or having children can trigger realizations for a couple that they did not in fact share or agree as much as they had previously reckoned. Such ability to revise or elaborate beliefs about each other and the relationship is seen as fundamental. Problems may be associated with couples becoming 'stuck' in their construings, tending to see the other in a particular way, e.g. a husband might see his wife as 'emotional', so that nearly everything she says or does is construed as related to her emotionality. This can set up a self-fulfilling prophecy whereby his actions and perceptions of her may frustrate her to such an extent that she becomes increasingly emotional, thus confirming his perception of her.

Accounts and narratives

Partners are frequently called, and call, each other to account for their actions, for example why they appear to be in a 'bad mood' or why they forgot to do something. The accounts that are offered contain three important ingredients:

1 *Time* A story or plot which serves to connect events over time. An account or narrative tends to have a beginning, middle and end.
2 *Justification* Attempts to explain events, and in particular personal accounts in relationships, tend to serve to justify, exonerate, protect and make excuses – in short to ascribe blame or responsibility.
3 *Interpersonal* The accounts given may differ, or may be adjusted according to who the account is being given to, e.g. different accounts may be given to friends, family members and the partner.

Accounts clearly serve various functions, including attempts to make sense of events in the relationship but also strategic purposes of influencing and controlling the other partner. Typically partners demand explanations when some event is seen to have occurred, either an action or something said which is construed as a transgression of the rules of the relationship. At such times there will be an appraisal or evaluation of the account given, whether it is reasonable and sufficient. Included in this process can be the acceptance of an apology when a legitimate account or explanation is considered to be unavailable or impossible (Harvey *et al.* 1992):

NEVILLE   The other night about the video . . . I swore at her . . . she got angry with me . . . next day it was over and forgotten.

BRENDA   No . . . not forgotten . . . I'd been away. Neville taped a few programmes that I wanted to watch . . . I asked which tape it was . . . he'd forgotten, he has to write things down, can't remember because of the Parkinson's . . . I said it's not here . . . he got into a muddle . . . he said 'You've fucked up the tape' . . . I said 'Just get on with it I'm not interested' . . . lost my temper didn't want to be spoken to like that . . . . He put the tape on and said 'Aren't you going to watch it?' and I said 'No' . . . to avoid a bigger row I became passive, I didn't react as much as I wanted to . . . knew it would become a slanging match.

NEVILLE   I had carefully taped the programmes . . . I went out to make the coffee and she unwittingly put the wrong one on . . . once I'd found it I was right but by now she didn't want

to listen ... such a stupid thing but that is how it developed
... I hate doing things wrong, being told off, can't do it
right ... I try to leave it in the corner to forget it but it
leaves scars.

BRENDA   We're like two dogs walking around the perimeter at a dog
fight sizing each other up ...

Power

In the extract from Brenda and Neville it is apparent that their explanations
and justifications are intimately tied in to a power struggle between them.
Construct theory as originally formulated tended to be individualistic in
assuming that peoples' construct systems are unique, for example that Brenda
and Neville's constructs were fundamentally personal and idiosyncratic.
However, constructs or discourses emanating from the wider societal context are influential, for instance Brenda describes how she becomes 'passive'
in the context of Neville starting to swear when he feels he is being 'told
off'. Also, it appeared that Neville saw Brenda as unreasonable and emotional. Such a perception of women as 'emotional', however, is not merely
idiosyncratic but part of a common perception in the wider society. Indeed
women have often been blocked from access to various kinds of power
because of this general perception.

Couples have to negotiate constantly about all kinds of issues in their
relationship and in effect this can frequently become a struggle in terms of
whose constructs or account prevails. Construct theory gives the impression
that this negotiation is somehow between equals, in an equal society, when
it is not. More precisely it may be that certain situations are defined such
that women are not expected, or allowed, to make equal contributions. As
we saw earlier women still tend to speak less in public discussions in the
presence of men but are more than capable of being articulate in other situations, for example in the company of other women. Generally, patriarchy
has essentially meant that men's construct systems have predominated for
many centuries in regard to all kinds of issues. One way of thinking about
power is to see whose constructs predominate in the relationship or indeed
in the wider society. The accounts employed within relationships can be
seen to be shaped by the internalizations of wider societal discourses, e.g.
about what is 'good', 'normal' and 'desirable' in relationships. The beliefs
and accounts, the narratives or stories couples employ can be seen as not
simply personally produced from within the relationship but as deriving
from dominant cultural discourses.

White and Epston (1990) have developed a model of therapy with couples
and families which attempts to discuss how their problems have evolved
and are maintained by the way they have come to regard each other within
such dominant narratives. More broadly a frequent assumption or 'myth'

is that 'problems' such as Neville's and Brenda's are predominantly due to personal failures or inadequacies and, associated with this, assumptions about their failure to meet standards of, for example, 'normal' sexual activity, or how a 'good' relationship should develop. Both what is construed to be indicative of 'failure' and what should be done about this may be shaped by the dominant narratives or discourses in society.

SYSTEMS THEORY

The three theories discussed, so far as can be seen, are widely employed by couples in their own accounts and explanations. Systems theory on the other hand is less frequently employed. In contrast to the frequently found suggestion that one or other partner is to blame in some way, systems theory emphasizes that relationships arise from the mutual, interconnected actions of partners over time. One strand of such thinking can be seen when couples state that neither of them is to blame or that things just escalate between them in some unexplainable way.

Systems theory proposes that relationships develop through a process of *feedback*. Consequently therapists employing a systems theory framework are concerned with such processes of feedback currently operating in the relationship and predominantly with historical factors, such as the childhood experiences of each partner. Each partner's actions are seen to affect the actions of the other, whose actions in turn affects them back – feedback. This feedback is seen to take two forms: *open* systems in which the feedback functions to produce escalation and *closed* systems which display stability and maintenance of existing patterns (Wiener 1961). In order to function effectively a couple was seen to need to alternate between both these patterns; some patterning, organization and stability are important in order to fulfil necessary tasks but periods of escalation, confrontation and negotiation are also needed to promote necessary changes. Jackson (1957) added the important idea that 'pathology' was a feature of a closed system which operated so that any change in the symptomatic member would be met by actions of the other which would have the effect of reducing rather than encouraging change. He gave an example of a couple where depression in the woman, despite her partner's statements to the contrary, appeared to make him feel powerful and in control. Evidence of positive change on her part (due to her individual therapy) led him to act in a depressed and moody way which in turn ensured her return to depression.

Jackson described this as homeostasis; symptoms were seen as serving a benevolent or protective function for families so that, for instance, a family facing disintegration might be united by needing to care for a symptomatic member. A system is seen as a set of communicating parts in which every action, or even inaction, by a member of a family is seen potentially as a form of communication. Watzlawick *et al.* (1967) suggested that in families people communicate both verbally and non-verbally and it is the latter, which is largely out of conscious awareness, that serves to maintain the homeostatic patterns in families. This idea connects with objects relations theory in that each partner's unconscious anxieties are seen as important but the emphasis is on the dynamics of how each person consequently influences the other, resulting in patterns of escalation. This also contains the idea that relationships are seen to have a *circular,* rather than linear, causation, for example, an argument is seen to develop out of the mutually interdependent responses of two or more members, rather than simply being caused by one of them.

The patterns of mutual influence in relationships are seen as displaying escalating patterns which are of two dominant types, complementary and symmetrical.

Complementary   In a complementary escalation the two partners (or groups) behave in ways that are dissimilar but 'fitting together'. An example of a complementary escalation according to Bateson would be if one partner was usually aggressive and the other usually submissive; submissiveness would promote more aggression and aggression would promote more submissiveness. To protect against this becoming too abusive the submissive partner might express anger or assertiveness, thus changing the dynamic temporarily to a symmetrical pattern.

Symmetrical   In a symmetrical escalation interactions consist of each individual or group 'exhibiting' like behaviours: for instance, if A shouts, so does B; if A cries, so does B; so their behaviours are similar. The escalations can contain a positive or negative sign. For example, the escalation might involve positive behaviours, such as mutual hilarity, the mutual escalation of sensual pleasure in sexual intimacy, or mutual feelings of rising excitement at a concert (Watzlawick *et al.* 1967).

Escalation can occur in either pattern. In order to avoid extreme abuse, the escalation in either form might be halted by one partner changing their behaviour so that the pattern changes to the other form. However, these opportunities may be governed by structural inequalities of power. The example of Brenda and Neville earlier shows an example of a symmetrical escalating process, some awareness of this pattern – 'dog fight, sizing each other up' – and attempts to halt or avoid a row.

Triangulation and conflict detouring

Systems theory stresses that couples rarely exist in a social vacuum and invariably a third element – a person, or in some cases even a pet, or a video recorder as in Brenda and Neville's case – responds in some significant way to the relationship between them. The concepts *triangulation* and *conflict detouring* embody the idea that a third person may be drawn into the conflicts between two others as a way of attenuating escalating conflicts. This may be at a 'cost' so that he or she comes to be attacked as the cause of the problems or even develops 'symptoms' (especially in the case of children of a couple), i.e. acts as a scapegoat and thereby preserves the stability or homeostasis. Individual actions, feelings and cognitions are seen as intimately linked to the interactions between other family members. Jackson suggested that conflict detouring is in effect the development of a family rule about how conflicts are resolved. This concept is also linked to an analysis of structures and coalitions. Similarly triangulation is seen as the attempt consciously or otherwise by each partner to draw a third person onto their side. In therapy this can be seen when each partner attempts to 'gain the sympathy' of the therapist.

Punctuation and interactional cycles

Systems theory, although offering a dynamic model of families, can be seen as being rather mechanistic. There is a need to reconcile a view of families as composed of human beings with the potential to make free, autonomous choices with the recognition that their choices often appear to fuse together into repetitive and predictable patterns. Watzlawick *et al.* (1967) introduced the concept of punctuation, which suggests that each partner usually tends to see only one part of the pattern of interaction between them, namely how and why they are responding to their partner's unreasonable behaviour. Both partners' punctuations, however, can interlock, like the pieces of a jigsaw puzzle, to produce patterns of repetitive and self-fulfilling actions, such as a pattern of approach–avoidance in a couple. Over time each forms predictions, not only of each other's actions, but also of each other's thoughts, beliefs and feelings. Since they are likely to spend considerable time together, share similar experiences and communicate continually with each other, they come to form a web of mutual anticipations.

A common interactional cycle or pattern between partners is one of approach–withdrawal (Watzlawick *et al.* 1967; Gottman 1979). If one partner seems to be becoming too distant for the other and for the relationship then the other may make an attempt to become closer again. Similarly if they are becoming 'too close' then one or the other may attempt to distance themselves. The balance between closeness and separation is likely to be idiosyncratic to the couple. Theoretically either partner may make attempts to keep an acceptable balance between 'closeness ' and 'separateness', according to systems theory. It is implicit in systems theory that such patterns may be driven by unconscious needs and anxieties similar to the account of the ambivalent needs for dependency and autonomy resulting from anxieties at the oral stage described by object relations theorists. The couple's explanations might include popular psychodynamic perspectives; for example, the woman might say, 'You are scared of getting too close because your mother rejected you'. Likewise the man may believe that she is too clingy because of her own family history. In effect each blames the other and justifies their own position in some way leading to maintenance of the cycle. It is much more difficult for a couple to see how, despite their protestations, they may both be mutually contributing to the maintenance of such a pattern by their current actions and communications.

Systems theory and power

Causality is seen to be circular not linear, so that one partner is not simply seen as causing the other's behaviour but that a pattern of action emerges out of the flux of action and communication between them. Each partner is seen as both stimulating and responding to the other in a continual cycle: what A says or does at a particular moment depends on what A and B have said or done previously and what A thinks B will do or say next or in the future:

> Unilateral relations between the parts are contradicted by the prin-
> ciple of wholeness. It is not possible to say that A causes B's behavi-
> our (unilateral control) but not vice versa, because to assert that A
> causes B's behaviour is to ignore the effect of B's behaviour on A's
> subsequent (and initial) reaction, each is the cause and stimulus for
> the other's communicative behaviour.
>
> (Hall and Fagan 1956: 1)

This implies that both partners invariably have equal influence and power to control each other's actions. However, this becomes a tenuous position in relation to abuse and violence in relationships or less dramatically where one partner clearly has more resources and the other is extremely dependent. As will be discussed in the next chapter some sources of power, especially financial and material, may be more influential in the relationship than others. Power may also be involved in the interpretations given to their own and the other's behaviour; arguably most interpretations, explanations and construings are male ones simply because their beliefs, their construings, even their 'psychological' explanations have more influence in the wider society than have women's (Spender 1980). From a feminist perspective the interaction is not simply idiosyncratic but an interaction between two unequal partners and, it could be argued, often functions to maintain a balance or homeostasis of inequality.

Similarly Haley (1976) has suggested that relationships inevitably involve power struggles, not simply in terms of who can get whom to do what but in terms of 'defining the relationship'. He suggests that a couple have to decide what behaviour is acceptable or unacceptable, negotiate behavioural rules, 'draw the line' around what is or is not to take place in the relationship. In effect all their actions are seen as communications which carry either explicitly or implicitly a number of potential messages about how they want the relationship to be and how they see each other:

DEIDRE   I was getting anxiety attacks every time he went away. I knew there was something wrong and even thinking about it was making me panicky.

STUART   There are particular problems because I like to go away and you don't want me to . . . I need the excuse now . . . whereas I used to go away more often for leisure . . . I feel I've repressed it. Deidre would say I've got a lot of free time, we both do. I feel terribly guilty, increasingly do less and less . . . would like to do it with the good will of the other, but nearly always it's a loaded situation . . .

DEIDRE   You always seemed worked up about it. I don't understand why, 'cos you've always done quite a lot of stuff really.

For Deidre and Stuart there is apparently a conflict about what the relationship should be like revolving around the construct 'close vs independent'. Each appears to wish that the other would accept their definition: Deidre appears to find it hard to see why Stuart needs to get away 'so much' and he finds it hard to see why she needs to be so close and 'panicky' about him being away. Their beliefs and feelings are also expressed in terms of bodily experiences and symptoms, for example Deidre having an anxiety attack when Stuart went away and Stuart feeling guilty. In effect their emotional states, Deidre's anxiety and Stuart's getting 'worked up' also function as communications and responses to each other's message that the other wants them and the relationship to be different.

Symptomatic behaviour and power

Frequently, as in Stuart and Deidre's case, attempts are made, usually by the more powerful partner, to define the other as having the problem, being ill, wrong – in short starting to pathologize the other. This ran through Deidre and Stuart's discussion, but not only did Stuart suggest that Deidre had 'problems' but she also repeatedly accused herself and absorbed all of the problems. This is not to say that symptomatic behaviour is inevitable but that pathologizing processes frequently occur and are related to inequalities of power. Haley (1976) and Madanes (1981) suggest that symptomatic behaviour can develop as an attempt to balance power in the relationship. This would seem to be most likely to occur if there is a great disparity in terms of power between the partners and if the couple cannot achieve an acceptable balance through any other means. Johnson (1976) and Komter (1989) suggest that the use of covert strategies is usually associated with relative powerlessness and therefore usually used by women (as in Deidre's case above) rather than men. This would imply that symptomatic behaviour is more likely to develop in women as they tend to have less power in the relationship than men and because they are more likely to have learnt to use covert strategies.

Hierarchical incongruity

Madanes (1981) has argued that in a couple the symptomatic spouse is in an inferior position because she is ill and needs to be helped; while the non-symptomatic spouse is in a superior position because he is well and does not need help. On the other hand, the symptomatic spouse is in a superior position because she can make her partner 'fail' at getting her better and can exert control over him through the inconvenience caused by her symptom. If the symptom is 'treated ' successfully then both lose power; the sympto-matic partner loses the power of the symptom and the non-symptomatic partner loses the power of being well. They are 'caught in an interaction which simultaneously defines their power and weakness in relation to each other; neither of them really wants the symptom to be 'cured' as they would both lose 'power' (Madanes 1981). If the symptom improves, both spouses stand to lose power in relation to each other, since equality is maintained by simultaneously defining both of them as inferior and superior to each other.

This implies that the symptom gives the symptomatic partner *equal* power, as both partners are equally inferior and equally superior. Both Haley (1976) and Madanes (1981) suggest that a symptom can almost totally 'organize' the non-symptomatic spouse's life, since the symptom can control whether, and with whom, the couple socialize; his/her freedom of movement away from, or towards, the symptomatic spouse; and decisions about work, promotion, moving house and who should take responsibility for the chil-dren and domestic needs. A symptom can be extremely powerful and influ-ential, especially since it is usually also defined as 'out of control'. The non-symptomatic spouse's behaviour is restricted, but since the symptom is 'out of control' he/she cannot really complain or blame the other without appearing to be bad or heartless. On the other hand, the non-symptomatic partner may become angry or very insensitive to feelings of guilt and may still complain and blame by believing, or pretending to believe, that the symptom does not really exist. Factors such as the partner's own childhood experiences may also be influential, with a repetition of patterns of feeling and behaving learned from his/her own family.

However, the idea of a symptom as functioning to gain power in a relation-ship resonates with accusations of blame, malingering or deliberately getting back at the other that some couples articulate. Consequently it is usually important that a symptom is labelled or given some external legitimacy, for example by a doctor as an 'illness'. However, systems theory does not imply that a symptom is in any sense a deliberate strategy and therapeutic work usually treads a fine line in not suggesting that this is the case. Instead, recourse to a symptom is regarded as a last, usually unconscious, resort by the relatively powerless partner in a relationship. Theoretically, it would be possible for the non-symptomatic partner to take steps to empower his/her partner. However, this may be the very issue that caused the symptom initially; i.e. the fact that the symptomatic partner is less powerful and that the non-symptomatic partner has refused to allow him/her to become empowered, or to 'give up' some of his/her own power so as to make the relationship more equal through fear of the consequences.

A problem with Madanes' (1981) proposition, and with systems theory more generally, is that it is more interested in pragmatic interventions to produce some change in the symptoms than in aetiology – e.g. why a couple are in conflict in the first place, why they could not correct the balance by some other means and how this is related to their relative power bases. This might suggest that, following systemic interventions, the fundamental power imbalance might reassert itself, leading to a return of symptoms. However, this does not inevitably seem to be the case and it is possible that at least some reconstruction of the internal power dynamics can occur due to therapy, even when change in the externally determined power differences are less obvious.

Symptoms as protecting the relationship

Fundamental to early systems theory formulations was the idea that symptoms operate to cover up unresolvable conflicts of power (Madanes 1981). Symptoms were seen to protect a couple from having to acknowledge conflict in their relationship and this may be important, especially if they hold a belief that marriage should be harmonious and romantic. Instead, they can maintain a 'myth' that things are satisfactory apart from the symptoms. This in fact resembles psychodynamic ideas of unconscious defence mechanisms, only here the myth is not just an individual process of denial but a shared or joint process so that both partners' unconscious needs are met. If the symptom is removed, the conflicts may be revealed again. If their inequality is overtly acknowledged, the more powerless partner will have to accept or resign herself to the fact of her subordination, or alternatively might have to accept that her position is intolerable and take steps to dissolve the relationship. If the former is the case, the relationship is unlikely to be satisfactory, since the more powerless partner will inevitably be resentful and is likely to try to gain power by other covert means, even if she is not symptomatic any more. Neither may wish for the latter.

Symptoms, sex and society

There appears to be some evidence to suggest that some symptoms are linked to gender, for instance, women are more likely than men to be inorgasmic and lose interest in sex. It seems likely that while there may be various 'causes' of sexual problems, one of the contributing factors may be wider societal discourses and images of men as more in 'need' of sex. The form of the symptom therefore may be linked to individual factors, but also to inter-personal factors and to wider societal factors. It may be that the form of the symptom is related to what symptom actually works in terms of balancing power in the relationship and what is acceptable in society. For some couples there have been other symptoms in the past but for some reason they have often gone almost unnoticed and have not been very influential. It may be that the 'choice' of symptom is related to the other's reaction, for instance one of the women in our clinical studies had been depressed in the past, but her husband did not seem to be particularly affected by this; however, when she developed a sexual 'symptom' he began to get worried and indeed, for the first time, was willing to come for 'therapy'. The sexual symptom 'worked' in a way that depression had not, perhaps because depression is widely regarded as common – almost 'normal' – in women, but complete sexual disinterest as 'abnormal' and demeaning to a man.

A sexual symptom may therefore be related to discourses and beliefs about sexuality and to structural differences in power between the genders. Men have tended to have more and different power than women for many centuries. One of the main female power bases has been their sexuality. The historian Stone (1977) suggests that female premarital chastity has 'long been a bargaining chip in the marriage market' and that men and women have bargained with 'different goods ... one social and economic ... the other sexual ... the withholding of sexual favours in women was the only source of power over men' (Stone 1977). Prostitutes have earned and still do, despite the so-called 'sexual liberation', earn their living by selling sexuality. Many women in the past have refused to engage in sex until the man married them in an attempt to ensure his commitment and some financial security. Offering and conversely withholding sex has historically been one of the major forms of power that many women possessed in relation to men. In fact in many societies virginity is still regarded as an essential requirement for a bride and women who have transgressed lose much if not all of their marriage potential.

It seems therefore quite likely that women, if they are relatively powerless in their relationship, will virtually have no choice but to 'use' their sexuality in an attempt to gain power. This can take various forms, for example being somewhat uninterested, complying but not enjoying it, complaining after-wards, making no effort to be attractive to the partner and so on. There is in fact likely to be a period of gradual or rapid escalation from such 'signs' of resistance and unhappiness with the relationships to all-out sexual with-drawal. What is important, though, is why this should take the form of a 'symptom' instead of being an overt, direct and open strategy? For instance, a wife could simply say, quite openly, that if her husband does or does not 'do' whatever she wants then she is simply not going to allow him access to her body. This directness seems to be a very rare occurrence and is probably linked to several factors; she may have learnt not to use direct strategies, or possibly she is not 'allowed' to be direct in the relationship itself, or it may not be seen to be 'legitimate' for her to 'use' sexuality so overtly. Traditionally, sex was seen as part of a wife's duty but more recently it is seen as something she should enjoy and if she does not then there is something wrong with either her or her partner. Within the traditional view sexual withdrawal was viewed as the woman not fulfilling her duty or punishing her husband. Within more modern views there is something wrong with her or she is abnormal. Either way this encourages the possibility of a covert response – a sexual symptom.

SUMMARY

In this chapter we have outlined some influential psychological theories of relationships. Though differing in their assumptions the theories tend to share the view that problems in relationships can be explained in terms of individual or relationship factors. Our suggestion is that the question is not so much which of these theories is more 'true' in any scientific sense (though this is important) but how these theories can also be seen to have a function as forms of popular psychology or psychological discourses. These situate problems at the personal and relationship level and thereby minimize the attention paid to societal factors such as material and ideological inequalities. In part we are suggesting that psychological theories to an extent derive from and support patriarchal ideologies which obscure such gender-based inequalities (Williams and Watson 1988). Psychology itself has been accused of effectively ignoring women's views and their relative position of powerlessness (Gilligan 1982) and of disconnecting subjective experience from the wider social context (Henriques *et al.* 1984). In subsequent chapters we will be exploring how material and ideological inequalities shape the experience, actions, feelings and beliefs of couples and how common relationship and sexual patterns derive from these.

3

Power bases and the social position of women

The difficulties of defining power have bedevilled research on its effects in relationships. As we have seen in Chapter 1, power can be seen not simply as influencing people's actions, thoughts and feelings but also what they do not do, what is made invisible. Power also functions at various levels so that the power that partners in a relationship exert over each other is not simply a personal or relationship matter. Men and women's positions of power respective to each other are, at least partly determined by their membership in the wider society. However, a useful starting point that has been adopted by some researchers is to examine what potential sources of power each partner possesses. How these sources or 'power bases' are employed is a complex issue, as we will see in the following chapter. However, it can be argued that the sources of power that each partner has available may shape and constrain the ways in which they attempt to influence each other.

One of the most influential attempts to develop a taxonomy of types of power was developed by French and Raven (1959). They proposed that it is possible to classify the sources of power available into six suggested categories:

reward	the ability to offer a variety of rewards
coercion	the ability to compel or punish the other into compliance
expert	having superior knowledge or ability
informational	the ability to communicate effectively
legitimate	the power invested by law and custom
referent	partner's status relative to each other.

This provides a starting point but some of the categories are very wide and general; for example, 'reward' can include the ability to offer a variety of material rewards, such as money, and also more relational and emotional ones, such as warmth, support, sexual attraction and so on. It is helpful therefore to distinguish two types of resources: objective vs relative power bases.

Essentially objective resources can be seen as all those which are readily and objectively apparent, for example, money, possessions, qualifications and so on. Relative resources, however, derive their power from the relationship itself, for example if one partner finds the other more attractive or values some aspect of their personality. There is some overlap between objective and relative power bases since, for example, attractiveness is subject to social norms as well as being a personal matter.

There are potentially a variety of ways that it is possible to categorize resources. It is also the case that these may mean different things to different couples, and it is not possible to predict the form of a relationship simply from an assessment of the differences in the profiles of resources that the partners possess. However, we suggest that to ignore the potential influence of disparities of their power bases is to ignore a fundamental factor which influences the relationship. Moreover, as we will discuss in Chapter 6, to do so may also collude with a common form of distortion, or false consciousness, which proposes that differences in these resources are not important, or that 'true love conquers all'. In fact we argue that it is most frequently the person who has most objective resources who is more likely to argue that these are 'not so important' rather than the subordinate partner who is more aware, for example, of their financial dependence.

Williams and Watson (1988) suggest that the dimension of objective vs relative captures some of the critical differences between men and women. In general they argue that men possess a variety of objective power bases and women in contrast possess relative power bases. In order to clarify this distinction they offer a more elaborated classification of power bases. They also suggest that there is generally a different profile of these power bases for men and women:

Women	Men
domestic	economic
affective	ascribed
relational	physical
reproductive	contractual
sexual	informational
	language

(Williams and Watson 1988: 303)

This distinguishes between different types of reward power and also helps to draw attention to the possibility that economic and emotional rewards may not simply be of equivalent importance. Men, they argue, tend to have more economic, informational, physical, ascribed, language and contractual power than women, who tend in contrast to have more relational, sexual, domestic, affective and reproductive power. The possibility that men and women have differing profiles of power bases implies that they are likely to attempt to influence each other in different ways. Obviously if one partner's physical power is minimal in comparison to her partner she is unlikely to employ this to influence her partner. It is also possible that these different sources of power are not simply equivalent, for example, as suggested above, women appear to have five power bases as opposed to six for men. But it may be that these are far from equal, for example, economic and physical power may be substantially more potent than any that women may possess:

> How are these power bases evident in negotiations and conflict? At what point does money talk? When are the children brought in as relational power? Is violence a 'covert veto'? What does it mean for a family that one person may be able to 'leave the field' because of his or her direct access to money? . . . These are some of the questions we should find ourselves thinking about if we are seriously concerned to see family problems and distress in the context of sexual inequality.
>
> (Williams and Watson 1988: 306)

In the next chapter we take up some of these questions and will offer some evidence about how the different power bases determine the ways that couples influence each other.

We have adopted Williams and Watson's (1988) taxonomy but have offered some elaborations. In particular we have expanded the language and affective/emotional categories and have incorporated a further category of *legal* power, which is similar to French and Raven's *legitimate* power. Language/communication power was subdivided into 'public informational', 'emotional informational', 'logical communicational' and 'emotional communicational' power bases. This latter subdivision was felt to be necessary in order to attempt to capture the distinction between various kinds of information and kinds of communication.

Three categories not widely discussed in the literature emerged in our study. Our interviewees mentioned types of power which could be categorized as 'social', 'coping' and educational. Social power was seen as an ability to get on with others, feel at ease socially, be relaxed in company and socially skilled. Coping power was the extent to which partners were self-sufficient in various ways, could manage by themselves. In a sense it was a combination of domestic, informational and other skills and related to the extent to which partners were seen to be dependent upon the relationships. Educational power was the extent of educational attainment, status, knowledge and skills of literacy, science and so on. It related to informational and language power. Finally, though not strongly articulated, there also appeared to be a power base related to class. This could perhaps be seen as a subsection of ascribed/legitimate power and conferred a sense of status, expectation of respect and subservience, for example defined by accent and lifestyle.

The following is our revised taxonomy, which has been developed as part of our research. We are not suggesting that any definitive system is possible but instead that recognition of the types of power base can help to draw attention to areas of inequality in relationships. Each category is briefly described and accompanied by illustrative extracts from the accounts of people who took part in an interview-based study which we have conducted (further details of this are given in Chapters 4 and 6).

ECONOMIC POWER

Many studies have revealed economic imbalances in families and relationships in favour of men. Men tend to earn more than women even when the women are in paid employment outside of the home. Furthermore, women's earnings may be partially or totally depleted by childcare costs such that for a woman who has young children going out to work may actually cost her family more (French and Raven 1959; Williams and Watson 1988). According to Marx it is the main source of inequality between dominant and subordinate groups, from which most other power bases flow. Women who work outside the home tend to have more power in their intimate relationships than those who stay at home; for instance, they have more decision-making power (Blood and Wolfe 1960). Within French and Raven's taxonomy economic/financial power can be used as a reward or a coercive power base in the relationship. For instance, the partner holding this source of power can threaten to withhold money from the partner in order to influence them. They could also use it as a 'reward', as a 'bribe', perhaps, stereotypically, offering to buy the partner something they want.

As many women are unable to support themselves financially, especially if they have children, they often tend to be dependent upon their partners, or the state, for financial support. This dependence gives men more of this power base in many relationships. Studies of domestic violence in particular illustrate how women may be 'forced' to stay in these abusive relationships because they are unable to support themselves financially. Financial power is also related to 'shelter' power i.e. the capacity to pay for accommodation . . . women in abusive relationships may literally have 'nowhere to go' as they are unable to pay for accommodation. Even in 'normal' non-abusive relationships the mere fact that women are financially dependent may affect their capacity to influence the partner to the same extent as their partner can influence them.

To illustrate some of the effects of unequal financial power on intimate relationships we can turn to the responses to one of the research questions: what effect do you think having differences in financial power has on your relationship? These responses included, for the women, feeling guilty, feeling dependent, having low self-respect, feeling angry and resentful and having less negotiational power. They tended to feel guilty about not contributing financially, often feeling uncomfortable with spending money on themselves.

Even when a woman does earn there is a general tendency for the money in the man's pocket to be his while the money in her pocket is the household's – the 'housekeeping'.

Sometimes the men complained about their wives not contributing. One woman who was financially dependent described her unease about her dependency and her partner's complaints:

> It makes me feel totally dependent on him, I have no self-respect, I feel very angry about him complaining, someone's got to look after the kids, they are not at school yet, I've tried to get part-time work but I don't have any qualifications and all I earnt would be taken up by childminders, I envy my mother's generation in some ways, my father never complained about it.

She went on to describe how he uses his financial power:

> He uses it all the time to get at me, if I try to bring up various issues and he doesn't want to talk about them, especially if I ask him to do something or other he just says I earn all the money so why should I do that as well. He uses it as an excuse for all sorts of things . . . I have to be careful about rocking the boat.

Another woman describes similar effects:

> I talk to other women, who are working, unlike me, and it makes me very angry that they can do things, say things to their husbands, that I can't do or say because he threatens to withhold money . . . I know he treats me badly, controls me while doing just what he wants, and I can't complain about it and I know if I could support myself financially he just would not get away with it.

The effects of unequal financial power seem to be more easily perceived when there has been a change, for instance when the woman was financially dependent but now is not. Their behaviour often seems to change and they gain more power in the relationship:

> Before, I had five children and was very vulnerable, I avoided raising some issues because I was worried that he would stop giving me any money . . . he threatened it a couple of times and that was enough . . . he who pays the piper calls the tune . . . now I'm earning things have changed, I'm not so quiet about things I don't like now.

Other women similarly report that when they became more financially independent they also became more assertive, more independent, more confident and more able to 'argue back'. They also report that their partners often found this change quite difficult. However, women who have always been financially independent view it positively, not only for themselves but see benefits for their relationship:

It creates a feeling of equality in the relationship. I feel positive about making a financial contribution to the family and I feel independent at the same time, I feel confident about myself and it gives me the same status as my husband.

One of the major findings regarding the effects of financial power is the effect on sexuality in the relationship. As this is one of the main emphases of this book it will be covered in more detail in a separate chapter. Directly linked to financial power is 'shelter power', defined in the research study as 'being able to pay for accommodation oneself'. Women who do earn may also be dependent in this sense; not simply at risk of being turned out into the street, but being unable to walk out. Walking out may be more expensive for a woman than a man because she has to house not just herself but also the children (since women are usually expected to take primary responsibility for them).

Generally our interviewees did not say very much about this power base, presumably because of its link with financial power; however, one woman described how it was used in the relationship. She says that 'he threatens to turn me out onto the street', and that her response was to threaten back through her domestic power, though she does not say whether this affects him or not; 'I say well I won't clean "your" house as you call it'.

ASCRIBED POWER

French and Raven (1959) define this in terms of its being seen as legitimate, in that it is power that stems from the partners' mutual acceptance of a given role relationship; for example, partners believing that one of them has the right to request compliance in a particular area, and the other is obliged to comply, because the request is regarded as a legitimate part of their mutual roles. To some extent coercion and expert power bases overlap or are inter-related with this power base. For instance, a husband may believe that his wife knows more about childrearing then he does, so he would therefore accept her making decisions about the children as legitimate. On the other hand, he might not accept that it is legitimate for her to expect to be involved in making decisions about his job or career. While it is less likely to be accepted at the present time in Western culture, use of violence or other forms of coercion, usually on the man's part, might have been accepted as legitimate in the eighteenth century, at least in some sections of society. It might also have accepted as legitimate that a man had a right to demand and coerce his wife into sex, even by use of rape if she was sexually reluctant. Conversely it was usually, and perhaps still is to a large extent, widely expected that a man should support his wife and any children financially, and that it was legitimate for her to complain if he did not do so.

Clearly, legitimate power is intimately connected to social norms and discourses. It rests for its effectiveness on both partners mutually accepting that they each have rights and obligations to each other. However, as a result of historical and social changes what is regarded as legitimate also changes. For example, violence and physical coercion by men towards women is no longer regarded as legitimate. However, to some extent parental violence towards children, such as physical punishment, is condoned – smacking, though debated, is still perfectly legitimate if not abusive or carried to 'excess'. Similarly, with the erosion of Christian religious beliefs the notion that the man should naturally be the 'head of the household' has altered and many couples prefer to see themselves as equal partners, perhaps in charge of different areas of family life. Williams and Watson (1988) suggest that ascribed power, since it is not necessarily earned in any way but merely allocated because of, for example, being male, reflects the value system of dominant social groups. Another example is the hereditary power of royalty or of the aristocracy.

There may be changes in what is regarded as legitimate for each partner during the development of a relationship. For instance, if the wife starts to work, she may no longer accept that her husband has legitimate power to make decisions about money or moving home. He may stop accepting her making decisions about the children as legitimate if he looks after them as well. This is similar to French and Raven's *legitimate power base*. Although Williams and Watson (1988) suggest that ascribed power is mainly a male power base, it may be that more couples are rejecting ascribed power bases than they were previously. However, it is still predominantly the case that women who work outside the home will continually encounter male power – their bosses, supervisors, foremen, senior nursing officers, professors, captains, bishops, government ministers and so on are much more likely to be male. It is possible, though, that women may also become critical and sceptical about the abilities, competencies and the right of these men to power and as a result become less likely to accept male ascribed power unquestioningly (Miller 1976). Also, there may be more or less acceptance of male ascribed power in some areas of work and subculture than in others. The only couple who talked about ascribed power in the research study were Christians who subscribed to the idea that the husband was indeed the 'head of the household' and the woman accepted this saying that he made all the decisions, and that she was happy about this because of her faith.

INFORMATIONAL POWER

This is similar to French and Raven's *expert power base*. Either partner may have an expertise that the other does not and may gain power through it; one may be good at gardening, the other at something else. In terms of less idiosyncratic expertises women have generally tended to be seen as having domestic and childrearing expertise and men as being good at 'technical' or 'building' tasks. Williams and Watson (1988) suggest that the influence of these power bases will depend on 'the social value associated with the information or expertise that is held'. For instance, domestic or childrearing skills may be less highly valued and therefore less influential than 'men's expertises'. This attitude may be premised on the idea that such work is 'unskilled' because the skills do not have to be learned, they are somehow biologically inherent in women. It is worth bearing in mind the counter-proposition that such caring skills are in fact enormously complex and sophisticated: they are essentially 'human' skills and cannot be automated or replaced by computer-controlled systems.

In relationships partners may or may not be influenced by the other's expertises; often they do not even accept that the other is the expert. Individual men may accept that their wives have superior knowledge to theirs, for instance, about childrearing and this will then allow the woman to influence through this power base by saying that a particular decision, for instance moving house, would not be good for the children and so on. Women are generally thought to have more domestic expertise than men; they can use this, Williams and Watson suggest, by withdrawal of domestic services such as burning the dinner or leaving the house in a mess; however, a study by Komter (1989) suggests that this is usually ineffective. Men are generally encouraged to develop 'technical expertises', thus making women dependent on men to service the car or washing machine, put up shelves and so on. This can be turned against men, for example, a man might be accused by his wife of incompetence in these areas and therefore of not being a 'real' man. Men can also use women's dependence on them for their skills to 'get back' at their wives; for instance by deliberately doing a job incompetently.

There were several predominant responses by the participants in the research study relating to what were regarded as examples of expert power and the effect of these in the relationship. Having an expertise did often give the holder a degree of power in the relationship, on the other hand this was often seen as 'double edged', for example being seen as the expert at domestic tasks or technical tasks often meant that the holder ended up doing these tasks when they would have preferred not to. Many people said that they thought their different expertises to be positive as they created interdependence between themselves and their partners; however, this was not seen as positive when the other did not appreciate their partner's contribution.

Having an expertise can give the holder some degree of power, for instance some control and decision-making power over the house, such as how it should be decorated:

> She always had exactly what she wanted, decorating the house for example, mainly because I was quite willing to acknowledge my total

lack of expertise ... I did not have the confidence or self-belief to assert myself and say it does not matter if it's the most ghastly, jarring blend of colours; I would just acknowledge her superiority ... if you like ... her better taste and accede to what she wanted.

Similarly another man describes how his wife and himself have different expertises and how these can be used to influence each other:

> In certain circumstance my wife does dominate, especially the home environment, she makes the decisions there ... she chooses the decor of the house ... the decoration and style is hers but it's very similar to mine. The finer details, plastering ... are up to me ... and the order in which it's done is up to me ... so that's power for me ... I can withdraw my labour until I'm ready ... the heavy work is done by me ... though maybe that's because M has never done it ... maybe that's her ploy for avoiding doing it!

Another aspect of this 'double edged' aspect of expertise was that because they were seen to be the expert in a particular area, for example in child-rearing or domestic tasks, this often meant that they ended up doing these tasks exclusively when often they would have preferred them to be shared. Power was often reflected in being able to avoid doing things that neither of the partners really wanted to do. Komter's study (1989) suggests that women are often seen as having 'domestic expertise' which then allows the men to avoid doing much in the house because the women are 'better at it'. As one woman commented:

> To me he's very inconsistent ... like he's often there during the day when I'm at work and sometimes I'll come home and he's cooked a meal. Other times he'll say I did not know what you wanted so I did not bother and when he does cook something he tends to make a big thing of it ... play on it more ... if you dare to say anything's wrong with it or if you're not hungry ... one day I just wasn't hungry ... he got into such a mood over it, he can't see when the boot's on the other foot, he's done that any number of times ... a classic ... I 've done *your* washing up ... I couldn't believe it.

Even where a man may do a fair share of the shopping, cooking, etc. it is usually the woman who has the planning of it, plans the week's food and is responsible for keeping the fridge and freezer stocked and makes out the shopping lists. Often men, as in the quote above, see themselves as 'helping *her* in *her* work'.

Although having different areas of expertise was often seen as positive, for instance one man said, 'It brings a balance to the relationship, one complements the other ... a combination of skills provides a more varied relationship', this was not viewed so positively if the other did not appreciate or acknowledge the other's experience or input. There are several aspects to this; a strict division of labour may simply mean that the other does not realize what the task involves, does not understand the other's experience, for instance the man may not actually realize how tiring it can be looking after young children all day or the wife may not understand how stressful working outside the home may be:

> I went away for a few days ... the first time I'd been away since K was born; six years, he got a shock, realizing how much time looking after the house and K took up ... when I got back he told me he had not realized and for about a week he was really good ... did a lot ... didn't last long though.

Another aspect is that some tasks may be seen as more important than others, thus giving the other more power and influence through their particular expertise. Childrearing and domestic tasks are predictably often perceived as not being very difficult, not being very much of an expertise. This sometimes affects partners' perceptions of equity/reciprocal contributions to the relationship; their ideas of what is 'fair'. One woman interviewee, for instance, described how her husband complained about her not contributing as much to the relationship as he does, despite her doing all the childrearing and domestic tasks:

> He says that I don't do anything, that he works and brings in all the money, that he supports us all, that he contributes the most, he even calls me lazy because I'm so tired at the end of the day that I don't feel like doing anything much. Yet I *am* tired ... looking after the children, worrying about them ... he doesn't have to worry about them because I do it ... at the same time I feel guilty about being tired and find it very difficult to explain why to him ... he just dismisses what I say ... implies that there must be something wrong with me ... perhaps there *is* something wrong with me.

Women in our study generally carried out most of the childrearing tasks and it was felt that they could use their expertise to exert influence in making family decisions. However, this also appeared to lead to men feeling somewhat peripheral, the women ending up being far closer to the children than the fathers.

> I do about 75 per cent of the childcare and I have to go to work as well. The children want me ... it annoys him ... questions over their homework or something else they come to me not him, but then they might ask him and he's not interested so that's why they do that ... his power really ... when they were younger he would only bath them or read them a story occasionally ... now he says he would do it but they never ask him.

The closeness between the mother and children sometimes appeared to lead to the children being closely allied to the mother and against him:

> She took the mickey out of me in front of the children, they'd join in as well so there were three of them.

Early systems theory approaches to family therapy noted a pervasive pattern in families which was described as an interplay between a 'peripheral' father and 'over-involved' mother. The mother was in a sense seen as preventing her husband being in touch with the children and he in turn was seen to maintain this by his lack of involvement and withdrawal. James and McIntyre (1983) suggest that this failed to take into account that being in an alliance with the children is virtually inevitable if one parent does most of the childrearing. Rather than simply being 'pathological' such patterns are simply the reproduction of a form of family life made inevitable by women being bound to the childrearing role. Furthermore being in an alliance with the children may help to 'balance power' in the relationship since women generally have fewer objective power bases than men. This can, of course, go 'too far' if there is an imbalance that is not easily remediable through other means, to the point whereby the children are being 'used' or become over-involved in the power struggle between the parents. 'Using' the children is a common reaction during and after divorce. Although this may occur even if the man is being 'fair' in economic terms, it seems to be even more likely that women will 'use' the children in various ways, such as trying to prevent the father's access to the children if the man is being 'unfair', for example in withholding maintenance payments. Using the children in this way is frequently met with disapproval but the 'other side of the story' is often neglected; that if she does not 'use' the children a woman may find herself and her children to be financially impoverished (this in itself can also be detrimental to the children). Women are often in a no-win situation here since, for example, up to 50 per cent of the men in such circumstances withdraw completely and cease to have contact with their children after the divorce (Bradshaw and Millar 1991).

LANGUAGE POWER

There are several aspects to this power base; on the one hand there is the literal meaning of 'language power' perhaps better described as 'communicational' power, whereby one partner is more articulate, better at persuading through verbal argument, more able to put over their opinions than the other and so on. Scanzoni (1979b), for instance, suggests that one partner may be a 'better communicator' than the other because they have had more practice. This might imply that men have more of this communicational power because they are more likely than women to be working outside the home and therefore liable to have more practice in putting across their opinions, negotiating, etc. However, this may depend on what their occupation actually is, some requiring 'better communication' than others.

Communication and language are not synonymous: communication includes language but also includes non-verbal behaviour and emotional expression. Men and women, as we saw in Chapter 2, are to some extent socialized into adopting different communicational styles, men typically being more prone to verbal/rational forms and women to communicate non-verbally or 'emotionally'. Non-verbal and emotional communication may be just as influential in the relationship as 'rational argument'. Noller and Gallois (1986) suggest that women are much better than men at 'reading' the likely effect of their communication on the other. Women give accurate non-verbal signals, such as smiling when they are pleased and frowning when displeased, and are accurate at 'reading' the non-verbal messages of men. Men, however, do not give accurate non-verbal messages, so they may frown when they are pleased as well as when they are displeased, for instance, and they are not as accurate as women at reading women's non-verbal signals. Miller (1976) suggests that most subordinate individuals/groups have to learn to 'read' the other well, whereas more dominant individuals or groups do not have to know much about subordinates (Miller 1976). Women may be better at communicating because they are unequal, since they may have more to lose if they 'get it wrong', such as being physically attacked. However, studies of who actually 'wins' arguments suggest that in communicational exchanges between men and women, men 'win', although it is not quite clear how they manage to do so (Howard *et al.* 1980). Men, however, are less likely to win arguments if the woman works outside the home, perhaps because the woman becomes more skilled at adopting verbal/rational argument, perhaps also because she is likely to be more assertive or perhaps because she is simply seen as more rational than a woman who does not work outside the home. In order to explore this component of language power the research study employed two categories; emotional communicational power, i.e. being able to persuade through the use of emotional argument; and rational communicational power, i.e. being able to persuade through the use of rational, verbal argument.

The content of the communication may also have an effect. In the initial study by Blood and Wolfe (1960) couples were asked who made the final decision in various areas. First, in 'male' areas they were asked to indicate who decided what job the husband should take and what car to buy; second, in 'female' areas, who decided whether the wife should work or give up work, which doctor to use and how much money they should spend on food per week; and third, in 'joint' areas, who decided whether to get life insurance, where to go on holiday and what house to buy. It was found that the husband always made the decision in his 'own' areas; for example, the husband's job was decided by the husband 90 per cent of the time; while the wife only always made the decision about her job 39 per cent of the time. The only issue that wives decided about that came near half the time was about food (41 per cent). These studies seem to show that if a wife tries to persuade her husband about something he perceives as his own area, he is unlikely to be persuaded, however 'good' a communicator his wife is. A husband, on the other hand, seemed more able to persuade his wife about 'her' area.

If men and women have learnt to communicate in different modes, this in itself may create problems in relationships. This may be further compounded by another aspect of 'language power'; that is, that men have generally had and still have, though perhaps to a slightly lesser extent, 'ideological' power. As suggested throughout this book men's beliefs, opinions, attitudes, 'discourses', 'narratives', 'explanations' have been predominant for centuries. The language and concepts prevalent in our culture are male (Spender 1980). When women challenge male dominance they may be forced to use language, concepts, modes which they have not learnt to use as effectively as men and which, it could be argued, often do not accurately reflect their experience. One example of this is the patriarchal tendency to dichotomize, for example to propagate the belief that women are emotional and non-rational, incapable of rational argument. This may mean that when partners are in disagreement, or even simply discussing an issue, what the woman says is not seen as rational even when, objectively, it is, and similarly what the man says is seen as rational when, objectively, it is not. There may also be an element of a 'self-fulfilling prophecy', for instance the woman is perceived as being emotional and non-rational, this perception is frustrating for her and she may become emotional. As she becomes more emotional he may become even more rational or alternatively he may become emotional himself, the discussion may deteriorate, often into predictable stereotypical mutual accusations, and the issue is not resolved. In order to explore this component of language power for research purposes two categories were employed: one was public informational, i.e. knowledge about work situations, career prospects, how to get on in the outside world, politics, economics, etc. This was an attempt to look more directly at 'ideological power'. One interviewee comments:

> I get pole-axed when it comes to current affairs, although I have the time to read the paper and he does not and he often makes dogmatic statements.

The second category was defined as 'emotional informational': knowing more than the partner about what is going on emotionally in the family, with friends and neighbours and how to help them. For instance:

> How many men can sit down and relate to a mother or a child in some deep emotional problem they've got, they say . . . oh it will be all right

... they don't seem to be able to listen or relate to someone ... my
daughter crying on the phone ... here you talk to her ... can we send
her some money or something.

Invalidational power

Linked to language power is invalidational power. This includes the capacity
to influence the other by dismissing their opinions, arguments, 'put them
down' and generally invalidate them, for instance, by attacking their 'personality' and so on. Couples often know exactly what to say to 'upset' their
partners, know each other's 'weak spots' and in serious arguments may use
them; knowing that their partners will feel invalidated, for example:

> J's trump card is you are being selfish ... which is something that is
> horrible to me ... though it does not work so well now ... before if
> someone said I was being selfish ... I would think 'Oh God perhaps
> I am' and I wouldn't do it.

Whilst there is obviously a high degree of idiosyncracy as to what partners
may experience as invalidating, there may also be an element of gender specific 'put downs' such as 'You are not much of a man, are you' or 'You are
a bit butch and unfeminine'. In the following extract a woman describes how
a perfectly reasonable reaction to her husband being financially irresponsible
is turned round to be an invalidation of herself instead, along predictably
'gender specific' lines:

> If I got upset about something from the courts or the bailiffs or some-
> thing about an unpaid bill that he'd hidden from me then I was being
> unreasonable and neurotic and I actually believed for quite a while
> that I was neurotic and I over-reacted and that it was him who was
> really calm and laid back.

Reactions to invalidation to some extent depend on how the person feels
about themselves, i.e. their level of self-esteem plus the extent to which they
have alternative sources of validation. Many theorists have found that women
have far lower self-esteem than men in general, such as Komter (1989). Therefore, theoretically men have more of this power base than women. There
may be many potential sources through which we can feel esteemed and
respected. Because of gender dichotomization, however, it has generally been
men who are esteemed and respected more than women, as women's constructed 'traits' and abilities are less highly esteemed than men's. Women,
especially if they stay at home, may be more dependent on their husbands
to boost their self-esteem than vice versa. Men have more sources through
which they might be esteemed and respected, perhaps partially for the simple
reason that they are men and partially because they live in the public world.

> We both put each other down in a row but it doesn't seem to affect him as much as it does me . . . water off a duck's back, really . . . He just goes to work or out with his friends and feels better about himself whereas I stay at home with the children and brood on it . . . wondering if he is right and I am how he says I am.

Work and friendships may, as suggested above, function to encourage the man's belief that he is competent and in control.

PHYSICAL POWER

There are two main elements to this. One, as indicated above, is that men tend to do the 'heavy work' because they tend to be physically stronger; the other is the potential for men to abuse their physical strength by using physical violence to influence and control their wives. Regarding the former this has been briefly illustrated above by the male interviewee who says that he does the 'heavy work' and how he can, if he so wishes, do it slowly, etc. in order to influence his wife. Regarding the abuse of physical power, the subject of 'domestic violence' has been documented in detail by many studies so will not be analysed in detail here (Dobash and Dobash 1992). It is related to 'ideological power' and to 'legitimate' and legal power. Many studies suggest that violence towards wives has, though hopefully to a lesser extent currently, been seen as legitimate and justifiable if the wife does not comply with her husband's wishes, is 'mouthy', or does not fulfil her 'role'; for instance, not having his dinner ready or not keeping the house clean and tidy, being sexually reluctant or 'flirting' with other men. The police are notoriously reluctant to become involved in 'private/domestic' disputes. Similarly violence has often been seen, not as a deliberate attempt to control but as an 'uncontrollable' reaction to frustration:

> One thing I notice that I go through everytime I hit her is my intense need for her . . . When things get to the point that I need her a lot and I can't get her, I want her. I want her, that's it. I want her love, I want her attention, and I'll get it. I'll get it no matter what.
>
> (Goldner *et al.* 1990: 361)

This may interlock with perceptions of women's roles in relationships: that they should not only control their own but should also control the man's behaviour because they are unable to control it themselves. Women are in a sense required to 'police' the family, though typically without the power to do so (Donzelot 1980). More broadly this is contained in the idea that woman's role is that she should cater for her family's emotional needs: women as mothers (to their husbands), women as 'therapists', and the belief that it is up to them to keep things harmonious. Violence may be seen as her fault not his, because she has provoked him in some way, or failed to fulfil her role as wife, mother, 'therapist'.

Physical power and its abuse is obviously one of the most influential power bases for men in general. In intimate relationships also, women may live their lives in fear, be too scared to do or say things in the relationship that they wish to say. Indeed they may be oppressed, controlled, exploited in the relationship and structural factors along with ideology may make it very difficult for them to escape the relationship or to prevent the violence occurring. Many women in the research study were not even aware of their legal rights in relation to violence from their husbands, perhaps because they had not been subjected to abuse so had not needed to find out more about it, but, perhaps more insidiously, because it is not the kind of information that most people are aware of, an example of subjugated or peripheral 'knowledges'.

CONTRACTUAL POWER

Contractual power is defined as 'the ability to leave the relational field – to 'contract out'. This could take the form of threatening to leave, threatening divorce or refusing to listen or talk to the other. Theoretically it is men who are likely to have more of this power base, as it is more difficult for women to leave easily, to contract out of the relationship and support themselves financially. This is borne out by research which indicates that women's economic well-being had fallen by 73 per cent one year following divorce. Men's in contrast had risen by 42 per cent (Goldner 1985). Contracting out can also be seen as refusing to talk or listen – a sort of 'take it or leave it' approach in which leaving the relationship may be more an implicit, ultimate threat. It is often the women who wish to talk, because they wish for changes, renegotiations in the relationship, particularly in terms of sorting out a fair arrangement for sharing domestic tasks (Komter 1989). Contracting out of talking about an issue implies that it will not be resolved because it has not been discussed, and so the status quo will therefore prevail. Komter (1989) comments that the husbands in her study were more likely to ignore their wives than vice versa – 'I don't want to hear it and then I don't hear it'.

It might be more difficult for men to contract out of sex, however, if they believe in the male sexual drive discourse (the belief that men cannot do without sex; discourses on sexuality will be covered in greater detail in a later chapter). Women may contract out of this to a greater extent if they believe that they need sex less than men. On the other hand if the women do contract out, the men may believe that it is illegitimate for women to do so, i.e. men believe that they have legitimate power to insist on sex with their wife. A wife may then contract out of sex in a covert way. Evidence suggests that it is unlikely that men will contract out of sex in their intimate relationships, even covertly (Foreman 1996).

RELATIONAL POWER

This is concerned with 'connectedness with significant others', either within or outside families. Friendship alliances, especially gender alliances and family alliances, can increase power in negotiations and bargaining. Women can gain relational power through alliances with their children in particular through the 'different but equal' discourse, which puts women in the role of the one responsible for nurturing and childrearing. Women may gain affiliation/relational power through belonging to a women's group especially if it is a feminist women's group (Gillespie 1971). Women who live near their (especially female) kin may have more power in the intimate relationship than do women who do not live near their kin. They can often get emotional or practical help from their kin thus rendering them less dependent on their husbands. Although men may have less relational power than women in terms of 'alliance' with the children it could also be argued that 'male bonding', for example meeting other men 'down the pub' or even more formal institutions such as men's clubs, is one avenue through which men maintain their dominant positions and reconfirm their patriarchal beliefs and ideologies. As one female interviewee commented, 'He has alcohol and the pub, I have my women's group'.

AFFECTIVE POWER

This could also be described as 'emotional power'. There are several main strands to this; first, a difference between partners in terms of who 'loves' the other the most; second, a difference in terms of who 'needs' the other the most emotionally; third, the capacity to meet others' emotional needs. The first may be relatively gender free; in any relationship one partner may 'love' the other more than vice versa; this may allow for the one 'who loves the least' to use this to influence the other; for instance by 'withdrawing affection', threatening to leave or divorce. These threats can be very influential:

> I love and need her more than she does me . . . I'm careful not to rock the boat too much in case she leaves me . . . I would miss her so much . . . I don't think I could cope without her.

> He's got so much power because I've been in love with him for as long as I can remember . . . I'm absolutely daft about him.

Although this is likely to be idiosyncratic to a particular couple, inequality may affect the perception of who loves the other the most; for instance it may appear that the man must love the woman because he does not have to stay in the relationship, whereas a financially dependent woman may be staying in the relationship not because she necessarily loves the man but because she is unable to support herself financially. The question of who 'needs' the other the most could be thought of as a general emotional dependence on the other, for instance preferring to be with the other, do things with them rather than do things on their own, being more upset about being separated, not being able to 'cope very well' on their own and needing emotional support:

> I need him far more than he does me . . . I need lots of reassurance which I don't usually get . . . I find it difficult to cope with the amount of time he is out of the house.

This sense of 'needing' is contained both within the psychodynamic and learning theory models (discussed in Chapter 2): the nature of early dependency, attachment and separateness from the mother and different patterns of gender socialization.

Being emotionally vulnerable and dependent can give the other partner power in the relationship. The other can influence in French and Raven's (1959) terms, reward is gained through satisfying one's emotional needs to feel competent and independent and simultaneously through rejecting and punishing the other, for example by 'putting them down' for being 'dependent' and 'weak'. Not to appear to be emotionally vulnerable is therefore to have more power, and, it might be argued, this is partially how men maintain their positions of dominance and why they are taught to be independent. Potentially, then, men are likely to have more emotional power than women.

However, whilst it appears to give men more emotional power and women less in that women are encouraged to be dependent and men to be independent there is also the assumption, based mainly in psychodynamic theory, that men, as well as women, do have emotional needs but that men are simply denying this. One effect of this is that men may appear to be independent, in effect are really quite dependent, but are unable to articulate this clearly. This can lead to a perception of men, 'really, underneath', being emotionally dependent despite, ostensibly, being emotionally independent. This may make it quite difficult for women to satisfy the man's emotional needs as they have to do it without it actually being acknowledged. Another effect may be that various behaviours on the man's part, which objectively might be described as 'controlling', are perceived as being related to his emotional 'blockages' or difficulties in expressing what his emotional needs are. It could be argued that men are often perceived in almost a 'pathological' light, as having underlying problems with emotionality, as 'needy children'. Women may therefore 'take pity' on men and tolerate all kinds of behaviours, including severe abuses of power such as physical violence, because they perceive the man to be vulnerable even though he is presenting himself as non-vulnerable. Women in our research study often saw their partners as rather like 'children' and thus were put in a position whereby they were having to be 'their mummies'. The effect of this on sexuality will be discussed later.

> Emotionally I think he's damaged from his childhood . . . he wants someone there . . . his mummy . . . someone he can rebel against and tell what to do . . . I'm not his mummy and I won't be his mummy.

> I think he's chopped off emotionally . . . I think he's had it so much from his mother he's just switched off . . . all stuffed down . . . he used to go out drinking when the children were younger, I used to moan and carry on and then I realized that was what he wanted . . . like a punishment sort of thing, they expect to come home and be told off . . . a naughty boy who gets punished and then everything is Ok . . . a mother–son sort of thing . . . if you don't tell me off I'm not being cared for.

> In terms of an emotional thing I think women are often more self-sufficient and blokes are more emotionally needy so they need the support, the confidence of knowing that there's at least one person in the world who loves them enough to go to bed with them . . . makes them feel more secure and confident.

An interactional effect might be that the man (usually) is attempting to be independent, separate, do things on his own and the woman is attempting to be 'closer', do things together. This interactional cycle does appear to be very common, gender specific and problematic, and, as will be suggested in later chapters, associated with female sexual 'reluctance'. For example:

> In the first years of our relationship I was very dependent on P, but he was always saying to me . . . almost . . . get off my back sort of thing . . . go and do something on your own . . . I felt very rejected. I wanted to be close, to be with him, but he always seemed to want to be off on his own . . . I cut off in the end, I suppose, and now he seems to need me more than I need him.

The 'ability to satisfy the other's emotional needs' has traditionally been thought of as something that women are more able to do than men. Women are thought to have fewer problems with others' emotionality, to be comfortable with their own and others' expressions of emotionality, to be aware of emotional needs, to be nurturant and so on. They may be more able than men to express their emotionality and are more able to have (female) friends who are supportive. They may gain power in the relationship through their 'skills' in this area, be the 'emotional experts'; articulating what they believe others' needs to be, able to satisfy the others' needs; make them 'happy and secure' and so on. On the other hand this may be a 'double edged' kind of power; as mentioned above men may be denying they have any emotional needs so that the woman's attempts to satisfy their needs might not be acknowledged or appreciated. At the same time it might be that women do not get their emotional needs met by their partners (Lerner 1983). Indeed Hite (1981) suggests it is a common complaint among women that the men are not emotionally supportive:

WANDA   I wish he were more romantic, a new man, more feminine and understanding, more caring, talking about emotions and all that.

RESEARCHER   Do you try to get him to talk about these kinds of things?

WANDA   Yes, we have these conversations for a little while, then he's had enough ... let's talk about something else.

(Foreman 1996)

SEXUAL POWER

This will be covered in more detail in later chapters, especially 4, 7 and 8.

REPRODUCTIVE POWER

French and Raven do not mention this power base, perhaps because it is no longer such a strong one for women. This may be partly due to changes in discourses about children themselves and partly because hereditary power has diminished in importance. In our own culture in the past, and in some at the present time, children, especially male ones, have been seen as a 'valued resource'. Women were also seen as necessary to look after their parents when they grew old; or as an addition to the family's finances, especially when the children were old enough to earn money or work in the family's farm or business. Children were also important to 'carry on the blood line' and to ensure that family wealth or position did not fall into the 'wrong hands'. However, despite the contribution that women offer, more cultures have required a dowry for women rather than a payment, or 'bride-price' for them. They have been seen as costly to marry off and as a financial liability rather than an asset.

Children do not appear to be perceived as a resource any longer. Because of the inadequacies of our culture's childcare arrangements, children may be perceived as less of a resource in themselves and as more of a 'drain' on other resources. Discourses such as those stemming from Bowlby's early work, or the assumption that women should be the primary caretakers of children, plus the assumption that the biological parents, rather than the community as a whole, should have responsibility for their own children, can all lead to women being blocked from gaining alternative power bases. Elderly parents are not solely reliant on their children any more, so children are not a resource in this way either, and children seldom work to help the finances of their families of origin. In effect, however, the elderly have become more dependent on their children again in Britain in the last decade.

For many centuries positions of power have been *ascribed*. Children necessarily had to be legitimate, therefore, in order to inherit power, i.e. power in terms of land, wealth and position. Women's reproductive power has been very high, but at the same time very much subject to the control of men. Women, after all, know without doubt that the child they are carrying is biologically and legitimately theirs, but men cannot be sure, unless they control women's sexuality. Part of the women's liberation discourse has been to 'put back' their reproductive power into their own hands, for instance in the discourse of women's rights to control their own bodies – to choose whether or not to have an abortion. This has only been partially successful, because men with power have opposed or obstructed them. For instance, the male dominated Roman Catholic church refuses to allow abortion or contraception. Similarly, the male dominated world of medicine has decided what should or should not be grounds for abortion. It may be men's fear of women's reproductive power that has led to male control of female sexuality for so long.

LEGAL POWER

Legal power may be linked to legitimate power although there is a distinction between the two, since legitimate power rests on one partner accepting the legitimacy of the other's request – i.e. on their belief systems – and carries informal, rather than formal, sanctions. It also overlaps to some extent with ascribed power but legal power emphasizes that the power includes the legal parameters of the relationship and the structure of this may be to disadvantage women in relation to men. It is also not open to negotiation by the couple.

The dominant groups make the laws, of course, and decide what is or is not legitimate to a greater extent than do subordinate groups. Men, as a dominant group, may decide which laws should be applied to whom and what should be accepted as legitimate for themselves and for others; consequently, they may make one 'law' for themselves and another 'law' for the others. Men have dominated the legal system, for example in formulating legislation and its enforcement through various sanctions. The following are some brief historical illustrations.

The law, gender and sexuality

A husband's legal and legitimate right to the domestic and sexual services of his wife was embedded in the Right to Consortium in the nineteenth century. A husband could claim damages if his wife was seduced or raped by a man other than himself. It was not until 1991 that it became illegal for a husband to rape his wife. Prior to this, the interpretation of the law was that it was the wife's duty as part of the marriage contract to provide sexual gratification for her husband and refusal to do so constituted a breach which made use of force a legitimate measure by her husband. Although it is now illegal to use violence against one's wife, and recent judgments make marital rape a crime, nevertheless domestic violence may still frequently be seen as legitimate. Studies of police attitudes and responses to violence show that the police may be affected in their decisions about what they should do if they are called into a case of domestic violence. They may well believe that the wife deserves to be treated with violence if her behaviour is difficult and 'mouthy' or if she leaves the house in a mess. It seems that some police officers think that it is legitimate for a husband to use violence against his wife if she is not 'behaving' herself. A study of social workers also found that some similarly accepted it as legitimate (Maynard 1985).

Theoretically, if women were aware of the law relating to domestic violence and if the law was properly enforced, a wife would be able to employ legal power to prevent her husband using violence against her. Unfortunately, many women are not aware of the law, so perhaps they lose out on this power base. Even if they are aware of the law they may be prevented from using it, in part because their husbands' violence is often seen as somehow legitimate. Furthermore, without witnesses the woman's unsubstantiated account of what happened in the home would not suffice any more than it would for violence committed in the street. Until recently women could be fairly sure of gaining custody of their children, and therefore of the marital home and maintenance. Now this is no longer so clearcut, as it is now more possible for men to get custody, and in general the wife only has the right to the marital home and maintenance until the children are out of full-time education. In some ways, then, wives have less of this power base now. Previously, the knowledge that in the event of divorce the wife would gain custody and that the husband would 'lose' the children to some extent, plus his home and some of his income, may have given wives some power. A wife's threat (coercive power) that she will divorce him, unless things get better or unless he complies with her wishes, may influence the husband, as he would lose out in various ways if they were divorced. However, she will not have this kind of coercive power if the law does not automatically grant her custody, the home and maintenance, and if both partners are aware of this. It is now also possible for men to claim maintenance from their wives if they divorce.

In theory, then, it might be valid to argue that wives, to a large extent, have had more legal power than husbands in the period from the mid-nineteenth century until the last decade. Unfortunately, there seem to be no studies that have looked specifically at the effects of legal power in intimate

relationships, except for a few studies which look at the effect of the awareness of the laws on domestic violence.

Most participants in the research study said that they did not even know
what their legal rights were, though several women said that they thought
they did have some power in the relationship through it because, if they
were to separate, then the women would be likely to get 'custody' of the
children. This was thought to affect the extent to which men would 'rock
the boat' as they were afraid of 'losing the children'.

SOCIAL POWER

As well as attempting to elaborate 'language power' and invalidational
power, we also added two other sources of power. As mentioned previously
these were added mainly because the earlier participants in the study had
indicated that these were important. 'Social power' was defined as being
confident in relation to other people. One of the effects of a disparity in this
power base was difficulties in deciding what to do socially:

> In some situations I feel more confident than him and in others he
> feels more confident than me . . . sometimes we put each other down
> for it . . . we're not very kind to each other . . . mostly we avoid situ-
> ations where only one of us would feel comfortable . . . that means we
> don't do a lot of socializing together.

Social power relates to several of the other power bases, for example the
more socially powerful person can be seen as more able to contract out of
the relationships, as being more attractive and therefore more able to find
another partner and perhaps as having more friends and allies that support
their views and position in the relationship. It can also imply that since they
get on well with others they may also be more emotionally healthy, reasonable and therefore in the right regarding disputes or conflicts of interest.

COPING POWER

Coping power was defined as 'being more able to cope alone emotionally
than your partner'. This is probably a mixture of several power bases: being
self-sufficient emotionally – so a type of emotional power, perhaps being
able to cope because of support from other people – so a type of affiliation
power, and perhaps also a type of contractual power.

> One of the differences between J and me . . . I know I have the cap-
> ability to survive on my own . . . I lived on my own for a time and I

really enjoyed it . . . he does not know whether he could or not, I've got confidence in my own survival, I'm not somewhere just because I have to be . . . one of my trump cards . . . a bit horrible, really . . . at the end of an argument I've sometimes said I'd really like him to move out . . . he gets upset.

Less disparity of this power base is generally viewed positively, if both are believed to be equally able to cope: 'there is the sense of being in the relationship because we want to be'; if neither is believed to be able to cope very well, 'it reduces fear of the relationship ending'.

Differences in power bases between men and women

We asked participants in our study (see details in Chapter 4) to fill in a questionnaire which first gave definitions of each potential power base and then asked participants to indicate which of them had the most of each kind of power. Financial power, for instance, was defined as 'A can earn enough money to support self, B cannot earn enough money to support themself, therefore A has financial power relative to B.' Invalidational power was defined as 'A has low self-esteem and is more easily put down, invalidated or upset by B than B is by A. Therefore B has invalidational power relative to A' (see Appendix 1 for questionnaire). This simple categorization was employed because people found answering these questions difficult. We had previously asked people to rank, put in ascending order how much of each power base they felt they had but this proved to be difficult. A simple comparison in terms of whether they felt they had more, the same or less of each power base than their partner proved to be more manageable.

The results were as shown in Table 3.1. Our findings lend support to Williams and Watson's (1988) suggested differences in profiles of power between men and women. We found there to be pronounced differences between men and women on financial, shelter, physical, sexual, emotional and childrearing power bases. Also, overall men were seen to have more power bases (14 per cent more overall). Men were reported as having far more financial, shelter, invalidational, public informational and physical coercive power bases than women. Women were reported as having far more sexual, emotional communicational and legal power than men. Men also had more coping, affiliation and technical expertise power than women and women had more social, domestic and childrearing expertise power than men.

Perhaps the more surprising findings were that men tended to have more emotional power than women, women tended to have more social power and that they were similar in terms of 'emotional informational power'. Regarding the former, as the next chapter indicates, there appears to be a

Table 3.1 Power bases and gender

	Male	Female
Financial	**62**	39
Shelter	**56**	29
Emotional	50	37
Social	30	43
Invalidational	47	32
Sexual	32	**52**
Coping	**53**	42
Affiliation	41	31
Language power		
Public information	**55**	43
Emotional information	42	**50**
Logical communication	**54**	**50**
Emotional communication	34	**53**
Domestic expertise	36	**48**
Childrearing expertise	36	**47**
Technical expetise	46	36
Legal	21	37
Legitimate	46	40
Physical coercion	**68**	14

Note: Based on 15 respondents. Maximum score for each power base was 75, and ranking of first six power bases are shown in bold, i.e. men are seen to possess most power of physical coercion, followed by financial power, greatest resource for women is seen to be power of emotional communication, sexual, and so on.
Source: Foreman (1996)

reversal on emotional power depending on whether the woman is financially dependent or not. Financially dependent women tend to be rated as having more emotional power than their husbands whereas financially independent women are often rated as having less emotional power than the men. There was a bias in the sample responding to this section of the questionnaire towards the women being financially independent. The finding that women tend to have more social power was consistent throughout; women were generally rated as 'getting on better with people' than men.

It might have been predicted that women would have more emotional informational power, awareness of emotions, supporting others and under-standing emotionality, traditionally thought to be a female skill. However, the scores for men and women were not significantly different. This may again be related to the bias towards financial independence in this sample; perhaps there was a preponderance of 'new men' in the sample who felt that they should be supportive. The men in this sample, however, do fall into more traditional stereotypical 'masculinity' in that they are lower than women on emotional communication; i.e. they perhaps do not express their

Table 3.2 Sources of power and financial dependency

	Financially dependent		Financially independent	
	Men	*Women*	*Men*	*Women*
Closest to children	0	7	1	3
More interesting	1	8	3	3
Physically stronger	16	1	14	3
Gives in least	2	8	1	2
More confident	10	4	8	5
Gets on better with people	4	7	2	12
Has more freedom	9	5	7	1
	42	40	36	29
Least sexually jealous	7	2	4	4
Least upset if divorced	2	8	1	2
More secure	9	8	7	4
More self-sufficient	7	8	8	3
Least emotionally dependent	7	7	7	3
Least in love with other	1	3	3	3
	33	36	30	19

Source: Adapted from Foreman (1996), p. 283(a)

own emotions, or do not react emotionally, or do not use emotional arguments to the same extent as women. Men still have far more financial power than women, despite most of these individual women working outside the home, perhaps reflecting the fact that women still earn less than men.

Before leaving this chapter we will briefly mention findings from an original questionnaire which had attempted to look at power bases in a less elaborated way (see Table 3.2). Some of the participants in our study were in relationships where the women were financially dependent on their men and some where they were financially independent. There were no couples in our study where the men were financially dependent on their partners, though of course this is increasingly common due to high levels of unemployment. Participants were asked to indicate their relative strength on each power base by answering questions in the form of 'Who is closer to the children?', 'Who is more confident?', 'Who gets on better with people?', 'Who has most freedom?', 'Who is more interesting?', as well as 'Who gives in more?', and 'Who is physically stronger?' and so on. They could answer 'self', 'partner' or 'the same'.

Women were reported as being closer to the children, more interesting and better able to get on with people than men. Men were reported as being more confident and as having more freedom than women. Regarding financial dependence and financial independence, financially dependent women were reported as being closer to the children, more interesting and less likely to give in than financially independent women. Financially independent women were reported as getting on even better with people than financially dependent women as well as men. There were no significant differences within the male group relating to their partners being financially dependent or independent.

An unexpected finding was that despite women often saying they had become more confident when they began to be financially independent (see p. 58), the women appeared to have less confidence relative to men even when they did work outside the home. This may be related to what Komter (1989) describes as 'invisible power' or a generalized sense of lower self-esteem possessed by women, in turn due to the low 'value' attached to female 'attributes'. Men were reported as having more freedom than women, this seemed to be related to their capacity not simply to influence the women to do things but to enable the men to avoid doing some activities, for example domestic chores and therefore more capacity to have separate free time. Men's greater freedom was also related to having more money, making them freer outside the home; for example, money is needed to spend time in the pub with friends.

Constraints on women's freedom on the other hand also appeared to be related to the expectations of women as mothers, responsibility for child-rearing and being closer to the children. Though potentially offering some power through the alliance with the children this also tends to tie women to them and the home, thereby limiting their capacity for freedom and independence. One women expressed this succinctly:

> The woman keeps the family together . . . her own needs are suppressed . . . a man does not have to suppress his needs . . . they do what they want to do but a woman has to think hang on I've got to get back for the kids. I was probably resentful of his freedom when the children were younger.

This chapter has attempted to show how men and women in general have different sources of power and has given some broad illustrations of the effects of these various kinds of inequalities. In the next chapter we will explore how these power bases may affect the ways in which partners attempt to influence each other in the relationship by the use of strategies relating to their respective power bases.

4

Interpersonal strategies of influence

In this chapter we will explore some of the implications of differing power bases for how partners attempt to influence each other. Following a review of some of the literature we will offer details of a questionnaire-based study conducted with a sample of heterosexual couples and some related findings from couples whom we have interviewed and some whom we have worked with in a clinical context (Foreman 1996). The aim was to explore possible differences between the types of strategies used when partners are attempting to influence each other and how these are related to partners' power bases.

A central question for this chapter is the effect of differences in material power bases, particularly differences in financial power in the relationship, specifically when one partner, most frequently the woman, is financially dependent on the other. As the previous chapter suggested, differences in financial power have an effect on which strategies are employed. At the most basic level this might be an overt threat to withdraw support or it may be a less overt, even unstated realization that this is a possibility. Material differences in power between partners do not simply determine how they will act with each other. Partners can be seen as active and reflexive in having beliefs, understandings and expectations about their relationships. It is also obviously true that many couples do discuss and negotiate their relationship and may even strive to hold to a principle of equality and fairness. However, the differences in power may, nevertheless, have a powerful influence, perhaps as an unstated background to the relationship or may surface quite dramatically at critical points in the relationship, for example when deciding who stays at home to look after a child or how money is allocated and spent. It is even possible that, though largely unspoken, both partners realize and are aware of the ultimate implications of inequalities and that this shapes not only what issues are raised but which are left 'off the agenda'.

Therapy and psychology have seen an emphasis on people's personal meanings, beliefs and ways of viewing the world along with an interest in how these are constructed from wider culturally shared meanings. As a consequence the material basis of relationships has been relatively ignored or under-emphasized. We will attempt in this chapter to explore how material inequalities shape and constrain the nature of relationships. We will start by exploring a range of empirical studies which have explored negotiational strategies in a variety of relationships, including intimate couples. Some of these studies are somewhat dated and tend to adopt an 'external' perspective which tends to under-emphasize the importance of partners' understandings and perceptions. However, they will be briefly explored because they pointed to the importance of power and offered some ideas on how it could be measured and investigated. Finally, we will consider how material differences also shape people's beliefs, expectations and identities and in turn partners' ways of relating to each other. In Chapters 5 and 6 we will explore further how material differences in power interact with discourses which underlie and maintain structural differences in power.

GENDER AND INFLUENCE STRATEGIES

Several studies suggest that men and women use different strategies of influence. This may be partly to do with their respective power bases and partly to do with socialization processes. Broadly, men have been found to employ more direct and overt strategies, such as aggression and coercion, than women, who employ more covert and indirect strategies, such as crying (Miller 1976; Doyle 1989). One possible reason for this general finding is that women are more likely to 'act helpless' because they have internalized gender expectations or stereotypes that they are less logical, rational, intelligent and capable than men and therefore under-estimate their chances of successfully influencing people, especially men. Scanzoni (1979a; 1979b) developed this idea by distinguishing two types of verbal persuasion: collective verbal persuasion includes saying that a course of action is best for the family or group. Individualistic styles include saying it is best for oneself. He suggests that 'traditional' women are more likely to use collective verbal arguments, stressing the needs of others. More 'modern' women are more likely to be like men and use individualistic arguments, perhaps because of the increase in influence of the belief in the right to 'self-fulfilment'. Similar findings have emerged in studies looking at the ways that men and women use speech. Women have been found to employ fewer commands in their speech, for example where a man might say, 'Close the door', a woman is more likely to say 'Would you mind just closing the door please?' Similarly rather than employing statements clearly expressing their personal views, preferences and desires, such as, 'I'd like to come here again', women are more likely to employ passive expressions using 'tag questions', for example by saying, 'We'll come here again sometime, *won't we?*' Differences in the use of such 'tag questions' have been found to be related to power more generally, so that not only powerless women, but also men with low power are more likely to employ them (Poynton 1989).

Such differences can be seen to be located within a wider pattern of differences between men and women in interactional styles. Scanzoni (1979a; 1979b) and Johnson (1976), for example, have suggested that women may be more sensitive to interpersonal cues than men; are concerned about what effect their behaviour has on others and concerned to keep things relatively harmonious and conflict-free. This could be due to both sex role socialization and relatively low power. Women learn to be relationship orientated, to be concerned with the well-being of the group. They also have to be more aware of interpersonal cues because they are generally in less powerful positions. In fact this falls within a general finding that less powerful partners in interactions are more sensitive to the reactions, non-verbal behaviour, nuances of meanings of the more powerful partner. The subordinate, or less powerful partner, needs to know much more about the more dominant partner. They need to become highly attuned to them, to be able to predict their reactions of pleasure and importantly . . . displeasure in order to avoid attack or retribution from them, (Rubin and Brown 1975). In effect this indicates that in many situations the 'weaker' partner is more reliant on her 'wits' to deal with the other than the more powerful one who can easily always turn to direct strategies, such as threats and coercion to get their way.

Consistent with this idea Scanzoni suggests that certain types of coercion, threats, verbal abuse as well as physical abuse, may be more likely when the relationship is one of disparity in power bases. If partners have equal power bases they have equal capacities to resist and counter-coerce so there is little point in either of them using coercion. However, if they have a disparity in power bases then the individual with more power will be less constrained in the use of coercion. Verbal persuasion may fail if partners are unequal since the partner with more power may not take the other seriously. Blood and Wolfe (1960) found that men who were dominant in the relationship did tend to be critical and dismissive in response to their wives. In unequal relationships threats are more likely to be effective as the other has less capacity to resist. Violence, or the threat of violence, may lead women to become hesitant to raise issues, or, if they do raise them, they will not pursue them too insistently; they may have to tolerate injustices and be less likely to use verbal persuasion or to respond with coercive strategies themselves. Coercive strategies of deprecation and verbal abuse (invalidation) may be more likely to be effective when the partner has low self-esteem. Attempted suppression – e.g. telling the partner to shut up, dismissing their argument, refusing to listen – is likely to be a strategy of the more powerful. If one partner tries to stop an issue being raised, it can be assumed that s/he does not want to talk about it although the other does. Consequently power is not only related to influencing one's partner to do something but also to prevent her/him doing something, such as raising certain issues which may challenge the status quo – the current arrangement which the more powerful partner supposedly prefers to maintain (Scanzoni 1979a; 1979b).

TYPES OF INFLUENCE STRATEGIES

An approach which has been informative in studies on influence and power is to attempt to describe and categorize the types of influence strategies that partners employ. Chafetz (1980) categorized influence strategies into authority, influence, manipulation and control. Authority was defined as 'feeling that institutional norms support the right to make decisions that are binding on the incumbent of the complementary role'; and is similar to 'ascribed' power. Influence was defined as attempting to persuade the other to agree, involving some form of negotiation. Control was defined as attempting to get the other to comply regardless of the other's wishes; including the use of coercion. Manipulation was defined as attempting to get the other to comply but covertly so that the other did not realize. Bell *et al.* (1982) tested Chafetz's categorization with 30 intimate couples in the USA, who were asked to describe what strategies they used to influence their partner. Their descriptions were coded as exemplifying control if they promised favours, attention, material goods, money, threatened physical harm, to leave, divorce, criticized the other or tried to make the other feel guilty; and as influence if they used 'special' information not shared by the other, 'skills' derived from their occupation, or tried to change the other's point of view by claiming that the other had less knowledge about the area. Manipulation was seen in strategies which covertly tried to engender guilt, for example by showing how upset they were by crying or withdrawing, if they lied or tried to change the other's mood (by joking, giving extra attention or gifts). Use of authority was seen to be evident if they simply stated what they wanted without using any of the above.

Participants in the study were also asked to indicate whether they had 'high' or 'low' resources. This was defined as anything you can withhold, give, promise, threaten, special information or skills, any way you can make your partner feel guilty, change their mood or get away with lies. Wives with low and high resources tended to use influence the most, closely followed by control; however, there was a difference in the use of authority depending on resource levels; wives with high resources used authority more effectively than wives with low resources. Men also generally tended to use influence the most, followed by manipulation in terms of frequency. Men were less likely than women to use control in general. When men had high levels of resources they were more likely to use authority. The use of authority appears to be related to high levels of resources for both genders. They also found that employment outside the home had an effect on 'winning arguments'. When only the man worked outside the home the wives were far less likely to 'win arguments' than the men or when they worked outside the home as well.

An important question is whether these findings relating to influence strategies are specific to heterosexual couples or are more clearly linked to power differences regardless of gender. In order to explore this Howard *et al.* (1980) carried out a similar study (employing questionnaires exploring their strategies of influence) with heterosexual and homosexual couples in the USA. They identified six main categories of influence strategies.

> *Manipulation* consisted of dropping hints, flattering, behaving seductively and reminding of past favours.
> *Supplication* consisted of pleading, crying, acting ill or helpless.
> *Bullying* consisted of threatening, insulting, being violent and ridiculing.
> *Autocracy* consisted of insisting, claiming greater knowledge and asserting authority.
> *Disengagement* consisted of sulking, leaving the scene or trying to make the other feel guilty and
> *Bargaining* consisted of reasoning, offering a trade-off or to compromise.

In general, bargaining, similar to the category of 'influence' described earlier, was the most frequently used strategy for all partners. Bullying and supplication were used the least. Also confirmed was the finding from Bell's study that control/coercion/bullying are not used very frequently. Generally, men were more likely to use disengagement and women were more likely to use supplication and manipulation. Interestingly, the 'less dominant' partners in homosexual couples were also more likely to use supplication and manipulation. Lesbian women were more likely to employ bullying as a strategy if their partner had children who were living with them. Unfortunately they offered no comparison of heterosexual and homosexual women with children, though it may be that bullying is generally more likely when there are children. Heterosexual women with dependent children were less likely to use autocracy and disengagement than those without children. Also, heterosexual women not employed outside the home were more likely than those who were employed to 'nag', use supplication and manipulation. Interestingly the men described 'nagging' as a form of bullying though clearly it is not coercive in the sense of being founded on the ability to use physical or economic threats. The partners of women who were employed tended to use bargaining less and manipulation more.

The use of supplication appeared to have some relationship to the degree of general dependency in the relationship; partners who rated themselves, or who were rated as more dependent tended to use supplication; this may go some way to explaining why homosexual partners also use supplication if they are more dependent than their partners. Heterosexual men tended to use supplication more than their wives if they were more dependent on the relationship than the women. In Howard *et al.*'s study manipulation was used most by heterosexual women, homosexual men, partners with a low income, those rated as less attractive or who felt more committed than their partners and male partners where the wife was not employed outside the home. With the exception of the last it appeared that manipulation was used by those with less power in the relationship. Men with dependent partners who employed manipulation may have done so because of social norms (especially in the more middle-class couples), disapproving of the use of autocracy and bullying as not acceptable behaviour from men towards women.

Interaction in relationships is perhaps inevitably strategic in that it involves beliefs and anticipations about potential consequences, outcomes and repercussions (Goffman 1972; Dallos 1995). Women (and others with low power) may predict and anticipate that more direct strategies will not work, or that they will be met by stronger negative reactions from their more powerful partner. Women who are 'direct' may also be punished 'psychologically', according to Johnson (1976); they risk being labelled pushy, unfeminine and even castrating.The labels are not only negative but also imply that those who have these attributes are unlikable and unlovable particularly to men. Whilst a woman who has sufficient power of her own, both materially and in terms of self-esteem, may not worry too much about being labelled in this way, women who are dependent may be swayed by the implication that men will not find them attractive if they are like that.

Leaving the scene may not appear at first sight to be a direct strategy but its effect can be to prevent the continuation of discussion so presumably the one who leaves the scene is the one who has least interest in change. Cutting short the discussion may also be attempted because the partner feels that they are losing the argument and possibly their power. Howard *et al.* (1980) found that generally men were more likely to use disengagement; sulking, making the other feel guilty, leaving the scene, than women. In addition those who were less well educated than their partners, and heterosexual women without dependent children, were more likely to do so. Level of education may be related to how well partners can articulate their point. Generally, men may perform less well educationally than women, certainly up to A level (the end of high school) but nevertheless still go on to occupy more prestigious and better paid jobs. Consequently, it is likely that some men feel less articulate, especially in the area of relationships and emotions but feel they should still be in charge. They may therefore become angry

and resentful and, being less able to articulate their views, or knowing that
they will lose if they do so, retaliate by threatening or withdrawing.

The level of commitment to the issues under discussion may also be
relevant in that men and women without children may be less bothered
about whether the issue is resolved or not, since, not having children they
may feel they are less confined to the relationship. It matters less whether
an issue is resolved, they can let it 'blow over' or even separate more easily
if things do not spontaneously appear to work. An obvious problem in
comparing these two major studies is that they do not categorize the strategies in the same way. Furthermore, Bell's study uses a vague definition of
high or low resources.

A wide range of studies adds support to our general thesis here that
differences in power significantly influence the nature of interactions in
relationships and the strategies that partners adopt. Blood and Wolfe (1960),
for instance, found racial differences such as that Black husbands had com-
paratively less decision-making power than white husbands, and that Blacks
of both genders were more likely to be co-operative than whites. This was
seen to be related to the fact that Black people generally possess less power,
occupy lower status jobs and so on. Vinacke (1964) found that girls of all
ages were more co-operative than boys. Girls have also been found to behave
in more accommodating ways, discussing problems with each other and seeking an equitable outcome, whereas boys tended to be more inclined to be
exploitative (Rubin and Brown 1975). Benson (1969) found that women were
generally more interested in the resolution of inequality and distributive
justice than males.

Lastly, Rubin and Brown (1975) talk about 'good bargaining'; bargaining
which they defined as 'good' if both partners end up *satisfied* with the
bargaining process and the outcome. It is important to note here that 'good'
bargaining is defined not simply in terms of some objective outcome but
partners' subjective perceptions of satisfaction. They concluded that the
'best' bargaining occurred if the partners were equal and had a cooperative,
interpersonal orientation to each other. An interpersonal orientation refers
to seeking out knowledge about the other, trying to understand their viewpoint. A cooperative orientation in combination with an interpersonal orientation means that partners tried to understand each other but did not use
this information to compete, upset or put the other down. In contrast if they
are competitive and interpersonally orientated they used the information
they have about the other to manipulate and exert power over them. The
'worst' bargaining was when the partners were unequal, competitive and
interpersonally orientated. This meant that they were sophisticated in understanding their partner, competitively trying to get the better of them, and
because one had more power they could abuse this and get away it. Swingle
(1970) argued generally that if the relationship is unequal the one with high
power is likely to be exploitative and the one with less power is likely to

be submissive or to withdraw. In agreement with this Thibaut and Kelley (1959) suggest that exploitation is more likely if the other has no alternative but to stay in the relationship.

SEXUAL INTERACTION

In the previous chapter we have seen that men and women are likely to possess differing power bases. More specifically, by and large, men are likely to have available not only different power bases but to have more objective power. This is an important difference since much of the power that women are likely to possess in contrast is relative, that is dependent for its effectiveness on the relationship itself. To some extent sexual power is also relative, for example in terms of whether the man finds and continues to find his partner sexually attractive or vice versa. Yet (as we will discuss further in Chapter 6) sexual power is given a sort of objective status by the fact that men are generally seen as 'needing' sex more than women. This is arguably a highly influential and dominant discourse which at least to some extent 'gives power' away to women in that men are positioned as needing women to provide sexual satisfaction.

What follows then is the likelihood that in relationships where there is a gross inequality of power favouring the man it is more likely that the women may resort, perhaps unconsciously, to using her sexual power to gain some power and influence. In our clinical work we have found a common pattern of sexual demand/sexual reluctance. Usually the woman has become reluctant in contrast to the man, who is demanding or seeking sexual contact. This asymmetry may be explained not only by the common assumption that men biologically need sex more, but also from the reverse that since women need it less, its withdrawal will not be as influential – the woman will be less bothered about whether it takes place or not. Accompanying this idea is also the perception that what women need more is emotional intimacy, and love and sex are almost secondary to this. This theme is powerfully illustrated in D.H. Lawrence's *Lady Chatterley's Lover* (1928/1960): Constance appears less concerned about her husband's sexual inadequacy (due to his war injuries) than he is. It seems that Clifford's sense of failure as a man drives him to bitterness, emotional coldness towards her and eventually drives Constance away and to other men. The novel is located in Freudian phallocentric sexuality, so the possibility that Clifford might have been able to satisfy his wife other than by conventional phallocentric sex is not entertained. (To be fair to Lawrence, it might not have made such a compelling story either). Ironically it is not just that men employ their power to gain sex with women but feel they need to recharge their power constantly, become a 'real' man by awakening and satisfying a woman through phallocentric sex. This fosters a vulnerability, relating to their identity and security as men, and thereby privileges sex as a central source of power in relationships. It is also likely therefore that issues of power, especially at critical times of conflict, will be conducted through sexuality.

A STUDY OF INFLUENCE STRATEGIES AND POWER

We conducted a study to examine the ways in which couples attempt to influence each other and how this relates to the different power bases that men and women possess. Couples can potentially employ a wide variety of ways of influencing each other but the choices may be constrained by the power bases that they possess. One of our central hypotheses was that the frequently observed pattern of sexual interaction (Hollway 1983; Hare-Mustin 1991; Foreman and Dallos 1992) – female reluctance/male demand – would be more likely to occur in couples where there was a clear inequality of power. More specifically we reasoned that this would be more likely to occur in cases where the woman was financially dependent on her partner.

Categories of influence strategies

In order to explore this question we designed a questionnaire which assessed the range of power bases partners possessed, for example their financial status, and explored the ways in which they attempted to influence each other (see Appendix 1, and Foreman 1996). Twenty married or cohabiting couples took part in the study. Each partner was asked about their own and their partner's behaviour. This provided some measure of consistency and validity since for each couple we could compare the agreement between their own and their partner's reports of how they acted. A specific area of focus was on the extent to which withholding strategies, especially sexual and emotional withholding, were employed and how these related to financial dependence. Ten of the couples were categorized as ones in which the woman was *financially dependent* and ten of the couples as ones in which the woman was *financially independent*. In none of our couples were the men financially dependent.

We employed six categories of influence strategies based on the work of Howard *et al.* (1980), Bell *et al.* (1982) and Chafetz (1980):

1 *Withholding strategies*   going silent, leaving the room, withdrawing affection, threatening to leave, going off sex, leaving and not listening;
2 *Involving other people*   saying it's best for the children, threatening to take the children, drawing a child onto one's own side (coalitions), complaining to others, saying it's not fair, saying it's the partner's duty, saying the partner is selfish;

3 *Verbal persuasion* bargaining, bribing, verbal rationalization, using work as an excuse, assertion, saying it's for own fulfilment, saying it's not fair, saying it's the partner's duty, saying the partner is selfish;

4 *Manipulation* bargaining, flattery, apologizing, complaining about something else, lying, withholding information, trying to get the partner to forget the complaint, making the partner feel guilty, evoking jealousy, waiting until the partner does something wrong then complaining, changing the subject, giving in but then not doing it;

5 *Bullying* attacking before the partner can accuse you, threatening to withdraw money, telling the partner to shut up, nagging, shouting, violence, putting the partner down, using ultimatums;

6 *Supplication* acting helpless, crying.

Although based on earlier work, these categories are different – especially in focusing on the category of involving others. These are clearly indicated in the family and marital therapy literature as *coalitional* strategies. There is obviously some overlap between the categories; for example, supplication could be seen as a subcategory of manipulation. However, the category of manipulation is in itself difficult. It could be argued that all these strategies are, in a sense, manipulative if employed consciously.

In contrast to previous studies we suggested that there are significant differences in which these strategies are employed, due to differences in their availability to men as opposed to women; for instance, physical/bullying strategies may not be available for women since they are usually physically weaker or because they fear violent reprisals from their partners.

Results

There were a range of differences between men and women and between financially dependent and independent partners, However, only a few of the results achieved any statistical significance (Foreman 1996). These significant results are presented in Table 4.1.

Women were found to be significantly (statistically) more likely to engage in the strategies of involving others, verbal persuasion (specifically in terms of complaining about fairness), supplication and bullying (specifically

Table 4.1 Gender differences in use of influence strategies

Women	Men
Involving other people	*Withholding* – going silent
Verbal persuasion – saying it's not fair	*Verbal persuasion* – work as an excuse
Supplication – crying, acting helpless	
Bullying – nagging	

'nagging'). In contrast men were significantly more likely to engage in with-holding (specifically in going silent), verbal persuasion (specifically using work as an excuse).

Involving other people

Women were reported as being more likely to do this than men, irrespective of whether they are financially dependent or independent. However, financially dependent women were more likely to involve the children in some way than financially independent women. It is possible that the children of financially dependent women were younger than those of the financially independent women, though it is arguable as to whether people are more or less likely to involve children depending on their age. An alternative inter-pretation is that the financially independent women did not need to involve the children because they have other sources of power. It could also be that women inevitably become closer to the children since this is a function of a division of labour in the relationship whereby childcare is the woman's domain or role and therefore is likely to become a source of power for her within the relationship. Overall financially independent women employed this category as much as the financially dependent women by virtue of employing the strategies of 'saying it's not fair' and saying it's their partner's 'duty'. Arguably there is some overlap so that some of the strategies in this category also fall within the category of 'verbal persuasion'.

Verbal persuasion (specifically, 'saying It's not fair')

Possibly this was not just a strategy but a statement reflecting the real structural and material inequalities in the relationship. Financially depend-ent women are in an unequal relationship even if it is constructed as being different but equal; financially independent women, according to several studies, tend often to be working outside the home and doing more than their 'fair share' of domestic or childcare tasks. Unfortunately the question-naire was not designed to extract information such as what exactly women are saying is unfair, though other studies suggest that it is usually some-thing to do with unfairness in the division of domestic or childcare tasks in the home. Perelberg and Miller (1990) also suggest that women are more concerned with issues of equity and distributive justice than men.

Supplication

This features the activities of crying and of 'acting helpless'. There was no significant difference in the use of this strategy between financially depend-ent and financially independent women, suggesting that the use of sup-plication by women (and the lack of its usage by men) is related to gender socialization rather than power. However, since supplication is a 'one down' type of strategy its usage may reflect a socialization of women into submissive strategies. Conversely the difference may also be related to constructions of masculinity, i.e. 'real men' do not cry or act helpless; or to the blocking of emotional expression in the socialization of men in our society (Doyle 1989; Farrell 1990).

Bullying (specifically 'nagging')

The greater reported use of this by women may in part be due to selective gender biased perception, in that similar behaviours in men (complaining, being pedantic and so on) may not be seen as 'nagging'. However, even if women do actually nag more this might involve socialization processes including the point that it is seen as a more legitimate strategy to use than other strategies for women. It may also be related to 'saying it's not fair', i.e. nagging is about trying to get their partners to share more of the housework. The problem with definitions, of course, is a critical failing that plagues questionnaire studies.

Men

Overall men were significantly more likely than women to employ the strategies of withholding (going silent) and verbal persuasion (using work as an excuse).

Withholding (specifically 'going silent')

Men with financially dependent partners were the most likely to do this. They also tended to 'not listen'. Again, the questionnaire was not designed to elicit information as to either the context of men 'going silent' or explanations as to why men go silent. It could be that men 'go silent' in the context of being 'nagged', i.e. the infamous systems theory description of a 'nag – withdraw' interactional cycle. It could be argued that men do it to gain or maintain power in the relationship. It is certainly an effective strategy to avoid doing the washing up or to avoid doing anything the man does not want to do including even talking or sorting out issues in the relationship. It seemed to function to block changes that the woman might want. At the same time men may do it because they think if they respond the interaction may escalate into overt conflict. Alternatively, it could be interpreted as a part of being socialized into being 'masculine', i.e. detached, calm and in control of their responses or reactions; being silent and reflective, with the implication that they are listening to what the woman is saying despite possible interpretations as to the contrary; 'You're not listening to me are you? ... of course I'm listening to you darling ... I'm just thinking about what you are saying!' In terms of power bases, 'going silent' may reflect the use of 'contractual power' and covert invalidation. Men can 'contract out' of talking about things they do not wish to talk about. 'Going silent' is also a type of invalidation in that it implies, or may be interpreted as meaning, that what the woman is saying is not really worth listening to.

Verbal persuasion (specifically 'using work as an excuse')

Men were more likely to do this than women even when the women were financially independent and working outside the home. This may reflect an assumption that women's work is not so important as men's; perhaps the men are still actually earning more than the women even when the women are ostensibly financially independent. Perhaps it is still somehow construed as legitimate for men to do or not do things because of the demands of work (a source of legitimate power). Interestingly, all women did complain about things not being 'fair'. Possibly women who work outside the home also tend to have to do most of the domestic and childcare tasks but without being able to persuade the men that this arrangement is 'not fair' because they have to work as well. It could also be to do with 'legitimate strategies' or the fact that the family is still generally more dependent on the man's wage than the woman's.

Men were also reported as having more freedom than women. Although the questionnaire does not give information as to what this freedom actually consists of it may be related to them being able to use work as an excuse to avoid doing household tasks or a reason for why they need to go out more than women do. Again this might have reflected men's capacity to 'contract out', this time in terms of contracting out of domestic or childrearing tasks, or be related indirectly to financial power and language power. If the man is the main 'breadwinner' he may be able to use this as a reason for having more freedom than the woman. It may also reflect 'language power', i.e. being able to persuade the woman verbally that his work is important and offer reasons as to why he should have more freedom. For the women, lesser freedom may reflect the 'downside' of childrearing expertise. Although they may gain power through being close to the children the other side of the coin is that they may have more responsibility for the children. For instance, if it was a question of the man or the woman going out for the evening it may have been more likely that the woman would stay at home because she was worried about leaving the children.

Confidence

A general finding was that men were reported as being more confident than women, women do not appear to become as equally confident as men, even when they (women) work outside the home. Though not a specific strategy

Table 4.2 Differences in use of influence strategies between men and women in the financially dependent vs financially independent groups

Financially dependent	*Financially independent*
Women	*Women*
More likely to withhold – sex	More likely to engage in verbal persuasion
Men	
Withhold – go silent	
Verbal persuasion	

Note: Results show significant differences between men and women within the financially dependent and the financially independent groups. There were very few differences between men and women in the financially independent group with the exception of women using verbal persuasion more than the men.

this can in a sense be seen as the contrast to supplication. It may imply that the man is stronger, more capable, more independent and serve as a strategy to keep the other feeling more helpless, inadequate and dependent. The fact that women do not necessarily become more, and act more, confident even when they are employed outside the home may reflect the effects of the general devaluing of women within a patriarchal society and the difficulties for women of working in a 'male world'. The fact that women are reported as 'getting on better with people' than men did not appear to coincide with an increase in their confidence.

Financial dependence

In addition to exploring the general differences between men and women it was important to examine how these were influenced by differences in financial dependency (see Figure 4.2).

Financially dependent women appeared to employ more withholding strategies such as 'going off sex' more and related to this they were less likely to 'complain about sexual frequency' than financially independent women. This effect may have been because these women were regarded as having more emotional power in the relationship than were the financially independent women. This may in turn be related to the fact that women who are financially dependent have less potential sources of power and hence some form of emotional tactics are their main avenues of influence. Interestingly, more women in the financially dependent group were also reported as having overall dominance in the relationship than women in the financially independent group. This, as we will discuss further in Chapter 6, however, may be a distortion of the real balance of power in the relationship and a perception which under-estimates the power, or the potential power, of men's sources of influence, such as physical force, money and work. Men in this group were also the most likely to use stereotypical male techniques, such as withdrawing by going silent. However, they were also seen to employ verbal persuasion more and to employ manipulation in the form of flattery or being 'especially nice' more than partners of financially independent women.

It is apparent that our results show that there are not always simple differences between men and women, or between financially independent and dependent couples in use of different categories. But there did appear to be interesting differences in the types of actions employed within categories of influence. For example, though both men and women in the financially dependent group employed forms of withholding these were different in that the women were more likely to withhold sexual intimacy and the men to withhold communication by going silent.

Verbal persuasion

Though verbal persuasion might at first sight appear to be mainly linked to how articulate and educated partners are, this showed an interesting variation according to power. When the women were financially dependent the men were reported as being more likely to use verbal persuasion than the women. On the other hand, when the women were financially independent the women were reported as being more likely to use verbal persuasion than the men. In part this may have been due to the fact that the men in the financially independent group were less likely to use any of the categories. It appeared in a sense that these men were a little more subdued.

There are various possible reasons for the apparent reversal of this important strategy. Possibly the women in the financially dependent group were not perceived to be using verbal persuasion but instead when they tried to discuss matters their attempts were construed as emotional 'outbursts' rather than rational. In contrast even when the men in this group were being irrational or emotional they may not have been perceived by themselves and their partner in this way. What counts as 'rational' is not only subjective but also subject to dominant male ideas of how talk and discussion 'should' be conducted. A rational argument therefore may be perceived as rational or non-rational depending on the gender of the person presenting it:

> It is not surprising to find that there are no terms for men talk that are equivalent to *chatter, natter, prattle, nag, bitch, whine* and, of course, *gossip,* and I am not so naive to assume that this is because they do not engage in these activities. It is because when do it is called something different, something more flattering and more appropriate to their place in the world. This double standard is of great value in the maintenance of patriarchal order. No matter what women may say it fosters the conviction that you cannot trust the words of a woman and it is

permissible to dismiss what she might say. By such means the dominant group exert control over woman talk.

(Spender, 1980: 107)

Financially independent women, though, may be more likely to be
expected to be 'rational' and thus be perceived as such. Alternatively, or in
addition, the financially independent women may indeed be more able to
present rational argument because they work outside the home and may
have had more practice in presenting opinions, arguments and pointing out
weaknesses in others' arguments. There may also be an interactional effect,
a cycle of invalidation so that the man's dismissive reaction to a woman's
attempts at rational verbal persuasion may serve to convince her that perhaps she was not being rational. Given repetitions of this cycle the woman
may 'give up' attempts at this form of influence or do so in such a hesitant
manner that she is easily dismissed. This form of invalidation through language may be an extremely potent and potentially destructive force. Since
language is central to a sense of identity, even how a woman talks to herself may mean that this sense of inadequacy becomes pervasive so that she
comes to see herself, and to be seen as, emotional, inferior and generally as
infant like. The frustration of not being seen as rational, the frustration of
being blocked from using rational argument, and generally feeling invalidated, may even lead to women becoming more 'emotional' in their attempts
to influence, thus confirming gender stereotypes.

Though the difference was not significant our observations of many
couples and families in a clinical context suggest that men in the financially
dependent group did appear to engage in more 'not listening' and 'going
silent' than any of the other groups including the men in the financially
independent group. Again, it is apparent that an activity such as 'not listening' can be seen to fall both within a category of withholding and also one
of bullying, in that the effect of dismissing or ignoring what a woman has
to say, along with the clearer bullying strategy of telling the partner to 'shut
up', can be a form of verbal intimidation which damages a woman's identity. In contrast the men in the financially independent group were generally less likely to employ bullying strategies than the men in the financially
dependent group. Possibly, the men in this group felt less able to engage in
this activity because the women were demonstrating their competence,
including verbal competence, in the external world.

It appeared that the women in the financially dependent group have less
material power but also less verbal power. This points to the possibility that
they are left with little alternative but to employ emotional power, including sexual withholding. In effect the strategies that are employed emerge as
a process of attrition. Though potentially a wide range is possible, in fact on
closer inspection these appear to be erased one after the other for the women
in the financially dependent group. In contrast women in the financially

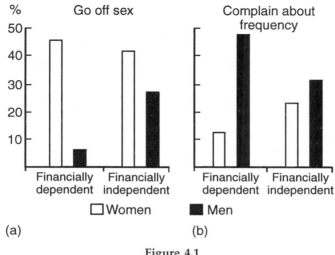

Figure 4.1

independent group had a greater range of power bases to draw on for their choice of strategies and were less likely to resort to emotional means and withholding of sex.

Withholding strategies and sex

The general results had indicated that both gender and financial dependence did play a significant role in shaping what strategies partners employed. We explored this in more detail to see if this was simply a general tendency for women and how it was linked to financial dependency (see Fig. 4.1). The results indicated that women were generally significantly more likely to 'go off sex' and were less likely to complain about the frequency of sexual intimacy. However, women in the financially dependent group were far more likely to avoid sexual intimacy and in fact the observed gender difference was a result of the highly significant difference in this group. The women in the financially independent group in fact were not significantly more likely to avoid sexual intimacy than their partners. In fact there was some evidence of a reversal in that women in this group were almost as likely to complain about the frequency than their men.

Either as a deliberate tactic or otherwise, 'going off sex' appears to be clearly related to inequality of power. When the couples were further classified in terms of being totally or partially financially dependent, for example, not being able to afford reasonable accommodation were they to split up with their partner, it was found that the women were even more likely to 'go off' sexual intimacy and there was not a single instance of the women in this group wishing to have more frequent sexual intimacy. On the other hand, the men in this group were more likely to complain. This appeared to support the view that where the women are financially dependent men regard sexual duties from the women as their right and therefore feel it is legitimate to complain. Also, the figures suggest that women are even more likely to go off sex when they are highly financially dependent.

Sexuality and emotional power

It was possible that 'going off sex' was related to emotional power in a general way, for instance as part of a broader category of 'withdrawing oneself'. This might indicate less dependency on the other and an ability to 'manipulate' the partner's sexual and emotional dependence in order to influence them. This was explored by a series of questions, such as which partner would be most upset if they split up, who was most sexually jealous, more in love with the other and so on. There appeared to be an interaction between emotional and economic power (see Fig. 4.2). In the financially dependent group, when the woman is also emotionally dominant, women are more likely than men to 'go off sex' and the men were more likely than the women to 'complain about frequency'. When the men were emotionally dominant in this group this pattern still occurred but to a lesser extent. In the financially independent group the pattern was not so strong, when the men were emotionally dominant women appeared to be as likely as men to 'complain about frequency'.

Summary

Overall it seemed that women were more likely to 'go off sex' than men in any circumstances. Women who were financially dependent were more likely to 'go off sex' than women who were financially independent. No (highly) financially dependent woman in this sample complained about frequency more than their partners. Men were more likely than women overall to 'complain about frequency'; however, men with financially dependent wives were generally more likely to 'complain about frequency' than men with financially independent wives. The differences between men and women in both 'going off' and 'complaining about frequency' were statistically significant when the the wives were financially dependent but not when the wives were financially independent. Those rated as having higher emotional power were generally more likely to 'go off sex' and not 'complain' than those rated as having lower emotional power. However this interrelated with financial power, so that when the wife is financially dependent and has high emotional power she is more likely to 'go off' and not 'complain' than when she is either financially independent or has less emotional power.

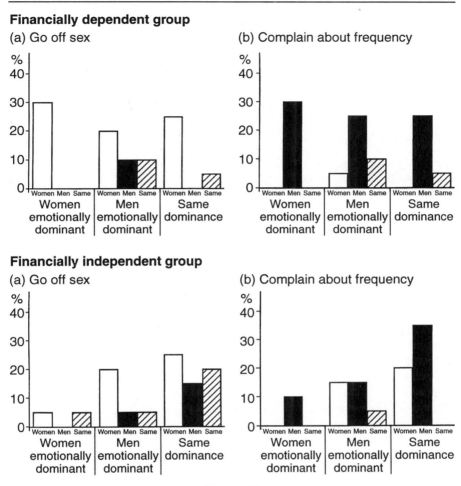

Figure 4.2

PERCEIVED IMPORTANCE OF POWER BASES

As we have suggested the influence strategies that are employed are related to the power bases that partners have available and importantly to their perceptions of the relative importance of these power bases. So, for example, if sexual intimacy is rated as highly important by partners, or one partner, then it is likely that this will emerge as an important sphere of negotiation and influence. In order to explore this partners were asked to rank their power bases according to the degree of influence each power base had in their relationship. There were 20 power bases suggested by the researcher and each partner was asked to rank these in terms of which they perceived

Table 4.3 Perceived influence value of power bases

Power base
1 Financial: able to support self financially
2 Sexual: needing sex less often than partner
3 Social: getting on with others, social confidence
4 Emotional dependence: being less dependent on partner than vice versa
5 Child rearing expertise
6 Technical expertise
7 Domestic expertise
8 Invalidation: high self-esteem, less easily upset than partner
9 Communication, logical
10 Communication, emotional
11 Coercive: able to punish, threaten, physical coercion
12 Coping: able to cope better than partner when alone

Note: Power bases shown in rank order, i.e. financial power is generally seen as the most significant source of power with which influence can be exerted, followed by sexual power, and so on. Based on answers to questionnaire, see Appendix 2.
Source: Foreman (1996)

to be the most important. Table 4.3 indicates which power bases were reported as the most influential in the relationship.

The summary presented in Table 4.3 suggests that financial, sexual, emotional, childrearing expertise and social confidence were seen to be the most influential power bases. Coercive/physical power was not ranked as very influential in our study, possibly because this was little used in the couples in our sample. Women and men were broadly in agreement regarding these influential power bases and also about seeing communicational skills and ability to cope on one's own as not so significant.

How influential these power bases are perceived to be appears to shape the influence strategies that are employed and in turn the nature of the relationship. We can see that financial and sexual power was seen as the most influential and in turn that these forms of power are gender related. Men typically posessed more financial power but men and women were seen to possess equivalent amounts of sexual power overall. However, when other dominant sources of power are not available, for example in the financially dependent group, then sexual power may become more important, by default. In fact this supports the finding that women in this group were more likely to withhold sex, perhaps because it was perceived to be one of the few influential power bases available.

If some power bases are seen to be more influential than others this may also imply that couples might perceive their relationships as equal. For example, if one partner appears to possess sexual power (and it is perceived to be one of the more dominant power bases) even though they have less of many of the others, and hence less overall, nevertheless they might by virtue of possessing this one powerful base be seen as equal. There was some indication of this. For example, the men in the financially dependent group were seen by the women to be more emotionally dependent, for example, reported as being 'more likely to be upset about divorce' than the women. In contrast, the men in the financially independent group tended to be seen as having more emotional power than the women. However, there were interesting differences in partners' perceptions. The women in the financially dependent group believed that their men were more worried at the prospect of divorce than they were, but the men did not agree with this. Likewise, the men in the financially independent group believed the women to be more emotionally dependent, but the women did not agree.

In effect both these findings suggest that some compensatory mechanisms may be operating but that these may be based on false assumptions. The belief by the women in the financially dependent group that the men were more emotionally dependent perhaps helped the women to feel that the relationship was more equal than it in fact was. This illusion of equality has been referred to as the 'equals but different' discourse (Hollway 1982, 1983). The position of the men in the financially independent group is interesting, perhaps suggesting that seeing their partners as more emotionally dependent was a way of gaining some reassurance that they (the men) still had more power overall, even though the women worked; in effect a reassuring perception that the relationship still followed the gender stereotype of men being more powerful. This finding, though, could also be related to women perhaps feeling 'insecure' and stressed at having to work outside the home in a potentially hostile 'male environment'. They may also have appeared to be emotionally dependent because the double strains of outside work and, probably, of having to do most of the domestic tasks led them to ask their husbands for support. It may be that the women in these relationships do 'turn to their partners' for support but they do not see this as emotional dependency rather as a request for assistance and equity of responsibility.

Emotional dependence and emotional power may be many-faceted and various forms of 'unconscious' dynamics may be operating; for example, women may detect forms of emotional dependence in the men but become aware also that the men deny these. Women may therefore be accurate in their view of men being emotionally dependent despite them denying it. Another possibility would be to do with 'choice' to contract in or out of the relationship. In the case of financially dependent women it could be that in some cases they are emotionally withdrawn and are mainly staying in the relationship because they have little choice.

POWER AND SEXUAL INTERACTION CYCLES

In general, then, our findings suggested that the more dependent a woman was financially the more likely was she to go off sex, and the more likely was her partner to 'complain about frequency'. Whilst women were generally more likely than men to 'go off sex' and men were generally more likely than women to 'complain about the frequency' this difference was not statistically significant in the financially independent group. This finding therefore offers some development to our understanding of the widely documented cycle of male demand/female reluctance. The discovery of this difference between financially dependent and financially independent couples also challenges biological or other accounts of 'natural gender differences' in sexuality as an explanation for this sexual interactional cycle. The findings do suggest that financially dependent women use sexuality as a way of influencing their partners in that they have relatively fewer material resources. In fact when we grouped our couples further into women who were 'highly' financially dependent, the effects became even more pronounced. It may also be the case that women in these relationships harbour some resentment about their position of powerlessness and this leads them to become sexually withdrawn. There was no evidence of any significant differences in beliefs about sexuality between the women in the two groups, and both shared the common view that men 'needed' it more than women.

A critical point is whether the women in effect 'used' their sexual power as a strategy or tactic, or whether they were reacting to a position of relative powerlessness. These may not be clearly or inevitably distinct. A variation was apparent according to the situation and circumstances. We can illustrate this by drawing on material from our interview study with people about power and sexuality in their relationships, and from our clinical case-study material. (This material is also presented in detail in Chapters 6 and 7.) On occasion some women said that they did employ sex in a deliberate way, for example, 'Well, if I want him to be nice to me then I will be nice to him in bed'. Another woman's comments implied that she experienced her sexual reluctance as a reaction, not only to inequality, but to the abuse of power by her partner:

> He thinks that he's not very good at it . . . I think he thinks he can't satisfy me. Well, if he does not it's usually because he's been so beastly to me . . . and the fact that he makes me feel so undesirable.

She clarified that this 'beastliness' included manipulating her by use of his emotional power, continually invalidating her and being irresponsible about money because he was the main 'breadwinner'.

Running through the accounts that women gave was a theme of 'going off sex' as a reaction to 'abuse' of power by the men, frequently early in the relationship, for example, men exploiting or abusing women's dependence on them, as well as more overt threats about money or physical violence. Many women said that they had wanted to be 'close' to the men, to be intimate and spend time pursuing activities together but the men had been reluctant and dismissive of this. In time this seemed to result in the women generally 'cutting off' emotionally and to sexual disinterest and reluctance:

He wanted me to be independent, he was always saying why don't you do this or that, I wanted to be with him, spend time with him but he seemed to reject me, in the end I sort of 'cut off'.

He was always going away, rock climbing or something, I used to say why do you have to go, why can't we spend more time together then he would say well you could come and sit at the bottom of the mountain . . . I was very dependent on him, felt that I had no inner resources to cope on my own, I needed him, wanted to be with him but he seemed to be pushing me away.

It was evident throughout our research, but particularly in the accounts offered by people in our clinical sample, that whatever the women may say when on their own, they never admitted to sexual reluctance as a deliberate strategy in the presence of their partners. However, even though the women appeared to take care not to say this many of the men did perceive sexual reluctance as a deliberate strategy:

She used denial . . . she would say 'No', long term . . . to get back at me for things I'd done to her . . . reduce the frequency . . . to punish me . . . I perceived her holding back as a way of getting back at me.

Conversely, women seemed to be less sexually reluctant when they had more equal power, particularly financial power. This appeared to be related to feeling that they had more autonomy and 'choice' about whether to engage in sex or not, and to feeling that the men respected or valued them more when they were working outside the home and were consequently less financially dependent. Consistent with this, the financially independent women were more likely than financially dependent women to use 'rational verbal persuasion' to exert influence than withholding strategies. Generally, this suggested a picture of the financially independent women as perceiving themselves, and being perceived by the men to be more confident and able to express their opinions in a similar way to the men.

Sexual reluctance also seemed to be related, in the case of financially dependent women, to a 'division of labour' which led to the partners not really having much 'rapport', having different day-to-day experiences and having different domains of 'expertises' which separated them. It seemed important to several women that there should be this 'rapport' for them to feel sexually interested. An unequal distribution of domestic and childrearing tasks, often associated with women attempting to persuade men into sharing these tasks more equitably but failing to succeed, was also associated with sexual reluctance. (This will be covered in more detail in Chapter 6.)

The important question remains of what strategies the men adopted in order to try to persuade women into sexual intimacy? Psychodynamic and feminist theories suggest that men may be more 'emotionally blocked', which leads them to feel and act rather like 'needy children' (Chodorow 1978;

Goldner *et al.* 1990). Sexual intimacy, or more accurately the prospect of denial of this 'need', is seen to activate a variety of childlike reactions. Examples of these featured in both the women's descriptions and some of the men's accounts, and included 'sulking', 'moaning', and more overt 'bullying', such as threats and attempts at control. Many women described that these actions significantly inhibited their desire, 'turned them off' sexual intimacy:

> He sulks. It's just happened actually, he spent the last two nights on the futon . . . He tried to cuddle me and I tried to say I really don't feel like this, at the time I thought it was my right to say it. I could sense that he was cross, so he went to sleep on the futon because he said he felt more comfortable . . . frustrated you know . . . I felt dreadful. I didn't get much sleep.

> He went into emotional blackmail if I did not . . . I was always living under this threat . . . Oh God I'd better do something . . . sulky, quiet . . . it would last all morning I'd try and jolly him along. He did not want to do anything, that was my punishment as we had so much that needed to be done.

In both of these extracts the men are perceived as being emotionally manipulative, rather childlike in their reactions to the women's sexual reluctance. The women were reluctant and the men responded by 'punishing' them by various means through their own power bases, for example: contracting out, withdrawal, sulking, refusing to talk or not doing something that the women wanted them to do. Both partners in these and other examples frequently appeared to be distressed by the cycle, and indeed this is often one of the main problems couples present when engaged in therapy. The women reported that they did usually 'give in' to the man but often did not enjoy the sexual activity. The women did not experience this as freely consenting to sex but instead felt the men had almost 'coerced' them into it; punishing them by various means for their reluctance. This feeling of a 'choice' seemed to be a central issue. Freedom to engage or not in sexual activity, not to feel pressured into it, appeared to make the women feel less reluctant. This view is supported by the lower level of reluctance shown by the financially independent women.

This problematic interactional cycle therefore appears to be complex and influenced by multiple factors. It appears to be related to differences in power bases, and the abuse of power by the men but also to the childlike way in which they respond to the women's sexual reluctance. This childlike response may be an aspect of men's socialization so that they become 'emotionally blocked', unable to express emotions and to articulate their vulnerabilities. However, it is also possible that this is also in a sense strategic, in that men may disguise their feelings in order to maintain power by not admitting their vulnerabilities to the women since this would give women power over them:

MIKE	I used to get very upset, I cried . . . just turn my back and eventually go and sleep downstairs.
RESEARCHER	Did you cry in front of your wife?
MIKE	Oh no.
RESEARCHER	Why not?
MIKE	I didn't want her to know, I thought she might take the mickey out of me for it.

One of the problems with this refusal or fear of showing vulnerability may be that consequently the woman does not know how 'upset' the man is. Several women indicated that had this distress been acknowledged they might have perhaps felt more powerful but also less felt less reluctant.

Sexuality may for many men be one of the only ways in which they can satisfy their 'need' for connectedness and intimacy. However, for many men this need also appears to trigger anxieties and vulnerabilities (Goldner *et al.* 1990). Instead of employing the kinds of actions that women said that they preferred, such as declaring their feelings, expressing love, admitting to needing the woman, wanting to be close, the men often appeared to choose coercion and sulking. This activity may appear perverse, in that it helps to ensure that men often do not succeed even in gaining mediocre and unsatisfactory sex, much less any love and affection. To understand why men act in a way that seems designed to aggravate their sexual frustration it is necessary to see this as part of men's socialization into patriarchal practices which maintain men in positions of dominance. However, though this might in one sense help men to feel more in tune with the patriarchal expectations of male dominance it appears largely to 'turn women off' sexually. In short it may frequently leave men feeling powerful but sexually 'empty handed', in fact in their own hands!

SUMMARY

Women and men have different power bases and various studies, including our own, do seem to indicate that these power bases are used in negotiations and shape the ways in which partners attempt to influence each other. Howard *et al.* (1980) had also found a low level of overtly coercive behaviour. However, there was frequent specific evidence of what could be construed as coercive behaviour on the part of the men in relation to sexuality. Throughout the chapter we have focused on the behaviour of partners as they attempt to influence each other in various ways. These strategies appear to be intimately related to the different sources of power – their respective power bases. These do not simply determine what strategies they will adopt but they do appear to shape and constrain their potential avenues of action. We are not attempting to offer a simplistic model that people's choices are totally determined. There is considerable variation between couples and this is related to various factors, such as their personal histories and the combination of their personalities. But it is also evident that there are considerable commonalities.

In the following chapters we will explore how these characteristic patterns of relating and sexual dynamics are mapped out by the shaped discourses in society which influence us all. As has started to emerge in this chapter these discourses have tended to be predominantly male ones. The singular lack of clearly articulated, and indeed accurate, discourses about female sexuality gives credence to feminist arguments that language is 'man made' (Spender 1980). Consequently male ways of thinking about sexual matters have been dominant. These may be internalized within relationships by both men and women, and come to regulate their beliefs, feelings, perceived needs and their actions. Most significantly they pervade people's thinking, shape their choices, offer an illusion of freedom and can set partners off on courses of action which lead to mutual conflict, sexual frustration and distress.

5

The role of ideological power in relationships

> The ideas of the ruling class are in every age the ruling ideas . . . the class which has the means of material production has the means of mental production, so that in consequence the ideas of those who lack the means of mental production are in general subject to it.
>
> (Marx and Engels 1970: 35)

In the previous chapter we saw that the ways that partners attempt to influence each other are related to the power bases that they have at their disposal. The profile of resources at each partner's disposal significantly influences how they 'choose' to act. We also started to see that partners have ideas about the relative value of their power bases in terms of the influence they can exert. The power bases differ in the extent to which they are defined in this way within the relationship. In short the beliefs that partners hold about their respective power bases at least partly determine how effective these will be. In this chapter we want to return to a discussion of the impact of societal factors in analysing how these beliefs are in turn constructed by prevalent discourses in society. A common example of this includes the biological discourses which suggest fundamental differences between men and women in terms of their emotional make-up and in particular their differing sexual needs. Another is the discourse that problems that arise in relationships are essentially personal or interpersonal. These are evident in psychological theories which propose that problems are due to childhood experiences or personality factors. At the interpersonal level this suggests that problems are due to incompatible personalities, faulty processes of communication or stuck dynamics. Such psychological discourses (as we saw in Chapter 2) appear to play an important part in regulating the thinking and consequent courses of action that partners embark on. In setting what counts as knowledge or truth, discourses shape people's lives and experiences. Frequently we are not even aware that we are holding assumptions which are shaped by particular discourses; instead these are frequently disguised as 'common sense' or as obvious truths.

However, discourses are intimately linked to power. The dominant groups in society have greater power to impose and maintain discourses which serve their interests at the expense of other groups. At the same time discourses also confer power since they can serve to legitimate certain structures, arrangements, roles and privileges in society. For example, the discourse that men are more rational and competent than women has served to maintain male privileges, including money, freedom, property, and access to education, skilled work and the professions and so on. Discourses are not static and unchanging but instead can be seen to change a bit each time someone takes up a discourse and brings it to bear on a set of circumstances. Since people's lives and circumstances are to some extent unique and varying so these continual new applications of a discourse will result in it mutating and changing. It may also be the case that discourses may be used in relationships according to the needs and strategies of the user, for example a feminist discourse may be employed quite differently and given a different gloss when a woman is speaking to other women, as opposed to men.

Partners differ in their material power bases and these can provide a leverage with which to assert one's chosen discourse and version of it. An example we will return to in this chapter is where men assert that women have emotional power, ability to manipulate their feelings, make them feel bad and so on which they present as equivalent to, or even more influential than, men's greater material power base. There is therefore a dynamic and recursive link between power bases and discourses: discourses serve to construct and validate certain arrangements and structures of inequality in relationships and these structures in turn provide the power to impose and maintain certain discourses as dominant. This makes the analysis of power and discourse all the more complex. At any given moment we might be prompted to focus on how the material bases of power are shaping discourses and at the other how discourses have served to construct the relative profiles of power in the relationship.

FUNCTIONS OF DISCOURSES

Foucault (1972, 1979) in particular has outlined the complex ways in which discourses shape various forms of practices. For example, relationships have been organized around discourses of the natural differences and complementarities between men and women. This provides a set of stereotypes of men as strong, competent, breadwinners, unemotional, confident and protective. In contrast women have been viewed as emotional, soft, nurturing, beautiful and needing to be protected. These discourses fuel a wide set of practices and structures that embody and maintain these differences, in the family, work and leisure activities. In suggesting that gender differences are natural men and women are not only allocated different positions of power – men protective/women dependent and needing protection – but it is implied that it is unnatural to alter these.

It is difficult to do justice to the complexity of these ideas and we cannot claim to do so here. However, we can summarize some of what appear to be aspects of the function of discourses in relation to our interests in relationships and power. In particular we wish to draw attention to some of the different ways that discourses may have an important impact on relationships. Foucault (1972, 1979) emphasizes that discourses may be both dominant and offering visions of truth, but also subjugating in that by offering these visions they also implicitly, or explicitly, diminish alternative views. In particular he has argued that in the twentieth century one of the most dominant discourses has been that of science. In various guises science is brought in to support the validity, the truth of certain views, for example of the natural differences between men and women or the nature of sexuality. By application of its methods of observation, measurement, descriptions, systematic analysis and experimentation science has been employed to offer proof or a claim to be able to establish what is true. However, this disguises the fact that science itself is a discourse and how it has been employed to privilege certain views of the world which serve the interests of some groups more than others. Psychology in particular has employed science to suggest, for example, that problems that people experience are essentially due to some personal dysfunction or inadequacy. In our research one of the clearest examples of this was the tendency to view sexual problems that people were experiencing predominantly in individual terms, such as their own inadequacies, biological make-up or childhood experiences. Scientific studies of relationships which have claimed to have identified causal factors, however, serve to distract attention from other possible causes, such as the impact of the experience of inequality and powerlessness on women.

It is possible to outline some of the components of discourses and the functions that they may serve.

1 *To construct truths and norms* Discourses offer views of events and areas of experience and suggest that this is the most satisfactory way of viewing them. Science may be imported to lend weight to the idea that a particular discourse is not just one of many alternative, competing ways of looking at something but is valid or true. For example, biological theories offer the influential idea that men need sex more than women, that women are more emotional than men, that women are naturally nurturing and maternal. These not only offer visions of what is true but also construct norms which then regulate how people 'should' act. So a woman who is not maternal is abnormal or 'sick'. Frequently, the discourse becomes separated from the evidence that is claimed to support it. As an example the biological discourses of sexuality often invoke scientistic concepts, such as hormonal differences

in testosterone, to 'explain' why men need sex more than women. Subsequent use of such concepts, for example in everyday conversations (and even in scientific discussions), often proceeds as if the contribution of these factors had been proven whereas they are, in fact, unsupported, or even unsupportable speculations.

2 *To divert attention to or away from certain areas of experience*   In specifying what counts as truth, discourses also selectively direct our focus. So discourses which hold that women are naturally nurturing in stressing the centrality of mothers for children's emotional development have also diverted attention away from the role of fathers, uncles, aunts and other family members. Likewise, psychological discourses that hold that difficulties experienced in relationships are predominantly due to personal or interpersonal issues have diverted attention away from a consideration of other potential factors such as inequalities between men and women embedded in society. This directing of attention frequently involves paying attention to some elements of relationships rather than others. For example, the focus on psychological factors, such as compatibility and personality, serves to ignore aspects of experience relating to material inequality, material deprivation, etc.

3 *Restricting access to or blocking alternative ideas*   In particular the discourse that men are more rational, logical and intelligent has constructed particular structures which have restricted women's access, for example, to education, professional and vocational skills. At its most extreme this can even involve censorship, for example the attempts to ban books which explored female sexuality and desire, or stories which might suggest that for many women mothering is not such a naturally delightful and fulfilling experience. Again the discourses about gender differences have tended to support family structures in which women stay at home with the children. This in turn has meant that women were not exposed to ideas or experiences which might lead them to regard themselves differently. At its most extreme some men have made it difficult for their partners to spend time with other women, especially attending women's groups and so on. Such blocking actions may in turn be supported by discourses that men are and should be naturally dominant in relationships. The blocking effects may also include the suppression or stifling of new ideas or discourses. If a discourse already captures the truth then new views are unnecessary and threatening.

4 *Creation of distortions, fabrications or untruths*   Discourses may contain versions of events which distort, fabricate or conceal. For example, discourses of female sexuality have typically portrayed women's needs and experience in terms of women needing sex less and placing women who do openly express their desire as 'loose' , 'slags' or 'tarts'. The experience for some women who freely engage in sexual intimacy, however, may be that they are doing this because they want to be 'nice' or 'close' to men. In contrast this biological discourse, certainly in the past, has come to label such generous women as deviant, for example as nymphomaniacs. Similarly, discourses of

power relations between men and women have frequently distorted the reality of gross material inequalities within a view of men and women as different but equal, existing in a complementary and harmonious balance. The fact that this does not represent their experience may then become distorted as a sign of personal pathology or deviance.

5 *Subjugation of alternative discourses* In asserting a particular discourse as true, discourse positions other or alternative discourses as less valid. More specifically, discourses may also contain within them ways of trivializing or marginalizing alternatives. Feminist discourses, for example, have frequently been portrayed as strident, offering a distorted picture of natural male and female qualities and so on. The effects can be that some alternative discourses are marginalized or fall into disuse.

DISTORTED CONSCIOUSNESS

Though we have itemized these various aspects of discourses they are not in reality so conveniently separable. Arguably, these aspects are invariably intermingled and it is possible that a discourse in a sense inevitably distorts by virtue of emphasizing one version of events above others. The issue of distortion is fraught with difficulties because it rests on the assumption of a true version of events which has been distorted. However, we will argue in this section that to an extent discourses do in fact distort aspects of material inequalities in relationships, in particular a minimization of the significance of the experience of financial dependency for women.

It has been argued by Gramsci (1971) that a dominant set of beliefs or an 'ideological hegemony' develops as the result of a gradual and slow social process in which consensus is developed between dominant and subordinate groups. Most importantly an eventual consensus is achieved wherein the subordinate groups come to accept and internalize as natural, self-evidently true or 'common sense' the dominant values, symbols, beliefs and opinions of the dominant groups. This resembles what Marx called 'false consciousness'. Postmodernist perspectives emphasize narratives and discourses in society as a shifting web of meanings created at a local level between people in groups, such as families. Similarly, Foucault's account and related developments in the study of discourses and their operation tend to under-estimate the extent to which some narratives appear to represent fabrications, denials or distortions. In contrast the idea of 'false consciousness' originally proposed by Marx and Engels (1970) suggested that ideologies are derived from structural inequalities. They serve a purpose and some are clearly more beneficial to some groups at the expense of others. It serves the interests of a dominant group therefore to promote and maintain certain versions of the world. This can, but need not necessarily, imply that some groups are 'deliberately' creating falsifications, or that they recognize their ideologies as false. Quite the opposite; in fact ideology may be most powerful when a statement or perception appears to be naturally and self-evidently true, so obvious that it hardly needs to be spoken.

False consciousness is not seen as something that is simply imposed on people but as a set of beliefs which are personally internalized and held to be true, i.e. people actively participate, by holding to such beliefs, in their own oppression and control:

> False consciousness [is] . . . the holding of beliefs that are contrary to one's personal or group interest and which thereby contribute to the maintenance of the disadvantaged position of the self or the group . . . Examples might include accommodation to material insecurity or deprivation, developing needs which perpetuate toil, aggressiveness, misery or injustice . . . deriving a kind of comfort from believing that one's sufferings are unavoidable or deserved . . . and thinking that whatever rank is held by individuals in the social order represents their intrinsic worth.
>
> (Jost and Banaji 1994: 3)

False consciousness can be seen to be evident when a set of beliefs are held which serve to justify an existing state of affairs which clearly operates at the expense of the individual's or group's self-interest. Research studies in a variety of situations (Jost and Banaji 1994) suggest that frequently people hold beliefs about themselves which are clearly counter to their best interests, for example:

1 Women tend to be described by terms such as passive, irrational and incompetent and these terms may be employed not only by men but also by women themselves. Men in contrast are more likely to be described as aggressive, competitive and selfish.

2 Working-class people and people who are poor have been found to be subject to stereotypes as lacking in abilities, unintelligent, incompetent and lazy, and a tendency to accept and apply these terms to describe themselves. Since the poor are predominantly women these negative perceptions can become part of a negative identity, low self-esteem and lack of confidence.

3 Victims of violence in many cases blame themselves for in some way having caused or provoked the attack. This has also been seen to a considerable extent in studies of domestic violence where not only the attackers (usually men) but also extended family, friends and professionals may support this distorted view.

STRUCTURES AND BELIEFS

Discourses and structural arrangements are inextricably linked. Once established the structures can themselves serve to validate the dominant discourses. For example, if women are regarded as instinctively maternal they are positioned in the home and are dependent on their partners. However, the very existence of this arrangement can then be turned around to argue that it is inevitable, in effect since it exists it must do so for a good reason:

> Once a set of events produces a certain social arrangement, whether by historical or human intention, the resulting arrangements tend to be explained and justified simply because they exist . . . the disadvantaged come to believe that the system is part of the order of nature and that things will always be like this.
>
> (Jost and Banaji 1994: 11)

Beliefs which support the interests of dominant groups are taken to be justified, inevitable or true because they are encapsulated in the systems in which they find themselves. The social arrangement of a gender 'division of labour' – for instance, men working outside the home to earn money, and women staying at home to look after the children and house – came to be explained, as being due to women and men having different needs and attributes. In fact historically both men and women worked at home, on the land and so on and with the rise of industrialization the poor, working-class women went with the men into the factories. The middle-class families could afford for women to stay at home and this was a class marker of respectability and reflected well on the man as head of the household. Subsequently this also fuelled the aspirations of the working classes, that a good man would not need to send his wife out to work. Because middle-class and later working-class women did stay at home this became described in terms of their 'freely choosing' to do so because of their attributes, their maternal instincts or their 'biology' and that therefore the arrangement must be in their and their family's 'best interests'.

Our belief systems and the narratives that we employ may be constructed by our more or less passive but continual immersion in and exposure to ideas; from our family and friends and through the media. The absorption of beliefs and ideologies may occur at a non-conscious level and hence people may not be aware of having been exposed to information which leads them to hold beliefs which are to their own disadvantage. A study by Devine (1989), for example, found that subliminal presentations (very brief presentations which preclude conscious perception and awareness) of racial stereotypes of Black Americans later influenced whites' judgements of an ambiguously described person. Those who are in a relatively less powerful position may as a result believe that they occupy these inferior positions because they are less able. If they happen to be a member of one or more of those groups then this self-labelling may function in a self-fulfilling way to locate them in those positions, and further support the false beliefs about their own lack of abilities:

People are apt to underestimate the extent to which seemingly positive attributes of the powerful simply reflect the advantages of social control. Indeed, this distortion in social judgement could provide a particularly insidious brake upon social mobility, whereby the disadvantaged and powerless overestimate the capabilities of the powerful who, in turn, inappropriately deem members of their own caste well-suited to their particular leadership tasks.

(Ross *et al.* 1977: 493)

Being or becoming a member of a particular group, for example the unemployed, single parents, wives, has attached to it a set of beliefs and identities. People may simultaneously be members of a variety of groups: woman, wife, mother, employee, student, friend, and though each may confer different aspects of identity these also overlap. Hence, the identity of wife and mother is inevitably, regardless of the local negotiations and attempts to alter definitions within a relationship, infused by the identity and role of being a woman as opposed to a man in society (Williams and Watson 1988). The beliefs that emerge to distinguish different groups may be quite restricted and to a large extent predictable from the power positions of groups in relation to one another. Low power and high power groups tend to be described in dissimilar terms; low power groups tend to be described in similar terms to each other and these descriptions usually imply some kind of inferiority to the high power groups. For instance, both Black people and women have been described as emotional as opposed to the description of whites and men as rational, at the same time emotionality is often perceived as negative. The descriptions and stereotypes are then used to explain why they are in more powerless positions. Yet, even if these groups are more emotional, which is a dubious assumption in the first place, there is a failure to see that their emotionality may be related to their positions of powerlessness rather than to anything intrinsic to their group.

As Williams and Watson (1988) suggest ideology can function to disguise inequality by ignoring or justifying violent means of keeping women in their place by saying that they 'need it' or 'deserve it'. It also functions to disguise inequality by describing reactions against oppression as 'madness' or 'mental disorder'. Ideology also disguises gender inequality by encouraging women to look to themselves rather than to their social position for possible causes of distress and misery and to blame themselves for problems created by inequality. In intimate relationships one partner may become defined as 'ill' or symptomatic often as a reaction to oppression and a lack of autonomy and choice in their lives. However, the symptom is not seen as related to their relative powerlessness but to their 'background' or their 'personality' – mad or bad rather than oppressed and justifiably unhappy. Once allocated to this position the members of the system will attempt to justify its existence and may even think of explanations as to why the individual is symptomatic. These explanations generally tend to locate the problem within the symptomatic individual rather than the interpersonal or wider societal system (Dallos 1991). Because the individual occupies the role of the person with problems they then become seen as having problems. This may lead to a circular process, the symptomatic person is seen as having problems, this in turn may increase the symptomatic behaviour and thus confirm the label of pathology and illness.

Any given society can be seen to contain a range of narratives which couples internalize in various ways and employ to map their experiences. These narratives are ubiquitous, often presented as obvious truths and may be absorbed more or less passively and outside conscious awareness. However, they are not neutral but are versions of events which may in some instances present distorted views of the world, which serve the interests of some groups of society more than others. This need not necessarily be seen as a conspiracy by some groups to deceive others, though it is a possibility that in some cases the distortions are deliberate. The dominant narratives are internalized by partners and serve to construct and maintain their own disadvantage. Falsifications and distortions may influence relationships in a variety of ways. They may distort the nature of the relationships between e.g. men and women in families. They may offer false or unrealistic explanations of events, for example, problems of mental health may be portrayed as either individual or relational problems.

Attempting to steer their lives employing a 'distorted map' may mean that couples in turn attempt to cope by distorting their own experiences and thereby compound the falsifications. Specifically, instead of viewing such 'myths' as a private phenomenon such distortions can be seen to appear as a response to an experience of powerlessness and negative framing, resulting from the internalization of dominant discourses which distort a couple's experience.

RESISTANCE

It is arguable that people may be passively influenced by dominant discourses and also that the dominant groups may actively promote discourses which suit their purposes. At the same time the discourses may also encounter various forms of resistance. This may be an explicit attempt to criticize or reject some discourses, or an awareness that some subjugated discourses exist and may possibly be of some relevance. It may also be a sense that the dominant discourses somehow do not fit with one's experience. Friedan's (1963, 1981) studies suggested, for example, that the conventional family arrangement was not actually experienced by many women as being in their best interests. Many women's accounts of their lives featured a sense of non-specific dissatisfaction; they were often unhappy or even depressed.

As Friedan suggested the lack of 'fit' between what might have been in women's 'best interests' and predominant ideologies, and structures which said that they should be happy with the arrangement, often led to a 'sense of unease', a feeling that somehow something was wrong, that the situation was not really in their best interests otherwise they would be happier.

Yet at the time there was no alternative discourse, no language (Spender 1980) that could reflect their experience in a clear and valid way. Inevitably this was likely to encourage them to believe that there must be 'something wrong with them'. In relation to the practice of psychiatry, it has been suggested that:

> Psychiatric theories can reflect and reinforce longstanding beliefs about women's status and role, contribute to her devalued status, blame her for difficulties, minimize violence against her and suggest that her behaviour should be shaped so that she can conform to the traditional role.
> (Penfold and Walker 1986: 9)

Yet as Friedan (1963) has suggested dominant discourses leave 'chinks of light'; parts of experience that cannot easily or convincingly be incorporated by predominant discourses. White and Epston (1990) point out that especially when people are experiencing problems the dominant discourses available do not sufficiently represent their lived experience, and most importantly, 'in these circumstances, there will be significant and vital aspects of their lived experience that contradict these [dominant discourses]' (White and Epston 1990: 40). In our therapeutic work and studies of couples (Foreman 1996) it appeared that many women similarly felt that dominant discourses similarly left out vital aspects of their experiences.

THE 'EQUALS BUT DIFFERENT' DISCOURSE

In order to explore the range of discourses employed, partners were asked whether they perceived themselves or their partner to be more dominant in the relationship, or whether they thought they were equal (Foreman 1996). The intention was to explore how these perceptions matched or were discrepant with reported or observable power bases. It was also thought that this question might generate some interesting ideas about what power is; how it is seen, whether there is a high subjective element to definitions and experiences of power or relatively less power. Further, it was hoped that this might also give some insight into the 'discourses' on power itself which may be prevalent currently.

The following section derives from the interview study (see Introduction). These consisted of semi-structured interviews with a broad sample of eighteen volunteers: ten women and eight men. The interviews covered demographic details, power bases, their current and significant previous relationships, beliefs about power and sexuality and the nature of their relationship dynamics. In relation to the 'equals but different' discourse the interview included an exploration triggered by the specific question: 'Who dominates in your relationship; you, your partner or do you think you are equal?'

Our subsequent discussion is illustrated by extracts from interviews. Some illustrative biographical details of the participants whom we quote from are given in Appendix 2.

What emerged from partners' accounts was that the men in particular tended to see their relationship in terms of each of them having different power bases but that these were equally influential, so that the relationship was balanced in terms of power. This has been called the *different but equal* discourse (Hollway 1989) and it includes ideas about difference and dichotomization, complementarity, division of labour, different areas of 'expertise', skill, or resources and interdependence. Generally partners tended to say that their relationship was equal despite them very rarely having similar power bases. If one partner was seen to be dominant this was usually explained in terms of individualistic factors such as 'personality'. There was a tendency to believe that there was an overall balance in their relationship whatever resources or power bases each might have. Different power bases appeared to 'carry' the same weight in terms of negotiation in the relationship; for instance being 'in charge' of the children was often seen to be as influential in the relationship as having financial power. The influence of financial power was only really evident when there had been a change in the balance of it between a couple.

This failure to see the impact of financial power is interesting, implying in effect that feminist perspectives on power were lacking and in fact very few interviewees seemed to adopt what might be described as a feminist discourse on power or relationships. Several of the women indeed appeared to wish to avoid being thought to be feminist; they would make comments during the interviews such as 'I'm not a feminist' as if being a feminist was somehow not acceptable. The only indications of the influence of feminist perspectives were women who articulated a sense of lack of fulfilment with being housewives and mothers. However, this was not specifically connected to a feminist emphasis on the importance of financial independence. This appeared to be related to a generally negative perception of feminism. It could also be seen to imply that female resistance to male dominance has to be covert, possibly for fear of reprisals for any more direct forms of resistance. One of the ways that some men appeared to block women from becoming more independent was by being 'awkward' about sharing domestic or child-care tasks, i.e. not being supportive of their efforts or enabling the women to become financially self-sufficient. Another controlling tactic was to 'label' the women's attempts to become more independent negatively, for example by teasing and making fun of them as well as outright criticisms.

The following extracts illustrate various aspects of the 'equals but different' discourse:

> I think that civilization is a very thin veneer, just below the surface we are very primitive creatures, the model of men being the provider, the hunter, the protector and the woman being the secure homemaker, the holder together of the family . . . is just below the surface for most of us . . . that does not deny equality of rights, interests, but the vast majority of women I've met want to put me in the role of protector and assume themselves the role of homemaker . . . the family bedrock . . . which I don't feel unhappy with . . . good for self-esteem . . . put in a position where one says this is my bit and I say I'm happy to do this bit and they say well you're doing a wonderful job and I say I think you are wonderful for what you are doing . . . you are stroking each other pretty well . . . in most societies it seems to be the case that men tend to be in the provider role and the women homemakers. Well just look at them, how they seem to enjoy their role . . . seems to suggest that they accept their role willingly. I've a strong belief in equality despite the fact I talk about difference, does not mean I think one is better than the other . . . the fact that they have different roles does not make one superior to the other.
>
> (Josh)

This extract exemplifies many of the points raised in the first section of this chapter. It is a good example of the 'different but equal' discourse and was more frequently articulated by men. Josh sees women and men as having different roles, as both being happy in these roles, as complementary and interdependent. Josh appears to be engaging in a form of system justification described by Jost and Banaji (1994). He attempts to explain and justify the 'existing arrangements' by reference to the existing differentiation of roles, which since they exist he assumes must be 'in the best interests' of all. He even suggests that women are choosing their roles willingly: 'Just look at them, how they seem to enjoy their role, seems to suggest they accept their role willingly'. Interestingly, he also suggests that it is women who 'wish to put him in this position'. He appears quite happy about it but he locates the 'push' towards the differentiation as coming from the women rather than from himself. Also, he appears to be implying that he 'goes along' with what women want.

Another male interviewee similarly described their different roles and resources in the relationship as different but complementary and equal:

> I had the job and the money, the power she had was looking after the children. I could not work and look after the children, she could not have any money unless I worked, it worked quite well, power over each other really . . . old-fashioned . . . I think we divided up areas so I was dominant in some ways; car, putting up shelves, finances,

mortgages and all that; she was in charge of the children, we worked well as a team.

(Bill)

Again the differentiation of roles is seen positively, each had some sources of power, they were interdependent and neither was dominant. Overall the arrangement was seen to have a balance; they 'worked well as a team'.

In answer to the question about 'who dominates', women very rarely spontaneously saw things in terms of different but equal and if they did refer to it it was not seen positively. Instead, women tended to talk in terms of being able to exert some influence on their partners, having more freedom, emotional power and personalities. Men's comments tended to be different, emphasizing biology, personality, emotional power, 'deferring' and 'acceding'. Many of the women expressed some unease when considering whether their relationship showed a different but equal structure. In particular what was frequently cited was a dissatisfaction with the specializations they had been allocated – domestic and childrearing. These were seen as double edged; women saw men as more powerful because they could manage to avoid doing the tasks that neither of them really wanted to do, such as the washing up, childcare, cleaning and cooking. Two female interviewees make these comments on the 'different but equal' structure and discourse:

> I feel a great sense of injustice, because I'm female I end up being responsible for the children which means that workwise it's so difficult to find something that fits in with the children so it ends up as my responsibility because I've got less earning capacity. Sometimes I get very frustrated; it's directed at society . . . I want to talk about it sometimes but he thinks it's directed at him personally and he says you want me to give up my job and stay at home, which is not what I want at all . . . I don't resent him being at work, there should just be better provision for childcare . . . I feel very powerless . . . ideally I wanted us both to work part-time and share the childcare.
>
> (Felicity)

Felicity makes the important point that even though her frustration is at society, to talk about this with her partner might be misconstrued by him as a personal attack. She therefore has to contend with managing not only her own frustrations but also protecting his feelings.

In the next extract May describes how she sees her and her partner's relative profiles of power as changing during the life of their relationship:

> He probably was more dominant but now it's changing in some ways . . . I answer back a bit more than I used to . . . changed since I've been working, studying and the children are not so young . . . I think he likes to think that he's in control . . . he does not like me challenging him . . . he does not like being contradicted . . . I do feel sometimes

that he tries to control me . . . that he'd like me to be different than I am . . . he'd like me to cook nice meals and cakes . . . though he knows by now I'm not like that . . . I get cracks about meals sometimes.

(May)

May's account reveals some of the processes whereby resistance and change is countered in relationships. Her partner in making a 'crack' about her meals can be seen to be exerting or importing social pressure for her to conform to a role of a 'good' wife and mother. Even through such apparently insignificant episodes of teasing partners may 'keep up the pressure' to conform by attempting to induce guilt in the other, by pointing out that they are not doing enough – not being 'good enough'.

Men were far less likely to complain about the negative effects of the different but equal discourse or organization on themselves or on the women; problems or difficulties in the relationship are not explained as being to do with patriarchal inequality but individualistic (personalities) or interpersonal factors, such as 'bad' communication or misunderstandings. It could perhaps be argued that, for the men, a different but equal discourse or structure is experienced positively. The women tended to describe the men as feeling 'threatened' when the women overtly attempt to negotiate a similar and equal structure or discourse, which often coincides with the woman going into full-time work, having been at home with the children for some length of time. Women in this position said that they tended to argue, challenge, 'answer back', stop trying to 'please' their partners and report that they behave more independently than they did before; their resistance is fairly overt. They also said that they did not like the position they were in before in the relationship; either that they were aware of their position previously but could not do anything about it or that they have realized now that their position was not satisfactory and was unequal. This is important in that it suggests that the influence of power bases such as financial power bases is not clear until something changes. Their previous necessary acceptance and resignation to their position could easily be interpreted as them liking and choosing it. This resonates with some of the work regarding the inferior position and beliefs of the Black populations in the Southern states of the USA (Dollard 1957; Jost and Banaji 1994). Most of those interviewed tended to see their relationships as fairly equal even though, from a more 'objective' viewpoint, they were not. Within a different but equal structure, women were often reported as being dominant if they had 'dominant personalities' or if they were seen to have more emotional power than their partners.

Individualistic discourses

A perception of power as related to individual factors such as personality was shared by both men and women. In effect for women to believe that their personalities could enable them to be dominant in the relationship would be an example of 'distorted consciousness'; i.e. women are believing something about themselves that is not in their best interests. The perception implies that if a woman does not have power in the relationship it is because of her and that she could potentially have more power if she had a different personality. Therefore it is her 'own fault' if she has little power. Similarly the man may be seen as dominant simply because of his own personality. One of the effects of this would be to attempt to change one's own or the other's personality and is liable to result in often pointless reciprocal individualistic blaming or accusations. At the same time this 'dominant personality' was also viewed somewhat negatively if it was a woman who was described in this way:

> I did not consciously acknowledge at the time . . . I was personally very discontented, very unhappy about being so submissive, but in the face of her extremely forceful personality . . . she maintained her dominant role partly by fear . . . I was afraid to confront her . . . I knew it would lead to an outburst.
>
> (Josh)

The above quote comes from a man whose wife was financially dependent at the time. Another male interviewee, whose wife was also financially dependent at the time, says something along similar lines:

> Overall I think the relationship was slightly dominated by her . . . in some ways she was very forthright and quick-tempered. I was slower, she had strong ideas about how things ought to be; politics and that, she'd say 'That's totally outrageous' . . . I'd be thinking well, there must be two sides to it . . . it's more or less a joke . . . that she was bossy . . . her mother was bossy . . . difficult to disentangle it from the joke.
>
> (Mike)

Josh seemed to be seeing his wife as dominant at some kind of emotional level; he was afraid of her, worried that if he argued with her it would lead to an 'outburst'. Mike, on the other hand, talked about dominance in terms of 'bossiness' and 'strong opinions'. Both implied a negative perception. On the other hand when the man is seen to be dominant because of his personality, this was not seen so negatively: 'I was the stronger character of the two . . . I used to organize things . . . going out at the weekends, the house, I was a good organizer in those days.' A similar 'good organizer', but this time female, describes herself in more negative terms: 'I'm more dominant . . . bossy boots . . . my power is organization, getting things done on time.'

The man is seen to have a 'strong character', his organizational skills are seen as positive, the woman in contrast is viewed above more negatively as 'bossy' and her organizational skills are not viewed so positively. In summary the individualistic discourses appeared to operate differently for men and women, in that the same 'individual' qualities are represented differently – as a sign of male competence as opposed to abnormal assertiveness for a woman.

Emotional power discourse

Josh, above, seems to be implying that his wife was dominant at an emotional level. This was a very common viewpoint; emotional power is rated as highly influential (see Chapters 3 and 4) and is usually attributed to women, especially if they are financially dependent. Emotional power also appeared to be rated as being as influential as other power bases such as financial power. Emotional power could be a component of the 'different but equal' discourse and structure or perhaps a power base that is more idiosyncratic to a particular couple. The finding that financially dependent women tend to be reported as having more emotional power than their partners and more than financially independent women, however, seems to suggest that it is not totally idiosyncratic and falls more within the different but equals structure (couples where the wife is financially dependent generally tend to have this different but equal structure).

Interviewees tended to see this as idiosyncratic rather than as being to do with gender and power:

> I suppose subjectively that I would say I had the power up until the point where my wife decided she did not want our relationship to continue . . . about two years before I left home. The relationship changed and I felt the balance of power was in her hands because I was the one trying to keep things going and so forth and I suppose before it had been her . . . the balance of power changed when she decided she'd had enough . . . reversal . . . whereas before it had been her that was concerned to keep things together as soon as she stopped doing that . . . it was up to me to please her . . . I was the one who was constantly monitoring her moods whereas before it has been the other way round . . . power lies with the one who values the relationship the least.
>
> (Josh)

Josh's description reveals how emotional power is frequently equated with, and becomes seen in stark terms as, who is more able to leave the other, who is more emotionally dependent. For many of the men the theme of monitoring and being wary of the women's moods which is evident in Josh's account was paramount in seeing the women as powerful.

In the next extract Pat indicates that even though apparently powerful in the sense of being the one responsible for 'sorting things out', subjectively her experience is of being powerless because she is so in love, 'absolutely daft about him'.

It's very difficult to say because he's taken the attitude that it's me who is very dominant because it's me that always has to sort things out or take responsibility and then he resents that but on the other hand he holds all the power over emotional aspects . . . so then I tend to feel that it's him who's got all the real power . . . its him that's really dominant . . . He's got so much power because I've been in love with him for as long as I can remember . . . I'm absolutely daft about him.

(Pat)

Emotional power can be seen as a discourse which is to some extent located within and validated by psychological and psychoanalytic frameworks. It emphasizes the power of emotions, of ability to influence another person by making them feel 'good' or 'bad'. This rests on various assumptions, the first being that emotional effects are as fundamental as financial and material ones. The second is that one person can 'cause' an emotional effect in another. Third, it is suggested that we are at the mercy of our emotions. They are seen as having control over us and if we love, need, depend on the other then we have little choice – we become slaves to our passions. This perspective is fuelled by psychodynamic notions of the unconscious as determining all of our actions and experiences – we are slaves of our unconscious.

This constellation of perspectives on feelings does several things; it draws attention away from the fact that men's anger or bad feelings may be a result of their expectation of dominance and reaction to resistance, it blocks and subjugates the idea that emotional power may not be of the same status as material power. It also distorts experience, particularly for women, in suggesting that their emotions are a strategy rather than a reaction to power-lessness. Individualistic discourses are very much located in psychological discourses. These focus attention on individual factors at the expense of inter-personal, material or societal factors. Individualistic discourses are prevalent especially for couples who are experiencing problems. Partners may make concerted attempts to attribute the causes of their problems, and blame and responsibility, to various individual factors; personality, personal and family history, biological make-up and so on. This subjugates alternative discourses that the problems may be related to inequalities of power and gender socialization. In effect ascribing emotional power to one partner seemed to be related to an attempt to view an unequal relationship as equal. In order to achieve this relative influence of emotional power, the value of emotional power seemed to be inflated or distorted so a balance of power seemed to be apparent.

SUMMARY: POWER AND DISCOURSE

Generally, the people interviewed tended to talk about power and dominance in terms of biology, personality and emotional power. They very rarely talked directly about material inequality though there was more likelihood that they would talk about inequality of opportunity. Women as well as men tended to see themselves as generally equal. Whilst often insisting that they were 'not feminists' these same women would talk, though often not very directly, in what could be described as 'feminist terms', e.g. about becoming more assertive, arguing back, becoming more independent or having more freedom and opportunities. Often this would be seen in terms of being more self-fulfilled when they worked outside the home. Despite this broad perception of equality women could, if they were specifically asked, think about the effects of financial inequality, especially if there had been some changes. This might imply that 'asking the question' had functioned as some kind of 'consciousness raising' for the women, or that they were aware, before being asked, that inequality was having an effect but had been 'blocked' in some way from articulating it.

What seemed to be happening was that some versions and elements of feminism were available as possible discourses, but that they were not described as being feminist nor were they very clearly articulated. They did seem to have more than a 'vague sense of unease', as women in the 1950s and 1960s seemed to experience it, according to Friedan's study. Women now seem to have more ability to articulate their areas of discontentment – greater 'language power'. Feminist ideas also tended to be rather 'peripheral', both in terms of the extent to which they existed in 'common discourse', and in terms of how strongly and clearly they were articulated. Women appeared to be adopting some elements of feminism but at the same time denying that they were feminist themselves. This implies that 'feminism' or overtly feminist discourse is not seen positively by women or men, and raises the question as to why this has occurred. Feminist discourse, in theory, should be in the women's 'best interests', in terms of both giving them more material equality and a 'language' through which to persuade and influence. However, feminists and feminism also seemed to be perceived negatively, perhaps along a dimension in which feminism is at one end (masculine, or non-feminine) and feminine at the other. So that by becoming a feminist a woman is seen as losing her 'feminine' qualities. This may be part, not necessarily consciously planned, of a reaction – of a male resistance to perceived challenges to their position of general dominance. As feminism became a more influential discourse and a potential challenge it was also distorted; 'feminists' became stereotyped and perceived negatively as 'man-haters' or 'lesbians' and essentially 'strident and unfeminine'.

At the same time perhaps there are various strands to feminist thinking which may also serve to diffuse its potential power to influence. Arguably the majority of 'feminist analysis' has been articulated by white, middle-class women and may at times contrast with, or not 'fit', the experience of Black or 'working-class' women; feminism therefore becomes diffused. However, this may be to do with the perception of power itself and the associated processes of dominance and resistance. A related problem may be that material inequality may generally be less important for the white middle-class women who have mostly been responsible for articulating 'feminist' perspectives. This in itself can lead to a diffusion of perceptions of power as related to material inequality. However, although it can be argued that the perspective of a white middle-class woman is not exactly the same as the perspective of a Black or working-class woman, and the perspective of a lesbian regarding gender is not the same as the perspective of a hetero-sexual woman, this may be more to do with the degree of oppression rather than a total difference between the experience of the various powerless groups.

More broadly perhaps, what have also become subjugated are discourses which argue about the centrality of the material basis of power. This is often dismissed as an unfashionable 'vulgar' Marxist position. Powerless groups tend to be described in similar ways and their attempts at resistance may be met with similar responses; their experiences and perspectives dismissed, ignored, distorted. Attempts at resistance may be blocked by the generation of negative perceptions or stereotyping. Women as a group have in a sense become divided and dichotomized into 'the feminists' and ordinary, or even 'normal', women. This may be similar to the ubiquitous dichotomization of the poor into 'the deserving poor' and the 'undeserving poor'. Thus the potential solidarity between individuals in a particular group, their com-mon and shared experiences of oppression and inequality, which could lead to an influential challenge to the status quo, becomes diffused; they are divided amongst themselves, which in turn allows those who are domin-ant to maintain their dominance – the ancient but effective tactic of 'divide and rule'.

The holding of financial power does seem to affect the degree to which 'ideological ' or 'language' power is influential. Financial and ideological power seem to be interrelated; for instance, financially dependent women were less likely than their partners or financially independent women to use 'verbal persuasion'. This implies that they are more able generally to influ-ence discourse than financially dependent women. Those who have been financially dependent and are now becoming or are financially independent reported that they are now more assertive, contradict, argue back, generally attempt to persuade and resist through the use of language rather than more covert means. They also reported that being financially dependent and being in a different but equal structure was having an effect on them; being cautious about what they said as well as what they did for instance; feeling that their behaviour was being controlled.

6

Discourses on sexuality

Discourses about relationships and problems, as we have seen, have a powerful role in shaping people's experiences. In this chapter we will focus specifically on discourses regarding sexuality and how these position men and women differently in terms of their roles, feelings, expectations, passions and desires. As Foucault (1979) suggests, discourses must be seen as historically located. They are not static but evolve, fragment, diversify and above all they are contested. Though at a particular time some discourses can be seen to be dominant and most influential they nevertheless encounter various forms of resistance, as we have outlined in Chapter 1. We will start this chapter with a brief historical overview of ideas about sexuality and how these have shifted. Ideas about the nature of sexuality, relationships and gender have altered historically with some traditions of ideas retaining contemporary influence and, alternatively, some ideas changing or falling into disuse. These shifts illustrate how malleable are our ideas about the 'true' nature of sexuality. This helps to highlight just how much contemporary beliefs and assumptions are not straightforward objective truths, nor even the most advanced forms of thinking about sexuality but not infrequently appear to be a recycling of earlier ideas. Furthermore, the dominant ideas at any given time can be seen as highly influenced by the current material and economic circumstances.

A HISTORICAL PERSPECTIVE: THE SOCIAL CONSTRUCTION OF SEXUALITY

One of the key tensions has been, and perhaps continues to be, the debate between explanations which view sexuality as essentially biologically determined, emphasizing its natural aspects, as opposed to socially constructed. In the eleventh and twelfth centuries Christian writings predominantly suggest a view of sexuality as a sin. Of course this may have predominantly been the Christians' view rather than what people actually believed or how they talked about sex. Judging by the amount and fervour of their preaching it might be speculated that ordinary people were not totally convinced, for example, that celibacy was seen to be preferable and to signify a closeness to God and salvation. 'Temptations of the flesh' were to be avoided. Although celibacy was the ideal it was also thought that human nature was weak and easily tempted; marriage therefore was acceptable in order to control these 'base impulses'. As St Paul suggested, 'it is better to marry than to burn with desire'. Marriage was also acceptable for procreation, sexuality that was not aimed at procreation, e.g. masturbation or homosexuality, was seen as a sin. Women's sexuality was mainly construed within the image of Eve, more weak and easily tempted than men and therefore liable to tempt men into 'sin'. The ideal man in contrast was ascetic and moral (Doyle 1989). From the twelfth to fourteenth centuries, often described as the 'age of chivalry', sexuality for both sexes was predominantly concerned with 'honour' and 'nobleness' (Doyle 1989). For men one of the ideal images was the knight; a new kind of man, a soldier, courageous but also honourable. Women's sexuality seems to have been construed in three ways: as like Eve, as above; as like Mary, Christ's mother, warm, compassionate, loving, good and non-sexual; and as an object of 'pure' or 'courtly' love. Women who were the objects of pure love tended to be married and unattainable, high born, someone to 'do battle' for but never to be actually touched, the relationship never consummated.

During the sixteenth and seventeenth centuries Puritanism emerged and part of its claim for power was an attempt to 'prove' that its ideology of discipline, thrift, sobriety, industriousness was morally superior to the ideologies of existing powerful groups, e.g. the aristocracy. This 'code of conduct' applied to all human affairs including the personal/sexual; 'Passion, unrestrained pleasure and personal extravagance had no place in Christian conduct' (Tawney 1926). During this time there appears to be the early development of a separation between sex simply for procreation and sex for pleasure. For instance sex, though only within marriage, was seen as beneficial in that it could 'lighten and ease cares and endear one to the other' (Tannahill 1980). The moral superiority of Puritan men was linked to the moral superiority of their women to other classes of women, e.g. aristocratic women. Aristocratic women were 'public ' women, extravagant and ostentatious, thought to be morally lax by the Puritans. The Puritan wife was to be very different, silent, passive, secluded, domestic, plainly dressed and non-extravagant. Leites (1986) comments that spouses were urged to 'take a steady and reliable delight in each other', a 'delight ' that was sensual as well as affectionate and spiritual. Their sensuality was, however, to have some degree of self-control and extreme emotions were to be avoided. Women were seen to be better able to control themselves than men, thus giving them the edge on moral superiority, wives were even encouraged to criticize their husbands for their moral and spiritual laxity (Leites 1986). This was in contrast to what was happening outside Puritanism, where women's sexuality was seen as rampant and in need of control. A young wife was seen to be invigorating for an older man but tales of being cuckolded also abounded, for example in the tales in the *Decameron* (Boccaccio 1995). In Puritanism we can see an early example of how women were to take on the role of 'controlling' men's 'base' impulses, presumably on the assumption that men are unable to control themselves. In terms of power it might be that to construct this role for women was to allow men to continue to do what they wanted to do and to put any responsibility on to the women. Donzelot (1980) points out that this idea of the sensible, restraining, controlled woman was spread to the working classes as a way of controlling working-class men in the nineteenth century.

Stone (1977) describes the eighteenth century, the 'Enlightenment', as a period of 'sexual laxity and licence; a release of the libido from the constraints of puritanism' (Stone 1977). Bouce (1982) suggests that this was evidenced in fashion: low-cut dresses, an exaggeration of female buttocks and breasts, the growth of pornographic literature and in open, public and unregulated prostitution. The upper classes were described as 'playing sexual, musical chairs'; men from this class were encouraged to boast about their sexual exploits. Sexuality was reconceptualized as part of nature and therefore 'good'. Nature was to be studied and understood, and being part of nature, sexuality was also a legitimate object of study; something that should and could be talked about, 'put into discourse' as Foucault (1979) suggests. Sex manuals were written and the first sex therapists appeared. The sexuality as sin and the self-control discourses were challenged.

Female sexual pleasure was acknowledged and thought to be important. The clitoris was seen to be important for women's sexual pleasure and orgasmic satisfaction expected, 'teasing to no purpose' was seen as potentially leading to nervous problems in women (Bouce 1982). Women could complain about men's 'hasty ejaculation'. There was also a belief that conception would not occur unless women enjoyed and gained satisfaction from sex, the clitoris was the organ that 'makes women lustful', orgasm was a sign that conception had occurred. Women were seen as more sexual than men because they were capable of multiple orgasms, a young woman might 'wear out' her husband (Bouce 1982). Like the Puritans, however, Enlightenment thought focused on moderation, too much sex was thought to make people physically weak; intercourse should not be too frequent and 'never on a Sunday'.

The structure of society changed in the nineteenth century. The new emerging entrepreneurial class, the bourgeoisie, like the Puritans, attempted to gain power partly by 'proving' that they were morally superior to other classes: 'the English became one of the most inhibited, polite, orderly, tender-minded, prudish and hypocritical nations in the world. They bowdlerized Shakespeare, Gibbon and other "obscene classics", inhibited every kind of literature save that suitable for family reading' (Perkins 1969: 280).

Women's sexuality began to be construed within a gynaecological as opposed to a religious discourse (Edwards 1981). The ovaries were regarded as 'autonomous control centres', women's behaviour and 'personalities' were seen to be essentially linked to their biology. Women were seen as going through various physiological and emotional 'crisis' stages, menstruation, pregnancy, childbirth, lactation and menopause that created a kind of 'trauma' in women, making them unstable and therefore not 'fit' to be involved in anything other than domestic tasks. They were thought to be subject to 'strange thoughts, extraordinary feelings, unseasonable appetites and criminal impulses' during any of these crisis stages and they might even make 'false accusation of rape' (Edwards 1981).

At the same time the ideal bourgeois woman was domestic and also desexualized. It was recognized that ovulation and conception occurred naturally and spontaneously which implied that female sexual pleasure was not necessary for conception. Men and women's sexuality came to be seen as different: female sexuality in all social classes was apparently controlled, the middle classes by the need to be 'polite and decorous; polite ladies do not move', and to be 'respectable and chaste' in order to be marriageable; the working classes by more direct means such as the Contagious Diseases Act of 1864. Men, however, were construed as sexually incontinent, as being 'driven' by their sexual impulses, bourgeois men were one of the main clients of prostitution, often bringing VD back to their wives. (This 'male sexual drive discourse' resonates with contemporary views.) In contrast since women were seen as more able to exercise control over sexuality they were also morally superior to men. This allowed women a strategy for challenging their subordinate position, if they were superior morally, why then were they prevented from being involved in 'public' life where their superior values could 'civilize men'? The unfairness of the Contagious Diseases Act was perhaps one of the instigating factors in the development of feminism, particularly the requirement that women should be examined physically to check whether they had VD. Interestingly it was the outcry from 'respectable' middle class women who were stopped (since the police had powers to stop any woman), questioned and had to prove that they were not prostitutes that called a halt to this. There was much less concern about the rights and dignity of poor or working-class women.

During the First World War women had worked outside the home, in 1918 suffrage was extended to women who were householders or wives of householders and over 30. The war had broken up families and in the post-war years sexual mores loosened, contraception became more widely available. A flood of moral criticism followed this period, there was pressure for women to return to the home. The 1920s–1940s saw the development of a suburban, white collar class embodying middle-class aspirations of home ownership, domestic comforts, women in the home and men as breadwinners. Gender inequality was explained within a 'different but equal' discourse, whereby men and women were seen to have fundamentally different but equal attributes. In the 1940s motherhood, still the main role of women, received a great deal of attention, because of the perceived social problems of delinquency and 'problem families' – 'latch-key children'.

The 'modern' discourses

According to Jeffreys (1990), in the 1940s and 1950s women were persuaded, because of the growing fear of feminism, that they needed a man for their own sexual pleasure. Sexuality was defined as phallocentric, featuring vaginal penetration and ejaculation. By the 1950s and particularly in the 1960s women were frequently construed as 'frigid' and 'uptight' if they did not enjoy sex. Sexuality was construed as 'natural' and anyone who did not enjoy it as 'pathological'. The emphasis on orgasm led to many women simulating enjoyment. Jeffreys argues that in a sense sex was not simply seen as 'fun' but as 'work', a 'skill', like housework, that women needed to acquire.

Within these beliefs to be a 'man' was to be responsible and mature, for men were expected to grow up, marry and commit themselves to supporting their families. Masculinity was virtually identical with a breadwinning role, if the man deviated then he would be thought immature, developmentally 'stuck' and possibly homosexual. Ehrenreich (1983) suggests that many men were unhappy with their role; white-collar work was seen to be emasculating. Most complaints, however, tended to be directed at women rather than the social system; women were seen as powerful, 'megalomaniac mothers' interfering in the lives of all the family. By 1956 *Playboy* was selling over one million copies; in this women were portrayed as 'gold-diggers', quite willing to 'crush a man's adventurous and freedom loving spirit'. The ideology of *Playboy* was to give the message to men that they did not need to get married, they were to carry on working and earning as much as possible but there was no reason for them to have to work to support families, they could 'buy' sex, and enjoy it without the hassle of having to become emotionally involved with women.

Also developing were the 'Beatnik' ideologies which included a challenge to conventional values of marriage, work, emotional commitment and to supporting their wives and families. Sexuality was seen within a discourse of 'freedom' and conventional marriage was seen as 'boring, dull and non-sexual'. It was also acceptable within the beat subcultures to have gender role-reversals, i.e. women who would support men. The emerging humanistic psychology in turn offered an alternative view of human nature, though generally male rather than female 'nature'. Instead of 'maturity', life and development were seen to be about 'growth' and 'fulfilling one's potential' (Perls 1969; Maslow 1987). If marriage was preventing 'growth' then it was perhaps better to get out of it; divorce was seen as a 'growth opportunity'.

In the 1960s, often described as the 'permissive era', male and female sexuality began to be construed as similar; it was 'natural' and 'fun', both sexes could and should enjoy it, even without emotional involvement. Those who did not were seen to be and sometimes accused of being 'uptight' and 'repressed'; the aim was to overcome these repressions and inhibitions (Jeffreys 1990). Jeffreys suggests that this emphasis on the importance of sex functioned to prevent women thinking about how to gain other kinds of power. Sexuality was separated from possessive and negative emotions; the most liberated individual would not be possessive, jealous or feel guilty. Single women were now construed as sexual in contrast to the 1940s and 1950s when they had been seen as 'dried up old maids' (Gurley Brown 1962) Women were expected to anticipate and turn themselves into a willing object and provider of sexual services to men:

> What the male turn on equipment requires is the exact reverse of a virgin or passively recipient instrument, but not a demand situation because that itself can threaten a turn-off from inadequacy feelings, but a skill situation.
>
> (Comfort 1994: 32)

Comfort's book is still currently one of the widest read sex manuals for heterosexual relationships, yet women's sexuality is hardly mentioned.

Feminism

Initially many feminists, from the 1960s on, believed that they had a 'true, essential sexuality' that had somehow been stolen from them by men. For the last 200 years men had been persuading women that vaginal penetration should be enjoyable and result in orgasm for women; they had been persuaded that they were masochistic, wanted to be dominated and, in the nineteenth century, that they were not really sexual at all. Furthermore, women's sexuality, it was argued, could be seen as 'superior' to men's because they were multiply orgasmic. The ideal male sexuality was 'potent, continually capable of sex and always desiring, able to separate sex from emotion and making use of all sexual opportunities' (Jeffreys 1990). The female version of this was epitomized by Erica Jong's 'zipless fuck' (1974), women's sexuality was construed in the same way as men's. When feminists began to look at the problem of male sexual violence against females, feminists began to question the acceptance of sex as positive. In the 1970s men's sexuality itself, for virtually the first time in history, began to be seriously challenged. Rape and child sexual abuse began to be construed not simply within the male sexual drive discourse but also to be analysed in terms of power. Rape and a patriarchal society's lack of an effective, concerted and convincing response to rapists were seen to be a method of exercising control over women, for example in suggestions that in many cases the woman was responsible because she 'led him on' (Griffin 1971).

However, in the 1980s there were various attacks on feminism, from both the political left and the political right: from the right for its perceived influence in the breakdown of families, from the left for its intolerance of pornography, its questioning of male sexuality and 'movements of affirmation'. Jeffreys suggests that most of the attack from the left came from socialist gay male intellectuals. Their attack featured the twin themes of freedom and naturalness: freedom included the right to sexual promiscuity and diversity, to engage in sexual activity of one's choice: paedophilia, incest or sadomasochism. Naturalness represented a disagreement with a feminist analysis of sexuality as being socially constructed. Gay men argued that the sexuality of the 'sexual minorities' was somehow natural and should not be questioned. Rather than challenging any of the conventional discourses on sexuality (male) this position of 'naturalness' can function to remove responsibility. The 'sexual minorities' – those who have a different sexual preference, according to Weeks (1985) – include 'transvestites, transsexuals, paedophiles, sadomashochists, fetishists, bisexuals and prostitutes'. Each of these groups is seen to have the right to express their sexuality in the way in which they prefer; morality or even 'pathology' are not part of the discourse. Jeffreys (1990) comments that male gay sexual discourses are simply a different version of the male sexual drive discourse and offer no real challenge to male sexuality, especially in terms of their emphasis on casual promiscuous relationships. 'Gay men do not just like other men they are like other men' (Stoltenberg 1978). However, these twin themes of naturalness and freedom are also contradictory since naturalness suggests that sexual orientation is not simply something we can choose but is 'natural' – biologically determined.

Eroticization of dominance

Alternatively, theories inspired by lesbian writers offered much support to the main direction of a feminist analysis in its challenge to a simple phallocentric sex and to male/female power relations:

> From the birth of lesbian feminism, lesbians have asserted that lesbianism is a fundamental threat to male supremacy. We have asserted that lesbianism is a crucial strategy for women to undertake if they wish to end their subordination . . . our energy must flow towards our sisters not backwards towards our oppressors . . . tremendous energies will continue to flow into straightening up each particular relationship with a man, how to get better sex, how to turn his head around into trying to make a new man out of him.
>
> (Radical lesbian paper 1970, in Jeffreys 1990: 290)

It was argued that 'heterosexual desire is eroticized power difference', so that the basis of heterosexual desire, what is experienced to be erotic, is founded on assumptions of difference and this 'difference' is predominantly an inequality power. Inequality becomes erotic so that men, it was suggested, tended to be attracted to women who have less power than themselves – younger, poorer, less qualified and less status. Conversely, women tend to be attracted to men who have more power than themselves (Jeffreys 1990). Furthermore, this 'eroticization of dominance' is learnt through exposure to a barrage of cultural stimulation from James Bond films to soap operas and Mills and Boon books (Wilkinson and Kitzinger 1993). This eroticization is not seen as a harmless preference but as embodying and perpetuating male dominance and oppression over women. Though it is beyond the scope of this book, there is a question of whether homosexual relationships can easily escape the trap of inequality and oppression. Research appears to be equivocal since lesbian and gay relationships can both demonstrate greater equality but can also exemplify gender stereotypes and patterns of dominance (Nardi and Sherrod 1994).

Lesbian discourses on sexuality are useful to heterosexuals both in advocating equality and in their challenge to phallocentric sex. Equality, they argue, encourages a mutual and non-abusive, non-exploitative approach to sexuality. That this is desired by many women is encapsulated in the quote below:

> 'More kisses, more time, more tenderness . . . why don't men like to be touched in other parts of their bodies . . . I do . . . I would like to see men with more imagination' and 'I would like to be able to sustain sexual activity indefinitely . . . I find a man's exhaustion after orgasm disappointing', and lastly 'I've never been able to say "yes" that's all I could have asked for, there's nothing more I want . . . I've always felt that my sexual encounters have been only beginnings; they've never been carried as far as I would like them to be.'
>
> (Hite 1976: 129–357)

In the following section of this chapter four main discourses, complemented by a historical analysis, will be examined as a framework for the analysis of contemporary thinking and assumptions about relationships, power and sexuality.

CONTEMPORARY DISCOURSES AND SHARED SOCIETAL CONSTRUCTS

This brief historical review reveals that ideas about sexuality and sexual differences between men and women have fluctuated over the centuries and within the twentieth century. Rather than being an obvious biological fact there is little hard evidence for any fundamental differences in 'need' for sex between men and women. However, some ideas appear to be extremely potent and influential, and it is arguably these which shape the nature of sexual activity and attitudes. George Kelly (1955) laid the framework for a theory which emphasizes that people's actions are guided by the constructs (Chapter 2). His concepts of commonality and sociality emphasized that in order to take part in social processes and relationships we need to hold some constructs in common and to have an idea of how others see events. Likewise, in order to participate in our society we need to be aware of the prevalent discourses and to agree to utilize these. We do not have to 'agree blindly' or conform but we need to know 'what is going on', how our society frames particular experiences and phenomena in order to be able to participate actively in society.

Specifically we can then ask what the common assumptions, beliefs, explanations, constellations of arguments – discourses – are about sexuality. These can be seen to be absorbed by groups, families and individuals and through their assimilation come to regulate the actions of couples. There will be a degree of personal and interpersonal interpretation of the constructs and also the possibility that individuals and groups do not simply passively absorb discourses but can engage in various forms of resistance. However, a related question that we will explore is the impact (or the lack of it) that, for example, feminism has had on popular notions of sexuality and gender.

Biology and sexual need

Hollway (1983, 1989) emphasizes that 'personal' experience is necessarily social, since it is framed by, given meaning by, the wider set of discourses that impinge on us. She has also indicated that there are a number of influential discourses regarding sexuality which shape sexual relationships. Inevitably these sexual discourses are fundamentally related to issues of power. Hollway has argued that perhaps the most fundamental of the popular dominant discourses is the idea of natural and inevitable differences between men and women due to their fundamentally different biological make-up. This leads men to need sex more than women, who in contrast are seen as wanting to seek intimacy. Hollway refers to this constellation of beliefs that men naturally have greater sexual urges and needs as the male sexual drive discourse (MSDD). In turn this may lead men to expect that they have a right to women's bodies, that it is 'natural' to put pressure on women to have intercourse, that if their desire is thwarted then it is understandable and legitimate for them to use force. If women internalize this discourse they may believe that they have an obligation to meet men's sexual demands, that their own sexuality and needs are less important, that it is 'natural' for men to initiate and control what happens, that women have a duty to satisfy those needs, that it is women's responsibility if things go too far. In contrast women are generally construed as wanting closeness and a relationship rather than just 'sex'.

Doyle (1989) suggests further that 'being interested in sex' is a major part of masculine identity. Such links between 'masculinity' and sexuality can create problems; there is a tendency for men to believe that other men are having 'better' sexual relationships than they are, and to believe that sex is 'straightforward' and problem-free; women rather than men are expected to have sexual 'hang-ups' and problems. Most men believe that they can never 'get enough' sex; that they will always feel like 'it' whatever the circumstance; that women, not men, are likely to refuse. One of the most problematic beliefs is that sex is all that really matters in a relationship with someone else; closeness, affection, 'cuddling', touch are not important. Furthermore, believing that sex is so important keeps men separated from full human contact. According to Hamblin (1983) men define what constitutes 'normal' sex, and this definition leads to particular expectations and therefore behaviour. She goes on to argue that if 'normal' or 'real' sex is defined as vaginal penetration and ejaculation, men may expect that the appropriate way for them to express their sexuality is through intercourse, and that all other forms of sexuality or sensuality are merely preliminaries; that they have a right to intercourse, that they are not real men unless they are having (regular) intercourse, that intercourse is what women really want. If women internalize this discourse they may believe that in sexual relationships with men intercourse is inevitable, that other forms of sexuality are not 'real' sex, that they should get satisfaction from intercourse and if they do not there is something wrong with them. The assumption that sex equals vaginal intercourse may also serve to confuse the issue about sexual desire. Various studies suggest that many women do not gain satisfaction from vaginal penetrative sex but do so from other forms of sex.

Hollway also draws attention to various levels of ambivalence and contradictions in men's dependency on sex. On the one hand men being defined as 'needing' sex more gives women power over men. However, this is diffused by making sex into an object, a commodity rather than a set of feelings or a relationship; 'once you have shown the other person that you need them you've made yourself incredibly vulnerable . . . now you've let them see a little bit that is you . . . it'll be rejected . . . the insecurity gives someone else power' (Hollway 1983: 132). Denying or suppressing vulnerability may be a method by which men have maintained their dominant position despite the fact that they deprive themselves simultaneously. Consequently defining women as more needing of intimacy, wanting a relationship, commitment – a have/hold relationship discourse – turns the tables to make women dependent. Women are constructed as wanting commitment, having expectations, liable to 'make demands', wanting 'closeness'; and men are the objects of this discourse rather than subject to it themselves. She comments: 'by reading himself as the object of the have/hold discourse he can suppress the recognition of his dependence on a relationship with a woman . . . if he succeeds he can sustain the relationship and meet some of his needs while both remain unaware of them' (Hollway 1983: 132).

The have/hold discourse can be seen to some extent as the other side of the MSDD discourse. However, it is perhaps clearest to see it as a separate discourse which emphasizes the concepts of emotion, connections, relationship and commitment. It offers a relational as opposed to biological landscape.

AN INTERVIEW STUDY: SEXUAL DISCOURSES

We had frequently encountered these discourses in the stories and accounts of couples in our clinical work and wanted to pursue them in more detail. In order to do so we included in the interview study (see Introduction and Chapter 5) an exploration of the extent and operation of these discourses, for example, whether men and women both accept the discourse that men, because of their biological make-up, need sex more than women. In this section we will outline further data from the interview study in which we interviewed ten women and eight men. Of this sample we will present extracts from 12 of these participants. Some illustrative biographical details for each person are provided in Appendix 2.

The interview explored in detail their views regarding relationships, sexuality and power. From this data we discerned four influential discourses (following Hollway's work), and a fifth, less evident strand, the 'feminist discourse', that appeared to shape their experience:

- The male sexual drive discourse, divided further into
  1 the biological drive discourse
  2 the phallocentric discourse
  3 the female as precipitator discourse
- The have/hold discourse or 'relationship discourse'
- The permissive discourse
- The 'new man' discourse.

We will briefly outline the key aspects of each discourse that we discerned in our study and give several examples as they appeared in people's accounts.

The male sexual drive discourse (MSDD)

According to Hollway (1982, 1989) the key tenet of the MSDD is that men's sexuality is directly produced by a biological drive, the function of which is to ensure reproduction of the species. Men's sexuality is understood through the MSDD; men are expected to be sexually 'incontinent' and out of control. Hare-Mustin (1991) adds that men's sexual urges are assumed to be natural and compelling; thus the male is expected to be pushy and aggressive in seeking to satisfy them; 'Male sexuality because of the primitive necessity of pursuit and *penetration* does contain an important element of aggressiveness which is both recognized and *responded to* by the female who *yields and submits*' (Storr 1970: 89–90).

Located within the MSDD there can be seen three different strands:

1 *The biological drive discourse* This is the idea of a biological *drive* that somehow 'compels' the male to seek physical/biological sexual gratification, the idea being that male sexuality is uncontrollable by the male himself. A further implication may be that he may be 'compelled' to resort to aggression or force in order to satisfy this sexual drive.

2 *The phallocentric discourse* This is a model of sexuality which emphasizes that it is a 'drive' whose aim is essentially penetration and ejaculation. That is, male sexuality is about penetration and ejaculation. The 'object' of this drive is female in so far as the goal is reproduction of the species.

3 *The female as precipitator discourse* In this, according to Hare-Mustin (1991), the female arouses and precipitates this drive; the female 'acts' as a stimulus; the male is responding to the female. This element is in effect distinct from the other three elements in that it is suggesting almost that the drive in the male is latent until stimulated by the female.

The following extracts exemplify the MSDD and aspects of these three strands (italics added for emphasis):

> I've been led to believe that a man's sex drive is not as *controllable* as women's . . . for a woman it is sort of controlled within oneself . . . because, I mean, there's nothing obvious about how we are feeling but for a man there is physically. It is evident for a man but for a woman there are no *outward signs* . . . a man starts down that road and then there's that ultimate end. It's predictable what is going to happen, but for a woman, well there is a climax, but there is nothing *visible* to show. A woman can *postpone* sex, a man cannot. Once he starts down that road he has to carry on until he's done it but a woman does not really have to, a woman could switch off half way after getting excited but I don't think a man could so easily . . . You have to be careful what you say, how you dress . . . lots of *signs* coming off that for men . . . it's difficult to put yourself in a man's place . . . they always say . . . there's such a strong sex drive for men that it's very difficult for them . . . I would not like to *provoke* a man by how I dressed or what I said.
>
> (Jan)

This extract contains strands from all three elements of the MSDD. Jan appears to be saying that men have a strong sex drive, and that it is uncontrollable: 'he has to carry on until he's done it'. She also adopts a phallocentric discourse focused on external 'outward' signs of arousal, (presumably) erection and penetration and ejaculation; 'until he's *done it'*. The woman is also seen as a precipitator: 'there are signs coming off that for men' and 'I would not like to *provoke* a man'. This also implies that she has to control her behaviour, for instance what she says or how she dresses, in order to avoid 'provoking' them. Sexuality is defined as penetration and ejaculation, and female sexual pleasure seems to be secondary or may even be ignored. The woman has less power in terms of the 'capacity' to get her needs met. Similar ideas about basic physical differences and this idea of pressure of sexual need for men are evident in the next extract:

> There are very clear differences between men and women on several levels, first the purely physical element; with men there is a *material physical product* in that they need to physically *reduce the pressure* that *builds* up . . . with women there are pressures that build up though in a different sense; they are not pressures that lead to a physical by-product . . . if a man who is accustomed to a regular active sex life suddenly finds himself in a period of not having a sexual *outlet* he will find himself physically pressured in a different way from how women find themselves pressured physically.
>
> (Josh)

For Josh the biological framework appears to involve a 'plumbing' metaphor; 'pressure' builds up and the man needs an 'outlet' for this pressure. This view potentially hands some power to the woman in that he sees himself as having a 'need' for someone to help reduce the pressure. There may also be the implication, however, that the pressure might 'build up' to such an extent that men might be 'compelled' to use force to reduce it, for example rape. In contrast women are seen in different terms. Howard, in the next extract, in fact indicates that he is aware that women are socialized into a different role regarding sex:

> A lot of women were encouraged in the belief that it is not nice to admit to any sexuality . . . as soon as a woman expresses any spontaneous interest in sex she runs the risk of being seen as a tart . . . it must make it very difficult for them . . . lots of men would not like it anyway . . . I know men who would be very uncomfortable with a woman who was 'forward'.
>
> (Howard)

Male sexuality appears to be viewed by Howard here as 'predatory' and *active*, with implications of pursuit, giving control and an active role to the male. Female sexuality in contrast is seen as passive and a woman who exceeds the constraints is 'too forward', risks being seen as a *tart* and many men 'would not like it'. The predatory, aggressive aspect of male sexuality is emphasized by Bill in the following:

I think the male because of his *physiology* almost is more *outward*, more *demonstrative*, more *assertive*, tends to feel he should take the *lead* some-how . . . also I think there is a *hormonal* difference between testosterone and oestrogen . . . testosterone very definitely produces more *aggression*.

(Bill)

In Bill's statement again there is the view of biology as determining behaviour but also of two types of biological explanations: phallocentric 'physiology', presumably referring to the penis and erection, and a reference to hormones. It is almost 'anatomy as destiny'; having a penis has a different implication for behaviour from not having one, having a penis signifies being 'demon-strative, assertive' and active. It also means that the man feels he should 'take the lead'. It is not clear, though, what the absence of a penis signifies – passivity perhaps. Secondly, there is a hormonal theory suggesting that testosterone produces aggression, and implying that male sexuality may be rather aggressive. In combination with the idea of being 'driven' sexually, this may imply that the man is liable to use coercive power in order to 'persuade' the women into sex with him.

The have/hold discourse

According to Hollway (1982, 1989) this discourse is not about sexuality specifically but about the Christian ideals associated with monogamy, part-nership and family life. She also suggests that female sexuality is seen as a 'lack' and is seen more in terms of 'relationship' with husband and family. Hare-Mustin (1991) suggests that this discourse is the 'under-pinning of the ideal family where monogamy is the rule and there is a commitment by both to have and to hold each other'. At the same time for a man to commit himself to a woman she must be attractive. She suggests that women are seen as needy of closeness and intimacy which are in turn seen as weakness, men are seen as necessary to support the weakness of women; masculinity is about strength and the concealment of weakness. Perhaps, put rather bluntly, this is summarized by the old saying that for men marriage is the price a man pays for sex, whereas for women sex is the price a woman pays for marriage.

The have/hold discourse emphasizes that sex should only occur in a loving, caring relationship and not until an acquaintanceship has attained the criteria for this can sex proceed. The male position on this may be in terms of 'how to prove to her that I want a relationship so she will have sex with me' in contrast to the female position of ' how can I be sure he wants a relationship not just sex before I will engage in sex'. It could be that the have/hold discourse also involves some game-playing or ritualistic aspects in that both men and women equally want sex and to be close but are expected to demonstrate different roles. A related and important point is that both men and women learn both discourses, so that MSDD and have/ hold can be seen as two ends of a continuum. In effect men and women choose, or are taught to choose, different preferred positions on this discourse but 'understand' and anticipate each other through this continuum, or construct.

The have/hold discourse as articulated above is rather difficult to unravel. The main elements appear to be about fidelity, commitment to each other and partnership. To some extent it appears to be a construction of women's rather than men's sexuality and makes a distinction in which men's sexuality is seen within a sexual drive discourse and women's sexuality is seen within a have/hold, or perhaps more appropriately a *'relationship discourse'*. Women's sexuality is not located within a biological drive discourse of 'pressures that build up' or as uncontrollable and requiring a necessary release; but is to do with relationships and relating, with wanting intimacy, closeness, commitment, involvement, 'love' and affection. The biological element may creep in as female sexuality is conflated with the maternal instinct: for example, the belief that women are interested in sex in so far as they have a 'drive' to reproduce and/or the belief that because they are women and therefore potential or actual mothers their sexuality is more diffuse, more nurturant, caring or affectionate. This also contains some of the fundamental elements of notions of romance and romantic love which stress closeness, emotional connection and spontaneous feelings of warmth from which desire flows:

> The statement 'I love you', whether spoken or merely implied, is not the statement of some primitive impulse, a kind of civilized moan of sexual excitement . . . Rather . . . a willingness and desire to enter into a certain kind of relationship, and if the statement is sincere, to meet the obligations as well as to enjoy the privileges associated with that relationship.
>
> (Averill 1985: 106)

The have/hold discourse, and within it the notions of love and romance, can also be seen, as in Averill's description, as focused on and constructing female experience. More simply it can be seen as representing a social control of sexuality and constraint of women's sexuality:

> I think people differ in their needs, not men and women necessarily but I think they see it differently. I think for men it's more of a *release* . . . more of a *physical* experience . . . for women it's more of an *emotional* experience . . . that's why I think you need to be *emotionally* close . . . for me . . . to enjoy the physical experience whereas for a man I don't know if that's necessarily true.
>
> (May)

Women and men's experience, including their use of the word 'love', may be different. For example, for many men sexual excitement and lust are central and the injunction that there are expected obligations is secondary, if not to be resisted:

> For men it's more *physical* and for women it's more *emotional* and *intellectual* . . . thinking . . . in the head . . . I think it's harder for a woman to make love if you are not feeling *in tune* with them whereas I think it's probably a lot easier for a man to . . . but it depends . . . we're all individuals.
>
> (Felicity)

In contrast to the playing down of sexual needs and lust in the have/hold and MSDD, the feminist discourse, which is discussed at the end of this section, is that women do have choices – to be lustful or seriously involved in a relationship, or both, or neither. Josh in the next extract summarizes how he feels men and women differ in their ability to express and act on their sexual desire:

> If I go to a party and meet someone who I find very attractive I can't think of any reason why I should not go back with her and make love with her . . . but I think most women in that situation would probably want to wait a bit longer until there was a more solid rapport built up because that is a fundamental part of sexual activity . . . in my view . . . for most women.
>
> (Josh)

Permissive discourses

The MSDD does not generally hold that women should actually *enjoy* sex; female sexual pleasure is not important; generally they are expected to accept, yield, receive, allow and satisfy the man's sexual drive. Women are the object of the MSDD; as long as they 'give him' what he needs or wants when he needs and wants it there is no cause for complaint. They are generally perceived as passive recipients of sex in the MSDD, any excitement being mainly a function of the man's ability to 'turn them on'. Reluctance to engage in sex may be put down as being due mainly to biology, women are not particularly interested in sex because they don't have the same sexual drive as men, they are almost naturally reluctant. The relationship discourse similarly almost ignores female sexual pleasure: women are construed as not really being interested in the physical component of sexuality but as having more concern with relationship and emotionality. Reluctance to engage in sex is explained as being due to feeling that there is a lack of emotional closeness. Women may or may not be 'active'; whether they are or not is seen to be related to whether they feel emotional closeness to their partner.

Within the permissive discourse, however, women's sexual pleasure becomes, ostensibly, important. Women are supposed to have the same sexual needs and drives as men. Reluctance is explained through the idea of female inhibition or repression; sex is 'natural', the enjoyment of sex is natural for men and women therefore a disinterest is unnatural; implying that there must be something wrong with her, that something has happened to her, perhaps due to an inhibited family background or sexual abuse, and this has led her to be inhibited and repressed. Women are supposed to take an active role because they want and need sex in a similar way to men.

> In the sexual revolution of the 60s, 70s ... women and men were supposed to be sexually active, equal ... that put on women the feeling that they should be enjoying it and incredibly responsive, go out and have a lot of fun and a lot of women are feeling it's not good fun, I'm not enjoying this, what's wrong with me. And an awful lot of the advice is that you should be liberated and if you are not liberated you must be repressed and why aren't I enjoying it.
>
> (Mary)

Deidre in the next extract articulates how she feels pressure to conform to the permissive discourse from her female friends:

> I have a problem ... started thinking about why don't I respond to sex ... I feel quite insecure about it, as if I should be better at it. Quite a lot of my women friends seem to really enjoy it, not the married ones mind you ... more initiating of sex than me ... more adventurous in sex than me. I was out with a group of them last week and they were talking about sex ... I felt very uncomfortable, could not join in. I felt very repressed and uptight, am I not adventurous? ... I've tried doing it in different places, a few different positions but not much ... Oral sex, I don't think I could manage that ... Is that *very repressed*? ...
>
> (Deidre)

Several men expressed a disappointment that they still had to take the initiative, perhaps that the women were still not permissive enough:

> Interestingly ... very often ... you know the evenings when you go to bed and you know this is a night when we expect to have sex together ... but I know it's down to me ... I have to make the first move ... I know she wants to make love but if I don't do anything I know we will just go to sleep ... she had a very Victorian upbringing.
>
> (Ken)

> I don't feel threatened by women who are sexually 'forward' ... this one woman seemed sexually liberated and extravert, active in arranging the situation ... very forward ... It was her that moved the relationship into sex but when it came to the nitty gritty she just lay there and did

absolutely nothing, she seemed to enjoy it . . . I did not take it as a sign I'd failed but I felt I was on my own . . . sex for her was something I did to her but sex for me is something you do together, equal; both taking part. She was not taking part . . . here I am, get on with it . . . I could not . . . I thought what's the point . . . if it's just physical gratification you can do it on your own . . . my ideal is that it should be an equal thing . . . though maybe I'm kidding myself . . . I want us to both be there for each other . . . both taking part . . . something you do together . . . not something one does to the other . . . I can't see the point.

(Howard)

These extracts summarize both the discourse and the problems to which they can lead. Women and men are supposed to enjoy sex and to be similarly motivated and active to men. They are expected to be 'liberated': free from sexual 'hang-ups', free and uninhibited about sex. Women who don't enjoy sex must therefore be repressed; 'why don't I respond to sex?' asks Deidre above. There is a danger that, in contrast to the MSDD where men may see themselves as inadequate and incompetent sexually, sexual difficulties within the permissive discourse are now blamed on the woman's sexual repression and inhibitions and not on the man: whatever goes wrong is probably the woman's fault. A further implication is that it is the woman who must change in some way, for example go to a psychotherapist, perhaps, or simply get more sexual experience and overcome their inhibitions by 'working them through' in sexual activity (with men). To be liberated or to prove a lack of inhibition also means to be adventurous, to try different things in different places and positions, to experiment.

There are positive strands to the permissive discourse in lifting some sanctions from women but in the context of inequalities and unsatisfactory conditions for women there are also many negative implications, especially in that the discourse may become used as a strategy of control. Deidre above had pointed out that her married friends were less likely to talk about how much they enjoyed it. This fits with the caricature of married women going off sex but the permissive discourse can be employed to ignore what some of the contributory cause may be to focus on the woman as at 'fault', not liberated enough perhaps if she is not enjoying sex:

We've talked and talked about it . . . he says it's my fault I'm repressed. We had a big thing recently . . . 'What's wrong with you?' . . . that's one of his trump cards, to say 'What's wrong with you?' Occasionally I've tried to put it back onto him but it always comes back onto me, maybe it is me? I'm adamant that it is not my problem but then perhaps sexual repression is my problem . . . I probably am . . . hardly surprising given our upbringing, white lower middle-class . . . and that is a trump card . . . my God what is wrong with me . . . is it my hormones?

(Mary)

There is also the related idea that the man's enjoyment is contingent on the woman's so that she is responsible for her own and his needs:

> ... women are responsible for what the man enjoys and it's important for the woman to enjoy it because that means the man enjoys it more. If the woman's not enjoying it that's not fair for the man because that means he can't enjoy it because it's got to be this wonderful, mutual, wonderful experience, and if she's not enjoying it she's spoiling it for the man and it's all her fault ... double, double her fault ...

> (Mary)

Mary makes a very subtle and important point here. The permissive discourse may intersect with the MSDD so that even though sex is supposed to be mutual in fact this disguises the fact that the man gains a sense of 'achievement' from knowing that 'he has satisfied his woman'. So a woman has to enjoy it both for her own sake and for his, and to 'really' enjoy it otherwise she is not really liberated. In some ways this almost suggests that the MSDD can be less pernicious: since the man does not really demand that the woman enjoys it, but just uses her to gain relief, she has the choice to enjoy it or not. In the permissive discourse she *must* enjoy it.

Feminist discourses

Discourses which clearly derived from feminists' ideas were little in evidence. Feminist discourses featured ideas relating to work, opportunity, freedom and equality in the relationship. They also contained the view that the problems were not simply personal or interpersonal but to do with general issues about men and women's role, attitudes and so on. These discourses were found to have three subthemes, the first stressing the woman's own needs as a person; the second relating to the idea that men could change – the New Man concept; the third the idea of sex as mutual.

The self-fulfilled woman discourse

One strand of this to appear in people's accounts was that of 'self-fulfilment' for women. This centred on women wanting to be more fulfilled in their lives, to gain self-respect and be more assertive about their needs. Women who are attempting to gain self-fulfilment or personal growth appeared to be 'taking a stand', or attempting to renegotiate various issues including sexuality. 'Refusing' sex or, perhaps, trying to ensure that the woman has some choice about it was seen as part of being self-fulfilled. The idea of 'self-fulfilment' was particularly common with women who had stayed at home to look after children while they were young but who now have no children at home. These accounts often featured women either returning to, or starting work and contrasting this to the sacrifices that they had made initially to stay at home with the children:

I used to do things to please him an awful lot and now I do things not necessarily to please him but to feel comfortable in myself. He finds that very hard, calls it selfish, calls that dominant and assertive, aggressive ... and that's very difficult to counter ... I've tried very hard to talk about developing myself as a person and what it actually is and why I don't want to hurt him if I do that, but I need to do those things ... do things that may not include him but will enable me to grow as a person ... I have become more assertive, but I was probably quite like that anyway ... If I had not had F. and had worked then I would have been assertive early on I think ... I feel I gave up quite a lot of myself for that and now I'm rediscovering it ... nurturing that side of my self ... the financial independence went hand in hand with other things ... being financially able to get out, meeting other people, doing other things ... internal growth ... and just realizing that if I'm unhappy about something it does not have to carry on that way ... what I'm unhappy with I can talk about and I don't have to put up with it ... it makes me feel I'm more in control of it ... that I can be more rational about why I don't want to have sex ... that it does not have to be pushed on me if I don't want to.

(Mary)

For Mary these changes were essentially things she wanted to improve in her relationships. She already had some independence and worked outside the home. Wanda, on the other hand, describes how a preliminary step for her was to gain some financial independence, and the freedom allowed by getting a car:

I've got a car to myself so I can go off and do what I want ... I felt less powerful when I was left at home but now the children have grown up and I'm doing things ... I was a people pleaser ... I pleased my parents, I pleased my husband, I pleased my children and especially I pleased my mother-in-law ... I did all this pleasing to my own detriment ... I began to feel about two years ago [this is the same time as she started to attempt to renegotiate sex] ... this is not me ... I'm not being true to me, being true to me is to say ... I don't want to do this ... I'm sorry but that's not how I feel ... I feel this ... He's not liked it much ... and then sex; the problem with me initiating it before was that I had on the surface a happy, an all right life, no hassles, uncomplicated, but inside me was this turmoil ... I'd done something I did not want to do ... I'd initiated it thinking I was doing it for the right reason, but the reason was that I would not get any backlash ... so it was not the right reason ... if I initiated I'd have this sinking feeling that it was not what I wanted but I better had ... I'm looking like I'm wanting it and I was lying ... the time had come ... a few weeks ... and once I had done it ... it was phew ... that's all right for a few weeks.

(Wanda)

The 'new man' discourse

The impact of feminist ideas had made an impression on the attitudes of some of the men, encouraging them to be less oppressive and more sensitive to women's needs. The popular, though slightly facetious, notion of the 'new man' was apparent in some accounts:

It always used to end up before we had K that it was always me that had to make the first move ... J was well into it but he's very aware of not wanting to *overstep boundaries* with women and *leaving them free* to make the first move ... not like other blokes going out and chatting women up ... He would not do that, he would not want to *invade* her *personal space, affront* her ... He's very aware of that ... I think that overlapped into our relationship.

(Felicity)

An important aspect of this discourse was that women felt a need to be able to state their feelings about sex and other matters – the right to say 'No':

I've never really looked at or asked why I seem to have a greater need than she does ... it's not a problem ... sometimes if I've made advances and I'm refused I can feel quite frustrated, angry ... but it does not create a battle ... I feel rejected but I can rationalize it afterwards ... I can accept that *she has a right to say No* ... I'm not pushing myself on her ... not as if I'm driven by I've got to have sex.

(Jim)

Sex as equal and mutual

This discourse showed some overlap with the permissive discourse but the flavour of it contained less of a demand or pressure on women:

I became aware that she was doing me a *favour* with sex ... as soon as I became aware of that there was no point for me ... I thought to myself, she's gone off it she's got a problem, maybe her father dying, I'd heard that sometimes happens. I thought the best thing I could do was not to make an issue out of it rather than face up to it and say is there a problem can I help ... which is something I should do but never do ... best thing to do was to give her room, not make an issue out of it, *pressure* her ... if she wanted to talk about it she would ... but of course she did not ... so I did not pressurize her and I think she interpreted that as *rejection*, I was not expressing *affection* I did not *need* her . . . turned my back in bed and went to sleep, never made any advances to her . . . so I set out to *prove* it did not matter to me either . . . if you get hurt the easiest way to avoid getting hurt again . . . don't put yourself in a position where you can get hurt . . . went on for a couple of years . . . a good antidote though is if you are angry . . . not worry about sex then . . . you just *set out to prove your point* . . . just need to talk to each other really.

(Howard)

Howard appeared to hold a discourse about mutuality and reciprocity in sex; so that if the other is not interested he 'can't see the point'. His account suggests that he did not want sex to be about him *doing* it *to* someone else as in the basic MSDD. Instead, he appeared to be employing a more 'feminist' discourse; that women should be 'given space' or not 'pressurized'. He said several times in the interview that he'd been trying to be a 'New Man' and to avoid being predatory about sex. However, some defensiveness and a power contest are also indicated in his account, especially in his description of setting out to prove that sex does not matter to him either. Apparent here also are some contradictions between discourses, since it appears that possibly his wife wanted him to 'make advances', since possibly for her making advances implies affection and that he needed her. Yet because he holds a slightly different version of the MSDD discourse, combined with his defensiveness, he fails to do that, and his action of setting out to prove that he did not need it may have been experienced as rejection.

PREVALENCE AND COMMONALITY OF DISCOURSES

In agreement with other studies (Hollway 1983, 1989; Hare-Mustin 1991) the most prevalent discourses in our study were the MSDD (biological drive and phallocentric aspects) and the have/hold discourse. There was less mention of the permissive discourse and virtually no mention of what could be described as a feminist discourse regarding sexuality. One of the most striking indications of our study was that there was no evidence that couples who had been presenting for therapy held different discourses from those in our 'non-clinical' study. Similarly, both groups shared the sexual interactional pattern of male demand/female reluctance and similarly experienced this as a significant problem. This raises the question as to why some couples present for therapy and some do not when ostensibly they have the same problematic sexual interactional pattern. This will be addressed in the next chapter.

This pattern of demand/avoidance appeared to be located in a wider context of '*the problem with no name*' (Friedan 1963, 1981; Komter 1989). Women, despite doing more activities they did not wish to do than men – domestic, childcare tasks and sex, generally indicated that they saw the relationship as equal. Though sexual activity was unsatisfying and unwanted for many of the women they did not articulate their feelings about this in terms of power relations or the oppressive nature of the beliefs and attitudes embodied in the MSDD discourse. Instead, many of the women appeared merely to 'feel a sense of unease' and articulated this in terms of preferring 'cuddles', or a general lack of satisfaction with the relationship. These statements can be seen as reflecting their internalization of the have/hold, relationship discourse and in effect negated their own sexual needs.

There seemed to be two possible interpretations of this:

1 Assuming awareness of 'feminist' arguments it is possible they are not articulated for fear of the consequences, such as conflict and rejection. For example, if a woman reveals that some aspects of her partner's sexual technique or attitude is 'unsatisfactory' this can be perceived as a threat to the man and he might retaliate. Since men usually have more power this is risky. More indirect complaints in terms of a have/hold discourse may be more acceptable and legitimate since they fall in with traditional notions of 'femininity'.

2 On the other hand it might be the case that feminist discourses, especially regarding sexuality, were not widely familiar in our sample or perhaps amongst the general population. However, there was no reason to suppose that this sample, who were above average in educational status, had less than average knowledge of 'feminist' ideas.

It is possible that the explanation lies somewhere between these two positions. Though feminist ideas have had an influence they have also received widespread critiques, or a backlash, not least in terms of stereotyping feminists as non-sexual, unattractive and 'strident' (Kennedy-Taylor 1994). Such attacks are located in traditional patriarchal discourses, stressing natural and inevitable differences between men and women and stigmatizing women who stray outside these. This can have a powerful function in encouraging women to distance themselves from feminism, especially since to be attractive, cuddly and 'fluffy' has been emphasized as part of women's socialization. Several women remarked in our interviews and clinical work, 'I am not a feminist', despite clearly being interested in having a more equal relationship and in fact supporting many tenets of feminist theories.

CONCURRENT BUT CONTRADICTORY DISCOURSE

Problems appeared to be linked to there being concurrent but essentially contradictory discourse available; for instance, in many cases both the MSDD and the have/hold or relationship discourses were employed simultaneously in people's accounts. This can place the relationship in a contradictory, even impossible situation; for example, if men are seen as largely needing sex and women as needing to relate and be emotionally close this inevitably opens up a chasm between them (Chodorow 1978). Likewise, the idea that sex is a commodity that can be 'bought' or exchanged for something else is in conflict with the idea that sex should be mutual and reciprocal. Similarly, within the permissive discourse women are expected to be uninhibited sexually but at the same time elements of the relationship discourse contradict this in that women who are uninhibited may also be labelled as 'easy'. Alternatively, women who are not interested in sex or are sexually unresponsive to their partners might be regarded, and may regard themselves, as 'frigid' or 'abnormal'. Perhaps more generally the idea that male–female relationships must be sexual in order to be healthy is an underlying assumption, partly coming from biological and the MSDD discourses – of sex as healthy release of tension, and men and women as inevitably triggering each other's instinctual lust.

Again, aspects of the MSDD, especially the emphasis on phallocentric, penetrative sex contradict 'feminist' discourses which emphasize the need for sexuality to involve broader sensuality, mutual touching and clitoral orgasm. In the former women are located as passive and dependent on the man for sexual gratification; in the latter they are more active and experimenting, thereby again potentially risking being seen as 'easy', or not interested in the man. There is also a contradiction between the idea that men should be able to 'turn women on', that it is up to them to ensure that women enjoy sex and are satisfied and yet within the permissive discourse (and perhaps the feminist discourse) women are supposed to be able to turn themselves on. The idea that men should be able to 'turn women on', metaphorically like 'the prince and Sleeping Beauty', assumes that women need to be turned on by someone else, rather than accepting that they may be driven to find their own sexual satisfaction. Furthermore, attempts to alter their roles are not necessarily an easy activity since partners may be frightened, that is, aware of the alternative discourses that may come into play and stigmatize them in various ways. For example, a man may fear that he risks being seen as 'weak' and effeminate if he shows his feelings too much, or as inadequate if he cannot satisfy his partner with phallocentric sex. Alternatively a woman may fear being seen as 'easy' if she clearly expresses her sexual needs.

POWER AND INEQUALITY

However, these contradictions may not be merely unfortunate but in part stem from inequalities between the genders and an attempt to maintain this inequality. Arguably one of the greatest contradictory messages is still to do with the 'double standard' (a combination of the MSDD and the have/hold discourses) in that it is more acceptable for men to be promiscuous than for women. Further a 'good' wife is expected to lack experience with other men, to learn to supress her own sexuality, to avoid being labelled as 'easy', but she should also be uninhibited with her husband. The man should therefore be the 'sexual expert', to be able to turn the woman on. Women are not expected to 'know what they are doing', nor to explicitly state what they want sexually because that would imply that they were or had been 'easy', as in the old joke that when asked about the man's performance the woman replies 'Wonderful', whereupon he strikes her, saying, 'How do you know I was wonderful?' However, not saying anything can mean putting up with unsatisfying sex which may lead eventually to attempts at avoidance and perhaps becoming labelled as 'frigid'. The double standard therefore has a negative side also for men. Not only is sex also likely to be unsatisfactory for them but several of the men were concerned and anxious about their performance. However, only one of the women in our sample said that her husband did not 'do it right' and most women appeared careful to avoid saying this.

Women are not supposed to be sexual, to wish for physical sexual pleasure but to be more interested in the 'relationship'. In terms of female physical sexual pleasure this is oppressive in that it becomes unacceptable for a woman to 'only be after one thing', i.e. physical sexual pleasure. Having to 'wait' for a 'good' relationship before they can engage in sex for pleasure may mean that they have to wait a long time. It may also be more difficult for them to use the threat of 'finding someone else' in order to influence their partners because of the necessity of having to have a 'good' relationship with someone else first. This is very paradoxical as well as being oppressive because in effect it would probably still be easier (given the prevalence of the MSDD) for a woman to 'get sex' with another man than it would be for a man to 'get sex' with another woman, as the following suggests: 'given that most women will usually say no to most men, while most men will usually say yes to most women, let women do the asking, without being branded as slags' (letter to *The Guardian*, 31 July 1993).

POWER AND STRATEGIES

The discourses described affect the relationship between partners in various ways. They explicitly or implicitly locate partners in certain roles in relation to each other and also define their power relations. In addition the discourses can be employed by partners to exert influence over each other. Most obviously they may be employed to persuade the other into or out of sex, and this in turn is related not only to the satisfaction of desires but to control over each other. In a sense discourses may be employed rather like an ally in an argument. Partners may fluctuate between one discourse or another, calling forth different discourses as strategies to win the argument: sometimes one discourse prevails; sometimes there is no resolution; so that they do not come to accept a shared discourse.

In the next chapter we will examine how discourses regarding power and sexuality operate in relationships. In clinical case studies it is apparent that couples sometimes turn to different discourses from one session to the next as they explore the possible reasons for their difficulties. Whose discourse prevails appears to depend on the relative power of each partner in a general sense in the relationship. The fact that one discourse appears to be accepted by both does not necessarily imply, however, that there is actually a shared view; generally it appears that whoever has the most power will also be able to persuade the other, ostensibly at least, to accept their viewpoint: 'He says I'm inhibited, I'm repressed ... he's saying it's my problem, I'm saying no it's not my problem, it might be both of us, or a problem of negotiation or something ... he says that my saying that, that it is in any way his problem ... is damaging to him ... hurting him'.

At the same time some discourses appear to be more widely accepted and more influential than others. Whose discourse prevails then may not rest only on the relative power of each in general terms but on the power of particular discourses. Women may well be at a disadvantage in this, because they generally have less power and because discourses that might result in them enjoying sex more do not appear to be widely shared. Feminist discourses, though generally presumed to have made an impact, appeared in our study to have been effectively marginalized. As we will explore in the next chapter this has negative consequences for both genders. The pervasive twin cocktail of the MSDD and have/hold effectively stifle sexuality. Though appearing to be to men's advantage the MSDD appears to keep many men anxious about their performance and sexually and emotionally dissatisfied. The have/hold discourse appears to prevent many women from exploring their sexual needs. The two discourses can combine so that both men and women can remain dissatisfied: men trying harder at the wrong things and women not being able to tell them what they want.

7

Clinical case studies: Sexual and relationship problems

In the previous chapters we have presented evidence to argue that partners' experiences in relationships are shaped by both the relative distributions of power between them and the common discourses regarding power and sexuality that they have absorbed. It seems that the combination of women having few tangible forms of power, being financially dependent and the pervasive discourses, especially that men 'need' sex more than women, is likely to result in a common sexual cycle of male demand–female reluctance. Evidence from the questionnaire and from the interview studies had suggested that financial dependence was critically related to sexual reluctance on the part of women in relationships. It would be over-simplistic to suggest that these twin factors of financial dependence and prevalent discourses simply determine how people will act. People are potentially autonomous and make choices about their courses of actions. However at the same time these choices can be seen to be constrained by these twin factors. The dominant discourses that people are exposed to can set limits on the potential choices they can envisage regarding their relationships and roles, and structural inequality can limit what choices they actually have.

In this chapter we want to explore in more detail what actually happens inside relationships: how these twin forces of material and ideological factors are played out in relationships and what kinds of dynamics are constructed. We will present three examples from our work with couples who had entered therapy with sexual difficulties as one of their key presenting problems. During our work with such couples we have been struck many times by the impression that the kinds of problems many of them were experiencing are variations on common experiences that many, if not most, couples go through. Goldberg and Huxley (1980) have shown that in fact many people who suffer serious forms of emotional distress, disordered thinking and sexual difficulties never attend for professional help. Our impression that this was the case was supported by the research data from the interview and questionnaire studies reported in the earlier chapters. Many of the couples in the research samples complained that their relationships were unsatisfactory and that sexual intimacy was either partially or totally absent and was frequently very unsatisfactory. In particular the extent of sexual dissatisfaction and distress was widespread. However, these couples were not formally involved in therapy but many had received some form of personal or relationship counselling.

PATHOLOGICAL DISCOURSES

The reasons why many couples do not seek therapy appear to be varied. Most simply there is the question of the availability of therapeutic services, awareness of these and knowledge of what they do and how they might be of help. People also differ in their attitudes to therapy, for example in terms of what they have heard from friends or family members. Quite simply many of the couples we worked with attended largely because their GP knew of our service, had a reasonably positive attitude to it and recommended to the couple that they come and see us.

Beyond these fundamental issues some couples feel too embarrassed to discuss their private, personal sexual intimacies with a stranger. Many people do not believe that therapy is or can be of any use generally, or that their problems are so bad and different from other people's that they feel it would be hopeless. Most significantly there are important gender differences in that women are usually more willing to seek therapy but many men are frequently less aware that problems may be 'brewing' and are more reluctant to attend for therapy to deal with these (O'Brien 1990). Even if problems are perceived many people reported that these were seen by one or both of them as individual faults or disorders and so there was no point both of them attending. Consequently there were many examples in the non-clinical sample where one partner, most often the woman, had attended some form of individual therapy such as counselling, but they had never sought any assistance together as a couple. Also, the pattern of referrals to our couples and sex therapy clinic was that typically women's referrals involved problems of lack of sexual desire, going off sex or not wanting to engage in it very often, whereas for men the problems featured inability to perform, such as impotence or premature ejaculation. In other words women's problems seemed to be related to their feelings and concerns about the relationships, whereas men's problems were to do with the state of their equipment and technique. In effect it seemed that women were more inclined to regard distressing emotional states as an outcome of some problem or potential pathology whereas men require some kind of outward sign.

Moreover there were many cases where men who had been reluctant to attend for therapy in relation to emotional problems, such as depression or anxiety on the woman's part, were keen to attend when the 'woman' developed a sexual problem. Getting 'her' sexual problems sorted out seemed to provide a much stronger motivation. We can remember vividly the time that one supposedly 'inorgasmic' and sexually reluctant woman stated after a few sessions, 'We don't have a sexual problem, we just don't talk about anything anymore . . .'

In addition to the previous discourses that we have discussed it seems that we can add the pathological discourse as a variant on individualistic discourses. These propose in essence that problems in relationships and sexual problems in particular are due to individual factors. This view has considerable support from psychology and the various psychotherapies. As we saw in Chapter 2 such explanations are embodied in psychoanalytic theories which emphasize childhood experiences, such as anxieties relating to attachments to the mother as the cause of later adult problems, faulty learning experiences, such as parents setting a poor model of adult relationships and intimacy, secrets and anxiety associated with sexual matters leading to later inhibitions, and so on. The widespread availability of individual therapy and counselling supports the idea that problems are in fact individual and can be treated at an individual level.

However, there are various criticisms of such an individualistic view: the first is that there are pronounced differences between men and women in the types of problems and symptoms they appear to experience. For example, women are more likely to develop eating disorders – anorexia and bulimia – and depression, and men are more likely to develop substance abuse problems such as alcoholism, and to show behavioural problems such as aggression and violence. This generally points to the possibility that problems are not simply or predominantly personal. Second, there is considerable evidence from interpersonal therapies that many problems are interpersonal in nature and are related to the dynamics of the relationships that people are involved in. Systemic approaches have made a valuable contribution in emphasizing that problems and symptoms need to be regarded as interactional phenomenon. Ordinary difficulties that are commonly experienced may evolve into major problems depending on a variety of circumstances, such as the reaction of the partner, the level of stress in the relationship relating, for example, to life cycle transitions such as birth of children, or crises induced by ill-heath, unemployment, and so on. The evolution is also influenced by the solutions that are attempted, including who is sought to give advice. Many couples have found for example that pursuing legal solutions can serve to fuel the flames and cause much emotional damage (and financial loss) to all concerned (Eron and Lund 1993; see also p. 45 above).

POWER AND SUBJUGATION

However, these interactional approaches, though valuable, have tended to be vague about issues of power. A significant exception has been the work of Haley (1963, 1976). Haley has vividly described how inconsistencies, confusions and contradictions in the power arrangements in relationships are intimately associated with problems and the development of symptoms. He suggests that conflicts and struggles over power are fundamentally related to struggles over meaning – whose definition is to prevail. Haley (1963) had emphasized that partners are continually attempting to define the relationship, in terms of roles, responsibilities, dominance in some areas, what activities they will undertake together and so on. Both have ideas about what kind of a relationship they want and what part they should each play. In order to function they need to achieve some agreement or at least agree to disagree on some issues:

> Difficult relationships are those where the two people cannot reach agreement on a mutual definition of areas of the relationship. When one bids for control of an area, the other bids for control and they are in a struggle. The struggle may be conducted by open battle, by sabotage, or by passive resistance, just as it may be crude and obvious or infinitely rich and subtle.
>
> (Haley 1963: 17)

This struggle over meaning has been regarded as an inability of partners to see that each of them may have an alternative way of describing or understanding the continual to and fro of actions and responses between them:

> Disagreement about how to punctuate the sequences of events is at the root of countless relationship struggles. Suppose a couple have a marital problem . . . In explaining their frustrations, the husband will state that withdrawal is his only defense against her nagging, while she will label this explanation a gross and willful distortion of what 'really' happens in their marriage: namely, that she is critical of him because of his passivity.
>
> (Watzlawick *et al.* 1967: 56)

In contesting the definition of the relationship partners may engage in various forms of influence, such as strategies of coercion, supplication, rational argument and involving others in order to secure their definition of what is happening. Failure to come to agreement may lead to a polarization of views, frustration and an escalation towards more extreme strategies, such as violent coercion, or symptomatic supplication, such as depression.

Similarly, Madanes (1981) has suggested that an important aspect of symptoms is that they are an attempt to balance the power inequalities in a relationship. However, a symptom inevitably places the partners in a position of 'hierarchical incongruity':

The symptomatic person is in an inferior position to the other spouse, who tries to help or to change him; yet the symptomatic spouse is also in a superior position in that he refuses to be helped and to change. While requesting advice and help, the symptomatic spouse refuses to be influenced.

(Madanes 1981: 30)

According to this perspective a symptom leads to both partners simultaneously having power and being rendered powerless. The partner who does not have the symptoms becomes powerless or impotent in the face of the symptoms which he can do very little to resolve. He is not even allowed to be angry since the symptoms are indicative of an 'illness' and are therefore 'out of control' – the partner cannot be blamed for them. The symptomatic partner on the other hand gains power by virtue of the fact that her partner is rendered helpless in his attempts to get her to overcome the symptoms and perhaps its inconvenient effects on him. At the same time the symptomatic person concedes power through becoming stigmatized as 'ill', having her autonomy undermined, decisions made for her, in short incurring a spoilt identity. Madanes' (1981) analysis connects with the results of the research we have reported earlier. Inequalities of power can be seen to enhance the likelihood that sexual and other relationship problems will emerge. However, the inequalities of power occur, we suggest, for two main reasons which systemic theorists have under-emphasized:

1 due to material inequalities of power which predominantly place women in positions of dependency;
2 dominant discourses which allocate women to subordinate positions in families and generally construct inferior and dependent identities.

Unlike some of the emphasis from systemic theories which seem to imply that partners are more or less equal and that their struggles are a 'fair fight' we suggest that this is typically not the case. Similarly the assumption that the 'interpersonal dynamics' or meanings, beliefs, punctuations that the partners employ are idiosyncratic to the couple is misleading. Recourse to sexual symptoms can be seen as a fairly desperate action which for many women deprives them of one of the few areas of pleasure and intimacy in their lives. The hierarchical incongruity described by Madanes can perhaps be better thought of as an attempt to resist or a reaction to the subjugation that the woman finds herself in. The man's inability to overcome her symptoms can be seen as but a token of resistance and not infrequently women incur various negative consequences, such as loss of rights, ridicule, anger and various forms of unpleasant or degrading 'treatment' and intrusion into their privacy.

INTERNALIZATION OF DISCOURSES

The struggles over meaning, how the relationship is to be defined, we suggest, are shaped by dominant discourses regarding power, sexuality and what it is to be a 'real' person. As we saw in the interview studies many of the partners had views regarding their relationship which featured individualistic and psychological discourses, for example, that one of them was dominant because she was 'bossy'. Likewise, other discourses that have been discussed are internalized and thereby shape partners' actions, including their attempts to define the relationships in various ways. As we have seen these discourses are not simply equivalent but some are dominant and influential as opposed to those which are relegated as peripheral or irrelevant.

Social and patriarchal processes not only subjugate some discourses but dominant discourses can also define men and women in relatively positive or negative ways. So, the dominant discourse that women are more dependent, more seeking of attachment than men can also imply that they are weaker or inferior:

> 'Dependency' is a problem that is presented to be 'resolved', and, in resolving this, people expect to reach a destination in their life at which they can 'stand on their own two feet' . . . Could it be that these definitions and these conclusions are informed by and reached through dominant cultural definitions of what it means to be a real person – that is, 'independent', 'self-possessed', 'self-contained', 'self-actualizing' etc.
>
> (White 1995: 104)

Dependency is constructed as problematic and essentially negative and usually attributed to women. Independence on the other hand is constructed as less problematic, positive and usually attributed to men. A 'mature' or 'real' person is independent, and since women are seen as dependent they are inevitably further perceived as non-mature and somehow inferior. Independence can be seen as equally if not more problematic in intimate relationships but this perspective, which is more likely to be articulated by women, is likely to be subjugated – dismissed or trivialized.

White (1995) suggests that discourses function not only by shaping ideas with which partners influence each other but are internalized and operate so that people impose self-criticism, even self-abuse, on themselves. Such internalization is constructed through the interactions and conversations between partners in relationships which are likely to convey the dominant discourses. One of the most pernicious forms of self-rejection may be the turn to pathology, wherein one or other partner starts to construe their feelings, their experiences of the situation not as a response to inequality but as due to their own pathology. Rather than seeing symptoms as a 'tactic' this suggests instead that they represent a reaction to relative powerlessness, a reaction of desperation accompanied by the acceptance of an individualistic discourse of 'pathology' which distorts the 'real' experience of inequality. It may be that in some cases the crisis that results may produce some change. More often than not, however, it is more likely to lead to one partner being pathologized and the relationship 'stuck' around the definition of the problems as caused by the 'symptomatic' partner's 'inadequacies'.

CLINICAL CASE STUDIES

Interviews and questionnaires provide a snapshot impression of what is happening in people's relationships. Clinical work on the other hand offers the opportunity to explore partners' understandings over a period of time. Therapy usually involves at least six sessions, usually at two-weekly intervals, and this allows a picture of the changes, developments and patterning of the relationship over a period of time. Furthermore it is possible to check ideas about a couple in a reflexive way by discussing the impressions we have formed of them, what we see as the beliefs and understandings that are guiding their actions. Perhaps most importantly clinical work provides an opportunity for both the therapists and the couple to test ideas and hypotheses. By attempting to construct some alternative ways of viewing their relationships and acting it is possible to see more clearly what is holding the relationships and the problems in place. Importantly it is also possible to see more clearly, when changes are attempted, how discourses have been internalized to form the basis of partners' implicit or explicit assumptions and explanations. Issues about power, inequalities, struggles may be concealed, denied or simply not a matter of conscious concern for many couples, who currently regard their relationships as relatively problem-free. In contrast couples in therapy have acknowledged that they have some problems and are willing to explore these, at least to some extent. Therefore case studies of couples in therapy offer a chance to obtain rich information about processes and content in relationships and the linkages to issues of power.

All the following couples gave us permission to employ material from our work with them for teaching and publication. However, we have altered their names and the details of their circumstances to try to ensure anonymity. Though at times our exposition may appear to present one or other of them in a more or less positive light we wish to make clear that it is not our intention to do so. In our view all the couples presented here were trying, like all of us, to make the best sense they could of their relationships. Blaming themselves and each other is what they had spent considerable time doing. Our intention was to assist them in some small way to do a little less of this. Thinking about the possible ways that structures of inequality and commonly shared discourses were shaping and constraining their options is, we think, a less blaming and even an empowering activity. Though we have throughout the book been critical of some of the consequences of patriarchy this is not simply to blame individual men and women. As we will see in these cases many of the men, though perhaps possessing greater power than their partners, were nevertheless also profoundly unhappy and distressed.

All the couples were seen by both of us and each partner was seen individually by the same sex therapist at least once. Though the therapists would share the individual disclosures from these individual sessions these were treated as confidential in that they were not revealed to the other partner without prior permission. The sessions included a discussion of power and sexual discourses but in addition attention was paid to a broad range of factors, such as childhood experiences, other adult relationships, beliefs and interactional dynamics. The therapy was orientated around a systemic approach which incorporated some sexual/behavioural techniques. The therapeutic needs of the couples were always given precedence over our research interests.

LOUISE AND MARK HATTON

Background

The problem presented was that Louise did not enjoy sex with Mark at all, she was not orgasmic, she did not like being touched by Mark, or even her children. She was happy to hold hands with Mark in public places where such affection did not threaten a prelude to sex. They reported, for instance, that she would never hold Mark, caress or cuddle him at any time even during sex.

Louise and Mark had been married for 20 years, and they were both in their forties. They had two daughters, aged 17 and 19; the eldest daughter had left home and the other was on the point of leaving. Though Louise was qualified as a nurse she had not worked since they had the children and therefore Mark was the sole breadwinner. Their main explanation for 'her' problem was that she had been abused by her father starting when she was 7 years old. Her case eventually come to court, eight years after the abuse had begun. In court her father had explicitly blamed her for the abuse, calling her seductive and denying that it was his fault. Louise insisted that she had not enjoyed sex with her father at all but instead was terrified of him and hated it. Despite her statements, and irrespective of the fact that as a child she could not be held responsible, the court had apparently implicitly blamed her. This left her in a sexual dilemma: to be sexually responsive or active would also have implied to her that it was her own sexuality that had caused her abuse; she would have been implicated in it; she therefore felt that she had to be passive sexually.

Relationship patterns and power bases

Mark would initiate sex with Louise four or five times a week. He would penetrate her as soon as he was physically ready, without any foreplay or mutual caressing, reach orgasm rapidly and then 'roll off'. Louise never overtly rejected his advances, but she never initiated or played an active part. She said she never rejected Mark even though she found sex aversive. Louise had more sexual power in that Mark was seen as needing sex more than she did. Originally Louise had been more emotionally dependent on Mark than he was on her and they agreed that she had loved him far more than vice versa initially. Also, Mark had had far more power than Louise: he was self-confident whereas she had very low self-esteem; she was shy, he was more outgoing; he was sexually 'normal', she had been abused and was therefore 'abnormal'.

Louise appeared to have power through the children and her domestic skills, and she was more articulate than Mark, was better educated and had worked as a nurse. Louise had given this up in order to stay at home with the children and Mark was the main breadwinner. He had a job as a driver which frequently kept him away from home. Louise had not returned to work when the children were older and now she felt that it was too late for her to 'start at the bottom' again. She said that she had felt better about herself when she was working. It was difficult to know whether it was her own choice to stop working or whether she had, like many women, 'just slipped into it' or whether Mark had positively discouraged her. What was clear was that Mark was disparaging about 'career' women, describing them as 'hard' and 'pushy'. As she knew that he did not find 'hard'/'pushy' women attractive the implication was that if she worked he would therefore find her unattractive as well.

She had gained power through the children but apparently this power rested on a view of her as damaged by the abuse – because of this she did not trust men with children and had been unhappy about Mark being close to their daughters. Mark said he was sad that he had become peripheral to their daughters but understood Louise's fears. Louise therefore gained power through the children; for instance, she had been able to use her 'childrearing' expertise to influence decisions. When deciding whether to move or not she could make sure her wishes prevailed by pointing out the potential effects on the children. Legally Louise did have some potential power though at the same time it would have been difficult to predict what would have happened if they had divorced. The children were too old for her to have gained custody and the house or maintenance automatically.

Sexual discourses and dynamics

It appeared that their relationship had aspects of an abusive pattern early on. They both said that Mark had been domineering and insensitive at first.

For instance, during the early weeks of their relationship Mark had gone out leaving Louise alone, and leaving her with a shoebox full of love letters from his previous girlfriends to read. It was not clear why he did this; he seemed to see it as 'bragging' to her about how attractive he was. It was perhaps also an implicit message to her about what he expected of her; a covert 'statement' of what kind of woman he liked or disliked.

THERAPIST	Did Mark tell you about having other girlfriends?
LOUISE	This is typical of Mark, one morning he went out to get the papers and he chucked this shoebox at me . . . there were all these old love letters from all his old girlfriends . . . I came across one who was my best friend at school . . . So Mark said, 'Oh slut that she is' . . . he was always telling me about his girls, all the time.
THERAPIST	Why do you think he did that?
LOUISE	I don't know. He was never sensitive. I can always remember when he asked me to get married. He said, 'I can tell you this. It's never going to be a rose garden.' And I thought, well, I was told.
MARK	Do you think Rudi, just man to man now, we're just bragging all the time? . . . I was terrible . . . I wonder how I can have been like that, I wonder really . . .
LOUISE	I think the letters were for entertainment, he felt he had to provide entertainment for me. I don't think he thought for one minute they would upset me . . .
THERAPIST	(To Mark) What could Louise have done to stop you (going on about other girls and being insensitive etc.), what did other women do?
LOUISE	I'd have lost him.
MARK	Probably, I didn't like to be serious, I was very carefree . . .
THERAPIST	On the one hand you let him walk all over you but on the other you put your foot down about sex, that you weren't going to be a push-over.
LOUISE	But I didn't. I just lay there and thought of England!
THERAPIST	Perhaps sex is very important to you two because it's the one area where Louise did make a stand. At the beginning, Louise, you put your foot down . . . so you don't have to let yourself be used for someone to stay with you. You probably won't be able to accept this yet but think about it.
LOUISE	(laughing) I hooked him . . . Of course Mark wouldn't be with me for twenty odd years if he didn't love me . . . I just can't seem to accept it . . .

From this extract it can be seen that a pattern of demand/deny had appeared very early on in the relationship and this in a sense is what had attracted Mark. As the above extract suggests if Louise had been sexually experienced or 'active' as opposed to 'passive', then Mark might have 'loved and left her', not married her. Louise was obviously not enjoying sex, yet they were engaging in it frequently. Mark's attempted solution to the childhood sexual abuse could be seen in a type of 'behavioural' framework; rather like an attempt to overcome a 'phobia' by 'facing' her fear/dislike of sex through constantly engaging in it in an ostensibly 'non-abusive' manner/relationship. He seemed to believe that he could enable her to enjoy it by continually 'doing it'. This however would only have 'worked' if the relationship had not been abusive at all, if she had felt secure and happy with him. Early on in the relationship it appeared that she had not felt like this at all in relation to him, indeed in some ways their relationship had some similarities to her relationship with her father.

They also shared a strong belief in the male sexual drive discourse. Louise, for instance, said that 'I would feel guilty about depriving him, he needs it, it would be unfair'. She also said that although she did not enjoy it she wanted to do it because at some level it did 'keep them close'. The belief in the MSDD discourse had been so strong that Mark's insistence on frequent intercourse had hardly been questioned, and even partly exonerated an affair he had engaged in. Although their relationship had been strongly located in the MSDD it now seemed to be changing, perhaps due to the influences of their daughters towards some aspects of the permissive discourse. Louise was now expected to enjoy sex and it was not enough for Mark simply to be allowed to do it. Within this mixture of the MSDD and the permissive discourse they both felt there was something wrong: Mark that perhaps he was less adequate sexually than he had thought and Louise that there must be something wrong with her if she could not enjoy it.

Though perhaps less prominent they also appeared to be operating within a framework of the different but equal discourse. It was agreed that Mark had greater structural power but that as a balance Louise had power in the home. Also, she said that she had given up her nursing career out of 'her own choice', though it was clear that Mark had wished her to do this and it would have been virtually impossible for her to return to it if they had separated. For Mark and Louise this discourse also revolved around the idea of being an ordinary couple with the 'normal' divisions of labour between them. The have/hold discourse appeared to be central to their relationship. Louise was regarded by Mark and by herself as a 'good' wife and in their courtship she had not been 'easy'. She agreed that she had tried to be 'attractive' to Mark and that she needed to offer him sex in order to hold on to him and this had been prominent in their courtship. Furthermore, she stated that he was a 'good provider' and had looked after her and the girls well, and worked hard.

Explanations and discourses of 'pathology'

Louise appeared to be caught between two sets of experiences and oppressive discourses: if she had been overtly sexually enthusiastic she would have felt that she had in some way 'contributed' to her own childhood abuse by her father. Initially Louise 'held out' on sex with Mark; she would not engage in sex with him until she believed that he did love her, at least to some extent. He could not persuade her into bed for some time. This he said had kept him interested in her, as she was not 'easy' like the other women he said he had been involved with, she was not a 'tart', she was a 'good' girl, a girl to marry. This also fitted with a discourse of being a 'good girl' rather than overtly sexual or a 'tart'. Mark did not like or respect women who behaved according to the permissive discourse despite having slept with them in the past. However, this meant that by not even being able to enjoy sex with Mark she was being trapped into a pathological discourse, that there was something wrong with her. Louise had told Mark about the sexual abuse early in the relationship, he was very sympathetic and confident that he could 'help her get over it'. When this eventually failed one way out for both of them was increasingly to see Louise as not 'normal', which fitted the already present view of Louise as having been damaged by the abuse in her childhood. Further, though Mark had presented himself as sexually confident this confidence was being eroded by his failure to be able to help Louise overcome 'her problem'. The construction of Louise as not 'normal' therefore protected Mark from seeing himself within a male discourse as inadequate. Also, it avoided seeing their relationship as problematic.

The effect of Louise's experiences seemed to leave her with a feeling that she 'could not help' finding sex aversive, that there was something wrong with her and that she needed and wanted to change. She could not say 'no' overtly and wanted to please. Neither of them construed Mark's sexual behaviour as problematic or questioned his sexual competence. What was not being considered was that the effect of the abuse on Louise might have been to leave her vulnerable to further abuse. Mark's attempted solution – to engage in sex as frequently as possible in the hopes that she would 'get over it', the lack of 'foreplay' and the emphasis on phallocentric sex – was consistent with an individualistic discourse but may in fact have contributed to and denied the possibility that she was again experiencing a form of abuse. This had been framed by Mark as helping her to get over her sexual problems, and previously framed by her father as showing 'love' for her.

However, the dominant construction of Louise as the sole problem was gradually beginning to shift to incorporate some subjugated ideas, especially that Mark's early domineering behaviour had caused problems in the relationship. This was in conflict with their main explanation, that the problem was due to Louise's sexual abuse. Mark remarked several times that he now disapproved of his behaviour in the past: 'I wonder how I can have been like that, I wonder really'. He was trying to be different and feminist ideas about equality and mutual sexual enjoyment were featuring in their thinking, perhaps prompted by the fact that their daughters were now adults and establishing their own relationships. Time was spent discussing different ideas about relationships, 'modern' expectations and so on. They both agreed that though they wanted things to be a little different they were both too old to become a totally 'modern' couple. For example, Louise said she wanted to stay at home and did not wish to initiate sex. Also, they did not want to appear 'odd' and too different from their friends. Changes in their dynamics appeared to accompany these considerations: Mark was less insistent about sex, they said they were talking more and also Louise felt she could choose to enjoy sexual intimacy, she did not feel compelled simply to tolerate it. She articulated many examples of Mark's 'insensitivity', for which he apologized, but she also praised many of his qualities, as he did hers.

DOROTHY AND TONY BIRD

Background

Dorothy had initially been referred via her family doctor to a psychiatrist for assistance with her bulimia. Some limited success had been achieved with this problem but Tony was more concerned with her 'excessive promiscuity'. She was constantly engaging in extra-marital affairs, for example at work and at the sports club they had attended. She said she did not enjoy these affairs, which Tony found distressing to the point of attempting to restrict her to the house (so she no longer worked), in order to avoid 'temptation'. Even this had backfired, however, because she had engaged in an affair with the central heating repair man who visited the house to carry out the repairs.

Dorothy had two children from her previous marriage. The younger girl (aged 9) lived with her and Tony, and the older sister (aged 13) lived with her father. Although she had held a variety of temporary or part-time jobs Dorothy had no formal qualifications and was not working currently. The couple had met at a local sports club and Dorothy had initiated sexual intimacy. Tony was the sole breadwinner and had a well-paid job in local government. Dorothy had been sexually abused by a relative as a child and felt betrayed by her mother who she felt knew about the abuse but did nothing about it. She had done the rounds of the psychiatric services, having been treated by a psychiatrist, attended a sexually abused women's centre and received some individual counselling. Again, similarly to Louise, her previous history meant she was was very vulnerable to a pathological definition of her actions.

Tony had not been married before and was said to be close to Carol, Dorothy's daughter. He had a responsible and well-paid job, and a good car, and they owned a pleasant house. Dorothy described Tony's background in contrast to hers as 'stable' but 'stifling', and said that he had been a 'mother's boy' who allowed his parents to thwart his ambitions. Tony more or less agreed with this analysis. Dorothy added that her own mother had 'ruled the roost' and that she was like her in this way, having 'dominated' not only Tony, but her first husband. She described Tony as 'neurotic' and 'weak' but she had hoped that she could in time 'change him into more of a man'. Interestingly this construct of Tony as emotionally weak distracted attention from the fact that he had a variety of considerable and essential forms of power over her, such as economic, shelter, knowledge and contractual. Apart from her housework at present she received very little stimulation, though she had worked for brief periods previously. These invariably resulted in her having sex with her employer or a colleague, whereupon Tony would force her to give up her job. She had become pregnant six months previously, but because Tony was not sure that he was the father he insisted that she have an abortion. She complied with this, consequently incurring disapproval and ostracism from her family, who were devout Jehovah's Witnesses.

Relationship patterns and sexual dynamics

The story emerging was that Dorothy was overtly sexual, would 'flirt excessively' in social situations, constantly make sexual innuendos and jokes and attempt to seduce virtually any man that she came across. Once she had seduced a man she said she would want no more to do with him. However, she claimed that the men would persistently phone her up, and though she wished to cease seeing them, she did not know how to say 'no' and end the relationship. Eventually she would ask Tony to intervene and 'sort it out for her', 'to go round to see the men and tell them that she was his wife and to leave her alone'. Dorothy appeared to be dominant in sexual matters, as she summed up by saying 'I've taught him a lot', with which Tony agreed. Their dynamics and in particular the interactional patterns surrounding Dorothy's symptoms appeared to be illustrated by the following sequence:

DOROTHY   I am getting all this help, I am doing my utmost to change. As far as affairs go, I haven't been out with anyone for several months now. I feel that I am doing my damnedest but he is doing absolutely nothing towards solving his problems.

THERAPIST   Are you talking about his eating problem? He has been to the hospital for examination hasn't he? What other aspects would you like to see changed?

DOROTHY	I wish he could be more sociable, not so neurotic about people looking at him. You know if he goes into a room with a lot of people he has to sit in the corner, he can't bear anyone behind him.
TONY	I'm very self-conscious. She's always telling me how puny I look, I can't bear to look in the mirror, how can you not be self-conscious?
DOROTHY	I'm only telling you the truth, you tell me to say what I see and feel.
TONY	Yes, but there is no need to say it and put the boot in as well.
DOROTHY	He's the nicest man in the world, really, but he's just got so many hang-ups – well I can't say nothing.

Power and relationship dynamics

The balance of power at first glance seemed to be in Dorothy's favour; she was having affairs with other men and seemed to be critical of Tony, who appeared to be frightened of losing her. On closer examination, though, it seemed apparent that the structural power was almost totally in Tony's favour. Dorothy's main area of power appeared to be her sexuality and greater confidence in social situations. However, these were cancelled out by designation as 'ill' as indicated by her bulimia and 'out of control' sexuality. She was totally financially dependent on Tony, he was better educated than her and was financially self-sufficient, she had no qualifications and saw herself as 'thick'. Tony was beginning, though somewhat half-heartedly, to threaten to divorce her if she did not cease her affairs. She would then have been in difficulties financially, particularly as her children were not his and legally therefore she would not be entitled to maintenance. He was also threatening her by suggesting that she might lose custody of her daughter Carol if she did not stop. Since she had already lost custody of her older daughter to her first husband, who had managed to persuade the court that she was an inadequate mother because of her sexual behaviour, this was a powerful threat.

On the other hand, Dorothy frequently treated Tony with contempt for his physical appearance, said he was small, 'weedy' and unattractive and laughed at the suggestion that another woman might find him attractive or that he might leave her for another woman. Tony agreed with this negative view of himself and lacked self-confidence in social situations:

DOROTHY	If no one takes notice of Tony they don't take notice of me either. I feel embarrassed that I'm the wife of someone no one is interested in, it means they are not interested in me either. I want to be the wife of someone so that I can be someone . . .

Both of them wanted the other to change but this appeared to be lead-ing to an escalation of the power struggle. As a result of the affairs Tony appeared to be so resentful that he refused to change in any way, and attempted to solve the problem by metaphorically keeping her chained in a 'chastity belt' at home.

Power and discourses

The male sexual drive discourse appeared to be influential. Consistent with the view of women as sexual objects whose purpose is to service and please men, Dorothy saw herself as trying to please men, by flirting and being sexually available, and gained some sense of status from this. This closely linked into the have/hold discourse in that Dorothy was extremely concerned to be 'attractive' to Tony and to men in general. In order to hold them she felt she had to be 'pretty' (in the sessions she took care to be attractively dressed and amply perfumed). She used her sexuality to bolster her self-esteem, sex was something she was 'very good' at, and this seemed to be confirmed in her boast that she had 'taught' Tony a lot about sex. Seduction for her was far more rewarding than anything else she could possible do and she gained more power from this than from anything else:

DOROTHY   I remember the first time I was unfaithful, it was with my boss, I was very innocent, he took me out in his posh car and bought me presents and gave me a lovely dinner. I felt so good ... so high ... We never had anything when we were young, nothing else makes me feel so powerful.

Her sexual behaviour was giving her power in a general sense in her world, power over men, something she could 'give' in exchange for other rewards. She had no legal power through her children as the children were not Tony's, and she had little support from her family of origin, who had rejected her because of her first divorce. Even in the home she felt powerless since Tony constantly invalidated her as a wife or mother, believ-ing that he was better at domestic tasks and at childcare. Though she had tried to be a 'good' wife, within the have/hold discourse, for example by cooking him unusual and highly nutritious meals, Tony invalidated these attempts; he was a finicky eater, preferred 'junk' food to her cooking, com-plained that she gave him too much to eat and this made his stomach bad. Dorothy, despite her protestations, also seemed to be behaving sexually according to the permissive discourse, she was having affairs, being overtly sexual, acting in a 'liberated way' but denied this, claiming instead that she wanted to 'please' men and that, 'apart from once', she had not been orgasmic with the other men. She appeared to think that her sexuality gave her power in her world, she felt good about herself when she could seduce and please men, they would give her 'little presents' and were always 'coming back for more'. Her sexual power, however, rested on her denial that she wanted any sexual pleasure, she did not ask the men to please her sexually nor make any sexual demands on them for her own sexual pleasure: 'I do almost anything they want, things that their wives won't do . . . anything that makes them happy'. To maintain her power she had to be able both to persuade herself and the men that she was not really interested in sexual gratification for herself. In effect she had to portray that she was not particularly sexual and was able to 'take or leave' sex.

A subtext to the MSDD discourse that they both appeared to accept was that men should be 'real men'. She had hoped that she could alter Tony but felt that he was too weak and insecure to change. Paradoxically her affairs were one of the areas where Tony did demonstrate masculine and assertive behaviour, since he would eventually put his foot down and see her men off by confronting them and telling them to leave his wife alone. Dorothy accepted this and did not insist on seeing the men after a confrontation had occurred. Consistent with the 'anywhere, anytime, with anyone' aspects of the MSDD discourse few of the 'real' men she pursued appeared to turn down her sexual offer, though she did say that she occasionally did not try to seduce a man if she thought he would not be interested. Many of the men were married but did not seem concerned about their wives' feelings. Within the sexual double standard Dorothy had to appear not to be a promiscuous, a 'tart', but achieved this at the expense of being labelled as pathological. Consistent with this framing of her as 'out of control' was the fact that she could not 'get rid of the men' once she had seduced them, and had to ask Tony to go and sort it out for her. Tony was thus compelled to be more assertive, more a 'real' man in telling the men to leave his wife alone. This was also proof to her that he cared enough about her to do it for her and overall supported the construction that she was pathological.

Explanations of the problems

The dominant explanations appeared to be located in individualistic pathological discourses. Dorothy in particular voiced criticism at Tony, accusing him of being weak but usually backed off this by taking the blame back onto herself, as in the extract above where she concludes, 'Well I can't say nothing'. Also, in addition to the discussion of the sexual issues she would frequently slide into more self-blame in terms of her problems with bulimia. Furthermore, this fitted with a dominant pathological discourse that, like her bulimia, her sexual promiscuity was 'out of control' – she could not help it and could not control herself. On occasion a subjugated discourse regarding the abuse of male power and the effects of her childhood abuse emerged. However, this would be dismissed as she remembered her parents' accusations that she was sinful because she had had a divorce and an abortion. Also, her religious background as a Jehovah's Witness led her to experience intense feelings of guilt, that her behaviour was wrong and 'sinful' and that she was a sinful person. In effect these two powerful discourses, the religious and the pathological, operated to frame her actions as 'mad' and 'bad'. These effectively subjugated possible alternatives, that she was rebelling against her position, or trying desperately to gain some sense of power and self-worth.

Tony appeared to see some of Dorothy's actions as attacking him and being cruel. Instead, he wanted her to be a wife and mother and to have his child and wished her to stop her affairs so that he could be sure the baby was his and not another man's. However, Dorothy explained that she had tried hard to be a good wife but Tony did not appreciate what she was trying to offer him. Most interestingly, although she did not fully articulate an explanation for this, Dorothy was reluctant to have a child as Tony wanted, partly because she would then feel trapped. Also, of course, it was possible that she resisted because she might not then be able to 'play around' with other men. In effect it seemed that the effects of the childhood abuse, condemnation by her parents and covert criticism from Tony had led Dorothy to internalize pathological discourses to the point that she had little sense of self-worth. She did not feel confident that she could succeed in education or skills training though she did attempt an evening class in German (which Tony accompanied her to!).

The dominant explanation in terms of Dorothy's pathology both enhanced but also disguised the power struggles. This framed her actions as 'out of control' and not 'responsible', without which her actions might have been seen as deliberate and for her own pleasure. A consequence of this might have been that she was therefore liable to retaliation from Tony. By allowing her actions to be labelled as 'sick' she could both exert some power in the struggle with him but avoid the worst consequences, such as Tony leaving and her possibly losing her daughter Carol. As Madanes (1981) points out, the sick position offers some power in that a degree of control, influence or attack can be exercised over the other person but at the same time power is lost because the person becomes sick, loses credibility as a person and is confined to a low status 'sick' role.

In the course of the sessions Dorothy appeared to become more confident and aware of the ways she had been invalidated in the past. She also recognized that her sexual activities were a way of attempting to gain some self-respect but that this was no longer working. The couple were able to validate each other to some extent and Dorothy even conceded that some women might find Tony attractive. She expressed some interest in pursuing some avenues for increasing her self-confidence but was unsure that she would be able to do much. Her sexual promiscuity did cease and she did eventually decide to have a child with Tony.

JILL AND PAUL SMYTHE

Background

Jill had stopped enjoying sexual intimacy with Paul and the couple appeared to be caught up in the common male demand/female reluctance sexual interactional cycle. Jill and Paul were both in their early forties. They had been married for 20 years and had three daughters, aged 19, 16 and 12. Paul was born abroad and following the death of his mother when he was six the family moved back to England where Paul lived with his aunt. His father remarried but Paul did not get on with his stepmother and was closer to his aunt until she committed suicide following the death of her husband. Paul was employed as an engineer, a job he had been finding stressful for several years, and he had experienced a period of depression for which he was receiving medication at the time the couple came to therapy. Jill, in contrast, came from a more settled background. She went from school to train and work as a secretary and met Paul when she was 16 and he was 18. They kept in touch while Paul was away at university and though they had some other platonic relationships they married when Paul was 23. Jill was currently employed as a secretary.

Relationship dynamics and sexual problems

The dynamics were similar to Mark and Louise. Paul would initiate sex two or three times a week – Jill expressed lack of interest but would eventually capitulate in order to avoid a 'bad atmosphere' developing in the family since Paul tended to become edgy and moody if 'deprived' of sex. Intercourse was described as clinical and without passion on Jill's part. There was little foreplay since Jill wanted to get it over with and Paul would penetrate and ejaculate quickly. Jill said she experienced little pleasure from this and had never experienced an orgasm with Paul. One of their explanations appeared to contain a learning theory/individualistic discourse that Paul had usually ejaculated prematurely in the early years. Jill had been quite enthusiastic about sex originally but the premature ejaculation had left her sexually dissatisfied and frustrated. Her frustration over many years had perhaps resulted in her losing interest in sex:

PAUL   What used to happen was there'd be a quarter-hour of foreplay but once penetration was made it would probably last a minute . . . knowing that I ejaculated early I used to delay penetration, tried oral sex but she very rarely wanted to do it . . . I don't so much suffer from it now. I can make myself delay . . . all she wants is for me to come quickly . . . not interested in foreplay . . . won't take her nightie off.

Power bases

There had been a change in financial power during the course of their relationship. Paul had always earned more and was more highly educated. Jill had stayed at home with the children for some years and had then worked part-time and was currently working full-time as a secretary. She was earning less than Paul but could have just about managed to support herself financially if they divorced, though she would have needed some maintenance from Paul for the children. Jill was highly likely to have custody of the children and therefore probably the house and maintenance if they divorced. Jill had originally been more emotionally dependent than Paul but this had changed, partly because she now, in contrast to Paul who was increasingly unhappy at work, enjoyed her job and gained support and stimulation from work and her colleagues. Paul was very good at 'technical/building' tasks, they described their house as being beautiful because of all the work Paul had done on it. Jill said she thought of the house as being Paul's. Jill had power through the children, child rearing, expertise and said she tended to make most of the decisions about them; for instance she wanted them to be privately educated, Paul did not, but her wishes had prevailed. Jill was more articulate than Paul and had high emotional informational power. Paul had higher 'public informational power'. Jill was perceived as being more attractive than Paul and had more 'sexual power' because Paul was believed to need sex more than she did. Her sexual reluctance, especially since she had had an affair, was very distressing to Paul and seemed to have been a contributory factor in his feelings of depression.

Some of their respective power bases and the changes they had gone through are illustrated by the following extract:

JILL	He wanted me to be independent, he was always saying why don't you do this or that. I felt I wasn't quite up to scratch . . . he's so perfect, so accomplished . . . if I walked away from that home the kids would be devastated but nothing would change, it's his home . . .
PAUL	Initially she'd gone through this emotional state . . . needed my type of strength. I valued my friends, big segment of my life . . . the children were young . . . I was playing golf . . . I said you must do something you like . . . become more independent. She relies on me less now . . . loves working . . . Her interests have been in different areas . . . I have definite views about the house . . . she has definite views about the children . . .
THERAPIST	Have your emotional dependencies shifted?
PAUL	I would say a rejection thing . . .
THERAPIST	Do you feel more dependent on her than she does on you?

PAUL   Yes, possibly.

THERAPIST   Did sexual changes accompany these emotional changes?

PAUL   We had a very good time sexually after the third child . . .
              she had post-natal depression . . . needed me for support
              . . . not that I gave a lot of support in discussing things
              but I was there helping with the children . . .

JILL   I make the big decisions . . . our roles have reversed . . . he
              earns more but I have made the larger decisions . . . when
              we were younger I was dependent . . . preferred really to
              work but the kids are important to me. He seemed very
              powerful in that situation . . . but he said do this [courses,
              etc.] . . . it felt like I was being pushed away.

Sexual discourses

They had a strong belief in the male sexual drive discourse. Hence, Jill
agreed to let Paul have his physical 'release'. Paul also believed that it was
up to him to initiate and satisfy women.

PAUL   I think it's the man's role to try to give a woman an
              orgasm. Early on I naively thought it was the same as a
              man's . . . that it didn't need the time . . . Generally it's the
              man's role to take charge. When I was young, I always
              initiated . . . different now sexual knowledge is far more
              . . . I used to view my girlfriends totally differently . . .
              separate to mates . . . young women are now initiating
              more . . . women talk about satisfaction . . . masturbation
              in women at our age was almost unheard of . . . Jill felt
              men masturbating . . . if you did that there was something
              wrong with you . . . she doesn't feel like that now but she
              has never masturbated herself, ever . . . when I suggested,
              when I was ejaculating early, that we use a vibrator she
              said No.

THERAPIST   Who would be most upset if sex stopped?

PAUL   I would be . . . physical need, if I get very frustrated . . .
              just a physical release . . . it's more satisfactory than
              masturbation.

Their acceptance of another aspect of the MSDD, namely that men should
initiate sex and that failure to achieve sexual satisfaction was largely the
man's responsibility, had implied that a lack of satisfaction was Paul's problem rather than Jill's; that there was 'something wrong with him' because
he could not 'turn her on' and satisfy her. At the same time sometimes the
'blame' would be put on Jill for being 'prudish' and for not being willing
to sort out the problem now by doing it more. This explanation, however,

had been rejected since she had had an affair and enjoyed sex with someone else which Paul saw as a personal rejection of him.

Jill felt that Paul had come to see sex as his 'right', since he provided for her and the children and he believed that marriage was not viable without a 'good' sex life. Paul at first denied this but then said he had come to think of it as his 'right' simply because he had come to feel 'powerless' in being able to generate desire in Jill and because he felt it was unfair that she could enjoy it with someone else but not with him, her husband. He was acting in this way as an attempt to extort some sexual validation from her but realized that it was not working and only making things worse. Running alongside this discourse there was the apparently contradictory permissive discourse; that they should both be able to enjoy sex fully. Not to enjoy it implies that there is 'something wrong with you'; that you are inhibited, prudish, abnormal in some way. This positioned Jill as having the problem. This definition of Jill as having the problem was challenged by the fact that she had enjoyed sex with someone else. In contrast this presented the possibility that Paul had the problem though he resisted this idea by asserting that sex had also been 'good' for him in his affair. One implication now was their relationship was problematic or even pathological and perhaps they should separate.

Explanations of the problem

Their explanations initially featured individualistic discourses, such as Paul's lack of experience and problems with premature ejaculation, Jill's 'prudishness' and her 'abnormal' lack of desire. Subsequently this shifted to feature Paul's 'abuse' of his emotional power early in their relationship, resulting in her feeling rejected and 'cutting off' emotionally. They also thought it was to do with their relationship and with Paul's 'personality', and more specifically his 'childlike' moaning and demanding approach to sex. They described their relationship as like a 'brother and sister': they got on well, did not argue or fight, enjoyed each other's company and had respect for each other but Jill just did not 'fancy' him anymore. However, there was generally little physical contact between them and Jill explained that Paul always initiated physical contact by 'teasing' her, tickling her, grabbing her bottom, and generally that he was a 'manic' and 'fidgety' person. Though she enjoyed his energy and enthusiasm she hated his teasing advances and said she desired a calmer approach to the initiation of physical intimacy:

JILL   I like men who are fairly 'laid back', confident . . . Paul is totally motivated all the time rushing around, not a man who sits back, always doing something . . . totally constructive and does everything very well . . . I find him 'spiky', if you cuddle him he is stiff . . . I like men that I find easy to cuddle . . . if you cuddle

them and they mould and you can relax into the mould . . . Paul
doesn't do that . . . he holds me tight and teases . . . can't relax
with him . . . I like men who are strong and successful but
weaker emotionally and look to me to be stronger . . . Paul is
emotionally dependent the wrong way . . . he is demanding,
attention-seeking in a youthful way not a 'manly' way. He has
an emotional age of 16 . . . that's how it's felt, a youthful
person's emotional dependency rather than a grown-up one.

They also subscribed to the view that Paul may have had difficulty in
relating to women emotionally because he had lost his mother and had an
ambivalent relationship with his step-mother. Jill thought that his teasing
may therefore have been a form of defence so that he need not clearly admit
he needed affection and served to protect him from the risk of rejection.

Shifts in power and discourses

Their explanations tended to fluctuate, during and between therapeutic sessions: sometimes one was seen as 'having a problem', sometimes the other.
These considerations of alternatives, though confusing, also seemed to be
potentially positive in that subjugated discourses were emerging along with
potentially new avenues of action. In the early years of the relationship Paul
had been more powerful. Jill's self-esteem had been very low, his was higher;
she was emotionally dependent, he was not; she had power through the
children, he had high financial power. This had gradually changed when
Jill started to work outside the home and especially when she began to work
full-time. One of Jill's main explanations for her sexual disinterest was that
originally she had been very dependent on Paul, wanting to be with him,
do things together, be 'close'. However, he had abused this by 'pushing her
away', leaving her feeling rejected and cut off emotionally and therefore sexually as well. Her career had 'taken off'; she loved her work, loved working,
his career was going 'downhill'.

The dominant discourse in their relationship up till that point appeared
to have been that Jill was abnormal regarding sexuality. Since she was relatively powerless and dependent she had been less able to resist this construction. However, as the power balance changed so too did her ability to resist
this definition. First, work had given her more self-confidence. Second, she
had had an affair during the last few years, at a similar time as her career
was 'taking off'. Paul became more emotionally dependent on her than vice
versa. At the same time Paul had felt rejected and hurt by finding that she
could enjoy sex with someone else. This partly threatened Paul's' sexual
self-esteem, though this was mitigated by the fact that he had affairs which
he said were successful sexually. The fact that they had both been sexually
'successful' elsewhere challenged the individualistic discourse that either of
them was at fault. What seemed to occur was that the blame moved 'up a

level' to a relationship discourse; that the relationship itself was problematic and they wondered if they were 'not compatible'. Interestingly, in therapy their concerns started to centre around whether they should split up rather than whether one or other of them was pathological in some way.

On one level this can be seen as a positive step but there are some drawbacks in that this obscures or subjugates alternative discourses, such as feminist ideas that the problems in their relationships are wider and commonly shared issues to do with the socialization of men and women and gender inequalities. In fact their adherence to conventional discourses about gender differences were apparent in Jill emphasizing that her lover had been a 'strong man' and she implied that she still did not feel it her responsibility to take charge of her own sexual desires and satisfaction. The final sessions revolved around a discussion of gender roles, expectations and the strengths and weaknesses of their relationship. It did seem that for Jill and Paul significant and potentially positive changes had been and were occurring. They ended therapy saying that it had given them a useful platform from which to continue working things out between them.

DISCUSSION: THE TABOO ON TALKING ABOUT POWER

The three cases differ considerably in the types of problems that were evident, the circumstances of the couples and the financial relations between them. Louise and Dorothy were both financially dependent and clearly had much less in the way of tangible power bases than their partners. Jill on the other hand was financially independent, and though her material circumstances might have deteriorated if she and Paul had separated this would not have been as extreme as for Louise and Dorothy. The sexual and other problems presented were different and do not appear simply to follow the line of argument that financial dependence induces sexual reluctance in the woman. Certainly, this did seem evident in Louise's case but it appears to be contradicted by Dorothy's case. Despite her extreme dependence she appears to engage in the very activity, sexual infidelity, which could lead to Tony leaving her. Furthermore, the couple stated that sex between them still was and had been good. However, Dorothy's case revealed that possibly sex was one of the main areas in which she could exert any power. Since she was not physically frightened of Tony she did not need to fear consequences of her infidelity such as Tony beating her. However, she was frightened of the consequences of divorce; she did not have a job, would not be able to afford the upkeep of the house and feared she might even lose custody of her daughter. Unlike Jill since she still engaged in 'good' sex with her husband the message was not that he was inadequate in this area, but that she was 'ill' and 'out of control' regarding other men. In fact despite criticizing Tony's looks and weakness she appeared to take great care not to attack his sexual competence, which seems a critical vulnerability for many men. She even seemed to gain some power from his competence by saying that she had 'taught him a lot'. Tony smiled with apparent satisfaction and pride as she said this. It was almost as if she was the 'teacher' in this area and her affairs could be seen as giving her greater skills she could share with Tony.

Of the three women Jill had most successfully overcome a pathological label. Early on in the relationship she had been defined as over-dependent and sexually abnormal or frigid. She had come to resist both these definitions by taking up satisfying work and by having an affair. She thereby proved herself to be competent, independent financially and emotionally, and sexually 'healthy'. Again, Jill was not physically frightened of Paul, who showed his anger not by physical threats, shouting or coercion but by sulking, withdrawing and occasionally threatening to leave and divorce Jill. It did seem that this ability to gain power and independence served to avoid Jill being trapped into a pathological identity. However, as with many couples a discourse that then becomes more dominant was that their relationship was faulty or pathological – that they were incompatible, couldn't communicate and so on. In contrast Louise and Dorothy were both relatively powerless and both apparently very much trapped by a pathological discourse. Despite the major problems these two couples did not, at least initially, talk about separation. It might have seemed obvious that both Mark and Tony for different reasons would have clearly wanted out of the relationship but they did not. Quite possibly the potential threat to the relationship was partly avoided by the women being pathologized as the problem.

What is perhaps most interesting, though, is that neither Louise nor Dorothy invariably accepted this pathological identity. In fact the men were more insistent that this was the issue. This fits with the idea that the concept of pathology, of an individual fault or 'illness' is a distortion of these women's experience. Instead, all three women appeared to have experienced considerable distress at various points in their lives. Some of the causes of these were fairly clear, Louise's sexual abuse by her father, Jill's sense of dependency and rejection and Dorothy's critical rejection and condemnation by her strictly religious family. However, the more insidious causes of women's distress relating to inequality, dependency, lack of power and lack of a positive identity were in a sense disguised. Instead, the distress experienced appeared to be interpreted in terms of the dominant discourses available, most compellingly the pathological discourse. This definition, however, invalidated aspects of the women's experience and did not fit the gnawing sense that something else was wrong; 'the problem with no name'.

This unease surfaced at times in the sessions when they did talk about their dissatisfactions in the relationships, lack of self-respect and so on. There was an interesting difference here too in that Mark continually validated Louise as a 'good' mother and home-maker and she correspondingly expressed no interest in 'going out of the home', for example to go back to work. For Jill and Dorothy, who both sought validation out of the home, in different ways, this validation was not evident. Paul did not exactly put Jill's domestic and maternal skill down, it was just that he was even better at these than she was, and was also excellent at house repairs and decorating. Rather differently, Tony invalidated Dorothy's attempts to be a 'good wife' by rejecting her cooking and intimating that he was better at domestic tasks and childcare. Louise, though validated in this area, expressed the view that she wanted more than this; Mark was away a lot and she wanted some company, some stimulation and to be able to talk to him and for him to take an interest in her, not just as a maternal and sexual object.

Therapy is inevitably a complex process and we are not suggesting that this is all there was to these couples' problems. We did in fact discuss many issues with them and also explored behavioural sex therapy techniques, their childhood experiences and previous relationships, and made concerted attempts to explore the men's feelings and experiences, as well as the women's. However, one of the most striking aspects of this work, and the other studies we have reported here, is the conspiracy of silence regarding power. It is almost as if a discussion of power, especially its effects in relationships, is one of the final taboos in our society. Many couples, after a little preliminary embarrassment (sometimes on our part) would, with some relish, launch into lurid and graphic details of their sexual problems, activities, needs and so on. In stark contrast our attempts to encourage couples to talk about power often met with much less success. We made several attempts to encourage these and other couples explicitly to consider their relative power bases, the potential consequences of these on their sense of identity and on their relationship. But most extremely the couples showed an apparent 'resistance' to discussing sexual problems in terms of power. They had difficulty in seeing that it was relevant. Again, we must qualify this by adding that the men showed the greatest reluctance in doing so. The women did articulate that they felt they had less freedom, were frustrated and so on, but this was not clearly seen as also influencing how they felt sexually.

In our view there are a number of reasons for this. The first is that ideas about sexuality, as we have seen, are dominated by discourses stressing men's greater biological need, women's greater needs for attachment and affection and the permissive discourse stressing mutual desire and satisfaction as 'natural'. All these discourses, with the exception of feminist ideas, strip sexuality from its relational and material context. In fact the permissive discourse is arguably the worst in this sense in that the discourses stressing women's needs for attachment and even the MSDD at least suggest that in order to enjoy sex women need to feel safe, secure and protected. When there is a sense of vulnerability, for example as a result of explicit or implicit threats of withdrawal of financial support, physical threats and so on this sense of security will dissipate. However, even a 'benign' dependence may still leave a residual anxiety and insecurity. Feminist ideas were evident in terms of women recognizing that independence, validation and so on were important but they appeared to be easily subjugated for a number of reasons. First, the portrayal of 'feminists' tended to be somewhat negative and also some of the middle-class bases of these ideas did not contact with the women's experience. For example, for many of the women whom we saw, satisfying, stimulating work was not a possibility since they had little education or money. For poorer couples women going out to work may involve yet another form of oppressive drudgery. Again Jill who had gone out and found stimulating work was middle-class, in contrast to Dorothy, who had little education, and Louise, who was a trained nurse but had not worked for many years.

Finally, it was also evident that the weight of psychological discourses, perhaps due mainly to the legacy of psychoanalysis, is that sexual problems are indications of an individual pathology rather than part of a wider state of distress. There is considerable evidence to suggest that sexual problems cannot be seen in isolation, for example lack of sexual desire and interest if viewed as one of the key components of the diagnosis of depression (*DSM III-R* 1987).

Some of the women did indicate some awareness of this and were more likely to voice it in individual rather than joint interviews. They also at times indicated that they could 'use' sexual denial as a way of 'getting back' at their partners. However, this was never voiced in the joint interviews, no doubt for fear of the adverse consequences. Rather than simply seeing this as oppression by the men it can be seen to fit with the male sexual drive discourse, which positions men as being in control of sexual matters, the initiators, and as responsible for 'satisfying' the woman. If the woman 'goes off sex' this must therefore imply that the man is no 'good' at it, if he was 'man enough' he could 'get her' to enjoy sex no matter what: she'd always want him to take her to heaven and back no matter what! In fact this also fitted with the 'honeymoon' story that many couples told us. Early on in their relationship sex had been good, or at least the woman had been willing. Later this deteriorated, and the men especially wanted it to return to the women wanting to do it. However, what was obscured by this story was the possibility that the many 'nice' things that the men had done in that period had stopped and this, along with the reality of the experience of dependence, especially because of the children, had allowed some of the inevitable dissatisfactions to surface. We frequently discussed this story with couples, exploring, for example, how the women had usually felt more free and powerful during this honeymoon period and perhaps this was generally linked to sexual desire and enjoyment. We started to see that it was one way that issues of power and its relations to sexuality could be more easily recognized and explored. The implications for therapy are the focus of the final chapter.

8

Implications for therapy with couples

> Without doubt, the psychologies and psychotherapies play an entirely significant role in the reproduction of the dominant culture.
>
> (White 1995: 45)

Throughout the book we have emphasized that power is a central factor in helping us to understand the nature of distress in relationships and how this relates specifically to problems of sexual intimacy. We now want to bring together some of our findings and offer some ideas for how couples can be assisted to make positive changes in their relationships. We will suggest some directions for therapeutic work which are broadly in agreement with White's (1995) emphasis that therapy is inevitably a political process in which power is a central concern. In Chapter 2 we outlined some of the most influential psychological theories and offered some ideas about how these are internalized and come to regulate the experiences: thoughts, feelings and actions of people in relationships. In a similar way these theories regulate the activities of psychotherapists. We are not attempting here to offer any simple critique of psychotherapies but to suggest that the therapeutic situation itself is imbued with power. Psychotherapists have power to impose their preferred frameworks on couples and sometimes inadvertently to pathologize one or both partners. An awareness of the extent to which problems are a product of inequalities residing in the relationships, but which are also socially constructed through the dominant discourses and structures of inequalities between the genders, can help to avoid such pathologizing practices.

In a sense we are describing our own realizations as a result of our research and experience with couples. Looking back on our work we can see times when we perceived difficulties as essentially to do with personal problems, for example that one partner was carrying emotional issues from their childhood into the relationship. We would spend considerable time discussing this and sometimes felt a rush of pride at having 'got it right' when one partner helpfully appeared to confirm this therapeutic formulation by revealing yet more details of their early difficulties. It seemed we were really getting to the heart of the problems and that these revelations were part of a process of healing. We are not suggesting that this is completely mistaken, but we are now more aware of the possibility that in some cases we were in fact colluding with the oppression of one partner and steering them further into a pathological identity. Furthermore, we became increasingly aware that our positions as therapists gave us considerable power to impose, or more correctly to support, dominant individualistic and pathologizing frameworks. One of the most pernicious ways that this occurs is that often it feels as if we are simply being respectful and going along with the ways that couples want to talk about their problems. But this respect for their wishes, though important, can easily miss how we are colluding with them in supporting dominant and oppressive ideas in our culture. In effect we started to see that in a sense it was our duty to work with couples to try to explore and challenge these dominant cultural ideas: '[as therapist] we can assist persons to challenge certain practices of power . . . We do not have to be entirely complicit with dominant culture – in fact, I think we should make it our business to ensure that we are not so' (White 1995: 45).

So, in this final chapter we want first to draw together our discussions and findings to offer a summary of our ideas about the relationships between power and sexual problems in couples. Also, though admittedly this is an ambitious task, we will offer some speculative ideas about the evolution of problems in relationships and some of the ways that the development of pathology in relation to sexuality may be avoided. Second, we will outline some implications for therapy along with ideas for how power can be introduced as a central rather than peripheral topic in therapy.

THE EFFECTS OF MATERIAL INEQUALITIES ON RELATIONSHIPS

One of the main aims of the book has been to explore the effects of material differences in power in relationships. We regard material differences to be a central factor, and one which has to some extent been obscured by the enthusiasm for constructionist approaches with their emphasis on the creation of meanings, beliefs and multiple realities in relationships. Rather than suggesting a simple materialist model of relationships, we have argued that power can be seen to have a double but related basis: the material differences between men and women and dominant discourses that shape ideas about power and sexuality in relationships.

We have indicated that one way that these two sources of power can usefully be conceptualized is in terms of the profile of power bases that each partner possesses. Both material circumstances and dominant discourses constrain the actual and perceived possibilities for action in relationships. We have also seen that the power bases that are available permit different types of influence to be employed by each partner. In particular it seems to be the case that when women are financially dependent they are more likely to be driven to employing sexuality as a means of exerting some influence. This is, in some cases, quite deliberate but more usually can be seen not as a deliberate strategy, but more as a form of desperation since it also deprives the women of intimacy and sexual pleasure. In contrast, women who are financially independent appear less likely to withhold sexual intimacy and are more able to exert influence in similar ways to their partners, for example through verbal persuasion. This pattern of male demand and female denial is made all the more likely by the prevalence of the male sexual drive discourse which constructs men as having a greater physical 'need' for sex. Women in contrast are construed as seeking emotional intimacy and commitment. The consequent pattern of demand/denial is so ubiquitous that it has even been enshrined in socio-biological theories which propose that it derives from fundamental evolutionary processes.

The second, and related, effect of inequality of power in the relationship appears to be that the less powerful partner is more susceptible to being labelled as pathological. In the previous chapter we saw that the effects of financial dependency are not always clear cut. In some cases a consequence appears to be that women withdraw sexually, in others that sexual intimacy remains but the women are more likely to be pathologized in various ways. In some, perhaps the majority of relationships, both processes occur. Women may withdraw sexually because they experience various forms of dissatisfaction with their lives, which is related in part to the inequalities in their relationship. However, this may be disguised or distorted in particular by the equals but different discourse.

The taboo against talking about power

The experience from our work and the writing of other researchers and therapists suggests that there is almost a taboo against discussing power in relationships. This may be related to 'romantic' discourses regarding intimate relationships whereby partners, women in particular perhaps, are not 'supposed' to be thinking about their relationship in terms of power or control but more in terms of 'love' and affection. Although women generally appear more willing to discuss some aspects of power this is likely to be in a general framework of wishing that they had more freedom to be able to engage in activities outside the home, or more freedom to avoid some of the mundane domestic tasks. Freedom and choice are relevant and important aspects of relationships but they were not typically seen as directly connected to power in the relationship. The assumption seemed to be that a woman could gain more freedom without the power balance in the relationship changing.

It seemed that to talk about power was only possible either relatively indirectly or in some narrow way, since talking about it more explicitly may be avoided because of possible expected repercussions. Talking explicitly about power tended to be seen as being 'feminist' and many women appeared to be reluctant to be seen as 'feminists' perhaps because feminism is seen so negatively. It appeared to be associated with various fears for women; that men would not find them attractive, but also that since it tends to be seen as a challenge to male power it is liable to meet with resistance and retaliation by the men. Since men are likely to have more power women appeared to wish to avoid overt conflict, which they (probably accurately) regarded as likely to occur given that many forms of feminism do represent an explicit challenge to male privilege. Talking explicitly about power with their partners appeared to be seen by many women as 'opening Pandora's box'; liable to release problems and conflicts, and likely to be met with resistance and counter challenges, conflicts that they were not in a position to 'win' and also going in a direction which they could not be sure would be productive and beneficial to them. Indeed the most likely prediction that they seemed to make is that it would lead to negative repercussions.

Given that being challenged is generally unlikely to be experienced as pleasant, it would hardly be surprising if the men were resistant to being challenged to talk about their privileged positions of power. Part of the issue here might be that both men and women find it difficult to see what the potential benefits of such 'unpleasant' discussions might be. The perceived costs seem to outweigh the benefits, for example the partner who is apparently symptomatic may resist talking about power because they fear that their 'symptoms' might be seen as a deliberate 'strategy'. In most of the case studies, for instance, it was quite clear that the influence of the symptom in the relationship was only acceptable when it was couched in terms of being 'out of control', an uncontrollable 'illness'. This assignation is frequently accompanied by suspicions that the 'symptoms' are not really signs of a 'genuine' illness but are manipulative. Even attempted suicide may arouse ambivalent feelings, for instance as an attempt to 'get attention', or a form of manipulation, or 'moral blackmail'. Likewise, a partner displaying a sexual symptom in a relationship may therefore encounter considerable surveillance of her actions and be expected to act in a way consistent with her pathological assignation. The research and our clinical work, however, suggested that in general 'going off sex' was more of a reaction to relative powerlessness than a conscious strategy. If symptoms were actually perceived as being to do with relative powerlessness rather than surrounded with a suspicion of manipulation or a deliberate strategy, then resistance to discussing power might lessen. It is important that couples are able to see the potential advantages for both of them in discussing and possibly altering their power dynamics.

As well as obvious resistance there appeared more generally to be a widespread view that discussing power was not central to the problems, that perhaps it was a consequence or a minor component. Most strikingly the grounds for dismissing the importance of power were the widespread acceptance of the equals but different discourse – that partners felt they had different but complementary and overall equal power. This tends to be so dominant that alternatives seem barely to exist in 'common discourse'. Although women were more likely to complain about the 'equal but different' structure and ideology, these complaints tended to fall within rather narrow parameters and were often dismissed or ignored. This lack of interest was in stark contrast to the willingness, for example, of our clinical couples to engage in a discussion of intimate sexual details. In our view this is a consequence of the massively influential individualistic and scientific discourses about relationships, identity and sexuality. The widespread availability of 'information' in magazines, newspapers, television and films fuels the discourse that sex is a kind of skill – how to have 'better orgasms', which can be acquired. The thrust (sic) of this is that likewise sexual problems are predominantly viewed in this way. This also constructs sexuality as an object, a commodity – to have sex, frequently and do it well – a little like good aerobics. Consistent with the male sexual drive discourse men were generally more committed to such a view. This was also reflected in the fact that a skills-based approach to problems, such as behavioural exercises, was generally more attractive to the men than the women. In contrast many of the women were more committed to the have/hold discourse and seemed to be saying 'There is something wrong in the relationship, I feel distressed and frustrated but I don't really know why'. By avoiding exploring issues of power not just at the interpersonal level but in terms of the wider societal context of gender and power most couples were caught in blaming each other, themselves or their relationship.

There is, however, an even broader reason that many people offer for not discussing power which is that it is impossible to measure, that it is such a slippery concept. We sympathize with this view to some extent but exactly the same arguments can be raised about almost any psychological phenomenon. How do we measure intelligence, leadership, extraversion, creativity and so on? Is power actually that much more complex to measure and discuss? We suggest that it is not. We have attempted to outline some of the ways that attempts have been made to measure power in relationships. The power relationships in couples can in our opinion be described with some confidence at any given point of time but this may have changed over the course of the relationship. For example, dependencies may alter with the arrival of children and their leaving home. They may also alter with events such as illness or retirement. In fact, though most people in our interviews and clinical work appeared to find it difficult or seemed unwilling to discuss power, they could do so more readily in terms of changes in relative power at different points in the history of their relationship. Though not perfect, we feel that a multi-faceted view of power, including material, emotional and ideological components, does offer a useful basis for research and therapeutic discussion.

The power to define the relationship

It is interesting that a number of interactional theorists and therapists have suggested that a central issue in any relationship is a negotiation, or a struggle over how the relationship is to be defined: who does what, what roles each partner will play, areas of responsibility, mutual obligation and rights, areas of trust and support and decision-making. However, earlier systems theory formulations, such as hierarchical incongruity have tended to be premised (perhaps implicitly) in the equal but different discourse. Madanes' (1991) perceptive and significant model of hierarchical incongruity correctly draws attention to the fact that the symptomatic partner is able to exert some influence through her symptoms. Unfortunately, though, this implies a mistaken view that therefore the relationship achieves some form of balance or equality. In fact there has been a general tendency in systems theory, inspired by Jackson's (1957) seminal paper on family homeostasis, to model pathology as a 'closed' system. In contrast we suggest that the emergence of symptoms in a relationship which is unequal is part of a complementary (Watzlawick *et al.* 1967) process, an 'open' system which will escalate towards increasing pathology and inequality. In order to sustain their effect it is likely that the symptoms will have to increase in order to overcome the adaptive processes in a relationship and as they increase there is an increasing chance that they will come to be construed as pathological. The emergence of a pathological identity carries with it a whole range of oppressions including stigmatizations, oppressive practices, such as becoming seen almost exclusively as pathological and being excluded from decision-making, losing respect for oneself and from others. In effect this can be a continuing escalation so that more and more aspects of the person's actions become seen as indicative of pathology – a process of totalization. Consequently, there is less chance that they or others see their actions in alternative ways, such as acts of legitimate protests or resistance to their position of powerlessness.

The construction of pathology

Not all unequal relationships develop sexual problems and not all sexual problems evolve into 'pathology'. It is obviously the case that couples will differ in significant ways on a variety of factors that can be seen to be related to the onset of pathology.

1 *Family history* There may have been experiences that one or other partner has had which leave them feeling damaged, vulnerable and bad about themselves. Traditions in the family may play an important part, for example there may be a family tradition of retreating into pathology as a response to distress. This may offer a form of modelling which, perhaps unconsciously, is activated in later relationships. It is also possible that the couples' families continue to play an important and in some cases an unhelpful role, perhaps dividing a couple, taking sides and offering unhelpful advice, making it more difficult for the couple to resolve issues.

2 *Life events and crises* In some cases problems may be related to 'bad luck', for example illnesses, loss of employment and so on which lead to enormous stress for a couple. Whether support is available at these times is a critical factor. If for various reasons, such as stresses and crises elsewhere in the family, such support is not available the natural and inevitable distress caused by these events may take longer to resolve and can easily become construed as signs of 'over-reaction', weakness or pathology.

3 *Effects of professional networks* Many of the couples in our research sample had received some form of help from some form of counselling or some assistance from a doctor, such as medication. These initial contacts can have a powerful effect in terms of starting to 'cast the die' of how difficulties are to be seen. If only one partner attends for counselling, for example, this implicitly defines the problems as predominantly to do with them. The content of the sessions, especially the typical focus on childhood emotional experiences, may further individualize and pathologize 'slightly extreme' versions of reactions to difficulties as indicative of pathology. These early definitions can have a powerful self-fulfilling effect. Alternatively, if they are seen as a couple this may be less individually blaming but serve to pathologize the relationship.

In our view these factors are important but perhaps what is most important is how they start to define signs of distress or difficulty within the relationship. As difficulties arise, and are apparently manifest more in one partner than the other then couples themselves attempt to formulate explanations. For example, if the woman is withdrawing sexually and appears somewhat depressed both partners appear to search for possible attributions of causes. Attribution theories suggest that these are predominantly either external or internal (see Chapter 2). Both partners may make attempts to blame and justify their positions. One prime candidate for such blaming is to attribute problems to personal inadequacies resulting from childhood experiences which have led them to being damaged in some way. In several of the clinical cases one partner had a history of 'problems' prior to the relationship, for example Louise and Dorothy had both experienced childhood sexual abuse. Consequently this ready-made pathological identity encouraged the likelihood of current problems in the relationship being defined as caused by their inadequacies or the 'damage' that they had incurred.

However, the emergence of distress and the subsequent definitions and attributions of this distress are related to power. It does seem to be the case that inequality is likely to encourage the emergence of some forms of behaviour and experience that indicate problems or distress. In our samples we found many cases where the women had experienced a variety of difficulties, such as depression, anxiety, stress, eating disorders and so on. In fact sexual problems were typically part of a wider profile of distress. This profile of problems has been documented in a number of studies; for example, Brown and Harris (1978) found that amongst the key factors involved in women becoming depressed were being confined to the home with young children and lacking an intimate supportive partner. One salient feature of depression is a loss of sexual desire. The predominantly poor working-class women in Brown and Harris's study typically experienced their lives as hopeless and themselves as having little power over their circumstances. Similarly, Friedan (1963) has indicated that many women's circumstances create a sense of powerlessness, distress and unhappiness. However, rather than seeing the emerging problems as related to power they may be construed as a form of pathology. White (1995) has argued that there is a very influential and damaging tendency in Western societies to employ a pathological/medical discourse to ascribe indications of distress as signs of pathology and weakness – a flawed identity. The 'ideal' self is typically framed within a patriarchal ideology as self-sufficient, independent and unemotional. In fact this model of a 'healthy' personality can be damaging for men as well as women since it offers an unrealistic, non-human image which conflicts with many men's experience of vulnerability and distress.

More broadly it appears that this discourse is 'employed' within relationships by each partner to define each other's, and also their own actions. The less powerful partner is more vulnerable to being framed within this discourse in the event of difficulties arising. The pathological discourse hangs over us all like a cloud, always there and ready to frame our distress, incompetence, vulnerability as weakness, abnormality and pathology. Women who are financially dependent and predominantly confined to the home are more likely to feel distress and also more likely to need the support of their partner to gain a sense of validation. In fact this need of a partner to ward off a potential pathological identity may be a vital ingredient of 'dependency' – dependency on the other to help us to feel good about ourselves.

The equal but different structure may lead to women feeling frustrated, depressed and consequently sexually disinterested; the man may then feel less likely to provide this support because of his own frustration and resentment. As the equal but different discourse is so dominant it may make it difficult for the man to realize or understand that the woman is experiencing distress in the relationship. The cessation of sexual intimacy, and associated problems, can lead to many men experiencing considerable anxiety about their own male identities, especially in terms of being sexually potent and not 'man enough' to satisfy the woman. Not infrequently the men become both anxious and hostile and this is likely to be exactly the worst response from the woman's point of view. Instead of desired reassurance, they experience hostility, frequently in the form of pathological attributions from the man and more generally from the wider culture which does not readily equate symptoms with inequality.

These dynamics are potentially likely to occur even if the man is not obviously abusing his power, though many of the men did, or certainly had abused their power in the past. One of the problems may be that the abuse of power itself is seen in narrow terms. Where it is obvious, as in violence, it may be seen to be legitimate to challenge it; indeed it is one area where feminist influence has had some degree of effectiveness and legitimation. However, there may be other kinds of more subtle 'abuses': being awkward and difficult about money, staying out of the home a lot implying a threat of leaving, complaints about work implying a resentment at supporting the woman, joking or 'mocking' as forms of invalidation, not listening or trivializing the other's ideas and so on. In the context of a woman's relative dependence and lack of power these actions can add up to a sense of oppression and insecurity. These patterns of abuse can increase if the woman reacts by 'going off sex'. Faced with sexual disinterest many of the men reacted resentfully, in part feeling that the woman was not keeping her part of the relationship 'contract' – critical and abusive behaviour in turn led the women to feeling worse and becoming more 'symptomatic'. At the same time it could be argued that many women are likely already to feel relatively powerless before they even begin the relationship. Even women who are financially independent in the relationship, although appearing to have more power in the relationship, are still subject to forms of oppression from ideological and structural factors, what Komter (1989) describes as the effects of 'invisible power'; lower self-esteem and less confidence than men.

Even if an abuse of power is not obviously occurring couples can be seen as caught in structures and ideologies which make it very difficult to act otherwise. Women who are financially dependent have few alternative sources of validation than the home. In effect for both partners there is a simple problem of finding convincing explanations for why problems may have arisen. Since the man is more likely to be at work it might seem evident that he is relatively 'healthy' since he can function in this context. Since many women lack this source of validation they may become increasingly lacking in self-confidence and may, at least in part, agree that the problem is to do with them. The couple can in fact be seen as caught in an attributional trap: the central relationships and source of validation for a woman who is financially dependent are likely to be the family and her relationships with their partner. But if these are problematic it is very difficult for her to rely on this to provide a source of validation to enable her to feel better about herself.

Of course the validity of competence at work as an indicator of mental 'health' is questionable. A person might well be able to function reasonably adequately at work but have extreme difficulties in relating to their partners in an intimate way. Many men can hold down a job yet will also 'batter their wives' or sexually abuse their children. Some of the responses of participants in the research illustrated how apparently well-functioning and competent men abused their power in the relationship, or tried to persuade their partners into sex by coercion or sulking. Irrespective of the truth that functioning adequately in work indicates mental health, it certainly does appear to be employed as an indicator of non-pathology, and may enable women who do work to resist the pathological label more effectively. These benefits are related to the nature of the work, and it may be the case that more validation is available for middle-class women who can gain considerable self-esteem and confidence from work. For poorer working-class women, on the other hand, work may be yet another source of oppression, not infrequently from male employers. On balance, in our findings many women found in work an opportunity for some friendships and support from other women, even if the job itself was menial.

History of the relationship

For many of our couples some reappraisals appeared to have been prompted by stresses and changes experienced by the men at work. The men in many cases complained that work had become stressful and invalidating. Several men were worried about possible redundancies and also the prospect of imminent retirement. This could lead to changes in the power balance which could in some cases be positive. However, it is also often seen as women's role to support men through such crises, to provide a haven from work, and hence a woman can be seen as inadequate if she is unable to do so. Many of the men were resentful that they had lost respect both at work and in the home, and that not enough consideration was shown for the years they had been the breadwinners.

At times it did seem to us that some of the women, especially in our clinical sample, appeared a bit 'tough'. The men were clearly distressed and vulnerable in part due to stresses at work, but the women seemed to be showing little sympathy. We came to realize that it was necessary to explore the history of relationships and to map changes in power and dependencies. This revealed, not surprisingly perhaps, that there were frequently legacies of resentments, for example memories of unrequited affection, abuses of dependency, and in some cases violence. These resentments often appeared to be playing out in the current relationship which appeared from the outside to be more equal. In some cases the women appeared to resent the men complaining and seeking support about their problems at work, loss of status and insecurities about life without work since they felt that the men had been less than supportive of their needs and distress in the past. Again these legacies were seen more in terms of personal faults and insensitivities, rather than due to prevalent ideas about gender roles or structural gender inequalities.

The interplay between the current relationship and its history appeared in many cases to resemble a form of 'strange loop' described by Cronen *et al.* (1982). The current state of the relationship was often viewed through the lens of the history of the relationship. Many couples would spend an enormous amount of time attacking their partners on a personal level in terms of their failings and inadequacies and recounting instances of their partner's cruelty, insensitivities and attacks in the past. Women would some-times attempt to talk about more obvious injustices and male abuses of power but it was extremely rare for the men to 'take this on board'. Mark, for instance, had probably been the most obviously abusive of all the men yet, because he did 'take it on board', was apologetic for his past behaviour, acknowledged that he had treated her badly, it was reasonably straightfor-ward to enable more changes in the relationship to evolve. For the other men, even when the women were quite explicit about various abuses that had taken place, the men seemed unable or unwilling to see that their behaviour had been or was currently related to problems in the relationship.

These memories served to define the current relationship as the product of this legacy and therefore as problematic. However, their feelings about the current relationship in turn were employed to define or colour how the past was seen. This in some cases appeared to be an escalating–symmetrical process whereby each partner produced more and more evidence from the past to frame the relationship as problematic. In the absence of a discourse that problems are related to inequalities, it may therefore be difficult for either partner to view the situation any differently. In the financially depend-ent couples this process often ended with the woman in tears, absorbing the blame and increasingly seeing herself as pathological.

Resistance

The weight of opinion from magazines, television, films as well as in the conversations of friends and family can lead partners to regard themselves as somehow deviant or abnormal. But pathology does not necessarily occur in all couples, and not even all couples where one partner is financially dependent. Financial independence seems to be less likely to result in the problematic demand–deny sexual interactional cycle and less likely to lead to a label of pathology. A key issue seems to be the extent to which women are able to resist pathological definitions of themselves. Women who are financially independent tend to have more power than financially depend-ent women; they were consequently less likely to be oppressed or subject to an abuse of power and less likely in turn to be symptomatic. They also seemed to be more able to resist pathological definitions of themselves. They both have less need to resist being labelled as pathological because they can exert influence by 'legitimate' means, and are more able to resist it should it be attempted. Alternatively, the combination of inequality, the resulting 'symptom', and the inappropriate and misguided responses, advice and information from others can lead to chronic pathology.

Perhaps one of the most important findings from the research was that women who are financially independent tend to 'argue back', become more assertive and use verbal persuasion in their relationships. This may indicate that they have more 'language' or 'ideological' power than financially dependent women. This may allow them to resist the label of pathology more effectively than financially dependent women. Financially independent couples were more likely to 'blame the relationship' than individual partners. They were more likely to be thinking in terms of 'incompatibility' and whether they should get divorced than the financially dependent couples. This may be another indicator of the power to resist individualistic pathological labelling, and is a 'step up' in terms of resistance and relative power, and perhaps a more 'fitting' explanation. However, even then they are more likely to think in terms of 'personal incompatibility' than gender inequality.

To summarize. Being financially independent will give women relatively more material power. Their partners will be less able to abuse their own power; several power bases will lose their effect if the woman is financially independent. The man cannot so easily manipulate his financial power or his physical power. If he is abusive she has more of a choice than a financially dependent woman as to whether to stay in the relationship or not. As well as affecting the use or abuse of material and physical power, being financially independent may also affect 'language' power including the capacity to resist the pathological label. Financially dependent women, on the other hand, have less material power, are more vulnerable to the abuse of power by their partners and less choice about staying in the relationship. It is more difficult for them to 'argue back' or be assertive. As they have few alternative sources of validation such as positive feedback from work colleagues, they may be less able to insist that they are not pathological. They may well be angry or resentful, especially if the partner has abused his power. This anger and resentment may be taken as a further indicator of pathology. The frustration of being unable to articulate their experience may similarly be taken as an indicator of pathology.

IMPLICATIONS FOR THERAPY

Just as the development of problems varies for couples so too do the pathways that they proceed along to attempt some change. In many of the couples we interviewed various forms of counselling had been attempted by one or both of them. Since nearly 50 per cent of all marriages end in divorce the solution adopted by many couples is to separate. It is interesting therefore to enquire why some couples make the effort to attend for therapy. Is it that they do actually want to see some positive change in their relationship? Is it that they are in some way pathologically glued together so that they cannot countenance separation? Or is it that in many cases the women are economically tied and dependent so that they tend to be in a position where divorce would be highly problematic? Alternatively is it that in these couples a process of pathologizing has started so that the solutions are seen in terms of one partner being 'fixed'? In our work we have largely dismissed the view that they are 'pathologically glued together'. Generally it seems that they want to try and sort things out and do not want to give up, that they are usually fond of each other and/or they do not really have the choice of divorce.

More contentiously we suggest that it is possible that some forms of counselling and therapy can, by ignoring issues relating to power, collude with pathologizing individual partners or the relationship, or both. Typically what appears to occur is that sexual reluctance in the woman comes to be seen as indicative of some form of pathology. If there are other 'symptoms' such as depression these are often used to confirm that the woman has some broader pathology. Involvement in the therapeutic system often means that the woman is given individual treatment or in some cases some attempts are made to work with the couple. However, the former may implicitly collude with the labelling of the woman as the problem; the latter not so much, but even in interactional therapies there may be a failure to address material inequality which either defines the relationship as pathological or even serves to uncover further 'evidence' that actually reinforces the designation of the woman as pathological. For example, discussions of each partner's families of origin and childhood experiences may appear to uncover evidence which corroborates the woman's pathology. If she is financially dependent, as we have argued earlier, she has less opportunity to resist this than similar evidence uncovered for the man. Almost certainly couples have engaged in trawling through their histories and the therapist doing the same may confirm that these individual histories are the main cause of the problems.

Power: imposing pathological frameworks

The therapeutic situation typically involves the therapist beginning by gathering information and asking particular questions in order to develop their own hypotheses about the causes of the problems. This is intended to help the therapist to start to formulate some ideas about what might be helpful interventions. But this is not a one-way process. At the same time the couple will be attempting to understand and interpret what the therapist is thinking. Why did she ask that? What does that imply about how she sees us? And so on. The fact that the therapist asks some questions rather than others may be seen to give some indication as to what factors are seen to be important as opposed to peripheral. If questions are asked about their early childhood, for instance their relationship with their mother, this may seem to imply that their backgrounds are relevant and central to their problems. Since most people are likely to have had some degree of problems and difficulties in these early relationships, it is relatively easy to 'pick out' possible causes of their problems stemming from their past experiences, especially if there have been traumatic events in their pasts. Unfortunately by focusing on these factors they can be assigned an exaggerated significance and centrality. At the same time, as soon as the focus is on their past experiences the focus is also on the individual, and is likely to be seen as being 'personal' and therefore potentially pathological.

There can be a real danger that the partner in the relationship who has already been partly or more fully conscripted into a pathological identity goes along with this line of questions to reveal further apparently corroborating evidence of negative past experiences, perhaps in the hope that they will be helped by doing so. Unfortunately this can be a 'blind alley' where instead of having uncovered the 'real' causes of the problems a collusive process is enacted. The men in these sequences may keep quiet about their own past problems or even if they do voice them their partner and the therapist may have become convinced that these are not central. There were clear examples of this in our work with Mark and Louise and Dorothy and Tony, described in the previous chapter. Since both women had histories of previous problems it was very compelling at times to become endlessly caught up in examining these events and by implication defining them as having the 'problems'.

This therapeutic direction is frequently unproductive for all concerned. Alternating between acceptance and rejection of this pathological identity, women frequently also express some 'resistance' since the definitions do not fit with aspects of their experience. They may resist quite overtly, for instance by disagreeing with the therapist's interpretations. For instance, a woman may disagree on the extent to which their relationship with their mother is the central 'cause' of the problems, or even that this is at all relevant. Rather than recognizing this as an attempt to bring alternative and subjugated experiences and explanations into the therapeutic discourse the woman's actions may be regarded instead as indicative of pathological resistance. Perhaps the most oppressive and collusive reaction would be to insist that such resistance indicates that there must have been real problems in their relationship with their mother and it is 'too painful'. In effect what they may actually be resisting is the therapist's explanation and the label of pathology, not only because the pathological label is negative but also because it is not actually an accurate perception of their position; it does not actually 'fit'. Such overt disagreement may be relatively unlikely because of the therapist's expert status and therefore power to impose their framework, and also because the woman may be concerned about turning the therapist against herself. Covert forms of resistance may be more likely, such as being upset in the session, being 'unable' to carry out tasks, and so on. All of which may of course reinforce the assignation of a pathological identity.

Power inside and outside the therapy room: the illusion of equality

Issues of power are also inherent in the therapeutic process: the therapist is in a position of power in relation to the couple. The questions that are asked or not asked may implicitly convey messages about what is seen to be important, relevant and where the causes of the problems are seen to lie. The dynamics of the therapy session itself must be taken into account. As we have suggested in previous chapters partners may differ in terms of the profile of power bases that they each hold. How these are played out in the therapy situation is complex. Many men are more able to present a rational image in therapy which can easily lead to a view of the woman as over-emotional, difficult and as the main contributor to the problems. This, though, is perhaps not the most common scenario. Instead it frequently appears in therapy that the woman is more able to articulate her feelings, able to talk about the problems and is more committed to therapy. The impression that this can convey is that the woman has considerable power in the relation-ship, or even that she is dominant. However, many women claim that this is not the case; instead they see the therapy situation as safe, a place where they hope that they can voice some of their concerns in the presence of a 'referee' without fear of reprisals.

In fact many therapists, including male therapists, often feel more empathy with the woman because she is more readily able to engage in the explora-tion of feelings which women (and therapists) have been socialized or trained to explore. Perhaps this is one of the reasons why not only couples, but many therapists, have not regarded power as a central issue, because in the therapy situation women operate within one of their few areas of power – emotionality and relationships. Consequently power does appear to be dif-ferent but equal in the relationship. In fact it is possible that the experience of the therapy situation may give a false sense of equality in the relation-ship, which drives a discussion of power off the therapeutic agenda.

The illusion of equality created in the therapeutic encounter may also serve perversely to promote the pathologizing of the woman. Resistance to being labelled as the pathological partner may include disagreeing with the therapist, refusing to do what they say, covertly or overtly, and attempting to articulate more subjugated experiences, feelings, thoughts to the therapist. However, this may be seen, for example within psychodynamic approaches, as evidence of the woman being overly controlling or even castrating. On the other hand if the woman resists more covertly by being silent or not co-operating with tasks, this may be regarded as evidence of denied hostility or anxiety, and so on. Either way once the relationship is viewed as equal but different (rather than as unequal, which it may be outside the therapy room) then a distortion of the woman's distress may be likely to occur.

Systemic or interactional therapies, though potentially less prone to individual pathologizing, can, nevertheless, also fall into a similar trap. It is frequently assumed that the dynamics of relationships show a basic consistency across various situations. Hence, the false assumption may be made that what is seen as the dynamics in therapy is what occurs outside. Interestingly, this assumption is definitely not made in cases of abuse or violence, quite the contrary. This is not to imply that all couples or all men deliberately set out to deceive in therapy, or that some women are not powerful outside. However, as Cecchin (1987) suggests, it is important to try to maintain a position of 'curiosity' about how things might be in other contexts.

A consequence of seeing the couple as different but equal, or of the wife as dominant, is that apparent 'resistance' to the therapeutic framework may be interpreted as to do with various forms of unconscious factors. However, this 'resistance' may be seen instead as due to the framework not 'fitting' their experiences, particularly of the less powerful partner. Since the less powerful do not experience themselves as equal or as having equal influence, they are therefore liable to resist the framework because it does not fit; it negates important aspects of their experience. It could be argued that as therapists it is important to be looking at disagreements with our frameworks, looking for subjugated discourse and experience, seeing resistance as an indicator of these subjugated experiences rather than merely reinterpreting resistance in terms of individual or interpersonal pathology. This seems important both because it should theoretically 'fit' experience, and because the pathological label is in itself disempowering. Imposing a theoretical framework that does not 'fit' one or both partners' experience has elements of an abuse of power on the therapist's part.

Some ideas for encouraging a discussion of power in therapy

It is probably the experience of many therapists working in a variety of therapeutic orientations that many couples are reluctant to discuss issues of power or are unable to see that it is relevant to their problems. We have explored a number of ways of introducing an analysis of power into our work with couples and families.

Making power visible

In some cases it is possible to tackle the issue of power and inequality fairly directly. One way that we have attempted to do this is to draw up a table, on a board or a piece of paper, of the different power bases that each partner possesses. This activity van be included or 'framed' as part of the assessment or information-gathering about their relationship. This can start to reveal some of the structures of power within the relationship and partners' beliefs about the relative value, significance and implications of these differences in their relationship. This activity can help to shift our implicit assumptions as therapists that the couple have equal but different power. However, whilst acknowledging differences in resources, one or both partners will frequently attempt to suggest that these balance out. In some cases it can be possible to confront or explore this assumption, in others the discussion may be more helpful if it moves to more indirect approaches. With Mark and Louise, for example, it was possible to discuss power openly. Without much prompting from us Louise recounted how he had been abusive to her and his previous girlfriends and Mark admitted to this and emphasized that he was attempting to change. However, he was less aware that he had perhaps abused Louise's dependency on him, for example by insisting on sex with her even when she was ill and was clearly not enjoying it.

In some cases it is possible to discuss the effects of powerlessness in terms of their past experiences with their parents, employers, school-teachers and so on. There are some drawbacks though; such a discussion might be taken to imply that the symptoms are a deliberate form of resistance and hence liable to some retaliation. Even more commonly couples may agree that there are inequalities but argue, convincingly, that there is little they can do about them if there is no work or affordable childcare available. It is often possible, though, to explore some possible moves, no matter how small, towards the dependent partner gaining some independence or self-esteem. In some cases it may be that a couple decide not to make changes but they may both still benefit from a sense of feeling potentially free, less oppressed and more empowered and supported by their partner.

Externalizing the problems

Often couples present their difficulties as unique and indicative of their own failings. In presenting a description of the problems partners can be encouraged to start to consider their explanations of the causes and how these attribute blame to themselves. This can reveal what dominant discourses underpin their explanations and also start the process of bringing forth some subjugated explanations. These explanations can be connected to or externalized in terms of wider societal discourses by asking questions about where these explanations came from? This can be assisted by questions about what advice they have been given and by whom – friends, relatives, colleagues and so on? Similarly it can be useful to explore what reading, television programmes and so on have influenced their thinking about sexual and relationship problems. Couples can be encouraged to bring along some examples from magazines and so on which have influenced their thinking or which represent some of the discourses that have been explored.

Such discussion can include acknowledging how we are all, including the therapist, caught in the common individual and pathologizing ways of seeing problems. If the therapeutic work includes live supervision a reflecting team format might be helpful in allowing a discussion of the similarities and differences in the couple's and the therapist's experiences of power and inequality. It can also be useful to include a discussion of the difficulty of resisting the barrage of 'truth' in the media.

Social comparisons

Another way that the problems in the relationship can be externalized is to work with couples to consider how their ideas might be shaped by their ideas about what other couples are like. This can lead to a discussion of the extent to which we are all influenced by social comparisons, evaluating our relationship in terms of what is seen to be 'normal' and acceptable, to what extent we are conforming to cultural ideas about relationships, gender and power relations between men and women. Couples can be encouraged to carry out an observational exercise to study what the relationships in other couples they know (friends, neighbours or relatives) are like in comparison to their relationship. What are their relationships like in terms of gender roles? What balance of power do they have? What appear to be positive and negative aspects of their relationships? How are they similar to or different from these couples? What aspects of their relationship do they want to be more like theirs and why? From such questions some general themes about the common discourses or expectations about relationships can be extracted. Along with this some discussion of the different arrangements in terms of power can be brought out and a discussion of the advantages and disadvantages of different power arrangements. Specifically, they can be asked to think about couples where the power appears to be more equal and what appear to be some of the advantages and disadvantages for the partners.

Difficulties of change

It can also be helpful in this context to share with couples our experiences, as therapists, of the stories of couples who have made changes, and the difficulties involved in attempting processes of change – the 'migration' to a new form of relationship. The difficulties for each partner may be discussed, for example the anxieties that many women face in returning to work and the possibility that the man might feel abandoned and jealous. It can also be helpful to discuss the long-term vs the short-term implications;

for example, the advantages of change for the relationship may be less than obvious in the short-term, if there is increased stress, or less time for each other. For the woman work may prove to be less than satisfying and not appear worth the aggravation it causes. Again the feelings that may be associated with these changes can be externalized, for example in terms of how they may conflict with the cultural norms, such as the woman as home-maker or the man as the primary breadwinner. This can reveal that the stresses that are experienced may in part be to do with the sense of not living up to these dominant cultural expectations.

CHANGES OVER TIME

An appraisal of the relationship and changes over time can help to reveal how the relative balance of power may have altered over time and how such changes related to changes in the relationships. There are many inter-connected facets of exploring such changes.

Development of the problem

A discussion of the problems can be guided towards an analysis of when the problems started and what was happening at the time. This starts to con-textualize the problem in terms of events and circumstances at the time rather than simply individual factors. This can be pursued to explore what the relationship was like before the problems started, in particular what expecta-tions they had at the start of the relationship about gender roles, sexuality, decision-making in the relationship, responsibilities and obligations, free-dom, how they negotiated important issues, and dominance and dependency in the relationship. Again such a discussion can be contextualized historic-ally in terms of how ideas about relationships and gender roles may have altered from when they first met, how they have attempted to deal with such changes and the difficulties in accomplishing such changes.

The 'honeymoon' period

It can be useful for many couples to explore the various stages of their rela-tionship, especially what they first found attractive about each other. Where couples are able to express some positive memories this frequently leads to a discussion of the 'honeymoon' period, a time when the relationship was good, sex was exciting and they were having a good time. This period can be explored to examine what made it good and particularly what aspects of the relationship were different then. This can lead to a discussion of free-dom, independence and power; for example, women often view this period of their lives in terms of having been more independent and free, and sex was not predominantly an obligation but something they could choose to do or not to do. Partners' early attitudes to each other and to other sexual partners can be employed to discuss wider questions about their expectations of dominance, dependency and power. What was erotic for them at this stage can also allow a discussion of issues such as the eroticization of dominance – was what made sex exciting to do with equality, choice, freedom and independence? Or the sense of the man being dominant and powerful and the woman submissive? Again this can also reveal the popular constructions of sexuality in terms of the dominant discourses, such as the male sexual drive discourse, have/hold and the permissive discourse and how these have influenced their experiences. An over-arching framework can be the extent to which it is possible or otherwise for the couple to return to this period. What would have to change? Would they need to have a more egalitarian relationship in order to achieve the same feelings of excitement and satisfaction?

Relationship life cycle

A discussion of the development of the relationship can frequently reveal periods where the relative power positions have shifted. Couples can be asked to describe periods when there were significant shifts in dependencies, such as the arrival of the first child or one partner becoming ill and needing to be cared for and leaving the other partner responsible for making major decisions. The discussion of such changes can be facilitated by using a visual representation (see Fig. 8.1).

Partners can be asked to think of two or three critical positive and negative periods/events/transitions in their lives together and to place these on the graph. These critical events and changes can be explored in terms of the relative changes in power, dependencies and how these relate to how satisfied each partner felt with the relationship.

The future

Couples frequently appear to be stuck in a focus on the present problems, supported by selective use of evidence from the past that things were always as bad. An exploration of what the future might hold can start to move away from this frame and guide the discussion towards an exploration of the implications of some important transitions, such as children leaving home, retirement, changes brought about by ill-health, arrival of grandchildren and so on. This can introduce a discussion of how roles will change, shifts in power bases, how different dependencies may arise and how these will be dealt with.

Start of the relationship	Present	Future
Relationship satisfaction	Critical +ve events/periods	
+5		
+4		
+3		
+2		
+1		
0	————————————————————	
−1		
−2		
−3		
−3		
−4		
−5	Critical −ve events/periods	

Figure 8.1 Life paths

Hypothetical scenarios

It is very easy to view the past as having taken an inevitable course and the problems as part of this. Various hypothetical scenarios can be explored, for example how might the relationship have been different if the woman had worked and the man had stayed at home? What difference would it have made to their relationship if the other partner had the symptoms? What difference would it have made, and might make in the future, if their power bases were reversed?

Family genograms

Drawing up a family genogram depicting both partner's families can be used to explore a wide range of issues relating to power and sexuality. It is possible to explore the context of their relationship in terms of the sources of support, involvements with family and advice that they have received. It is possible to compare and contrast the couple's relationship with that of the parents and even the grandparents. This can easily lead to a discussion of how ideas about relationships, sexuality and power have altered across the generations. The relative advantages of conventional gender relationships as opposed to more modern egalitarian forms can be evaluated. Frequently partners will reveal through this that they had chosen not to have a relationship like their parents'. This can generate a view of the relationship as not simply inevitable, as something that they passively have ended up with but as representing some active decisions. This can be pursued further to explore what model of relating they learned from their parents and how this may be colouring their current views. For example, a man might have a view of his father as having been weak and oppressed and this may be driving him to be more assertive, even abusive, of his power in his relationship.

CONCLUSIONS

One of the effects of patriarchal ideology is to subjugate or make peripheral the effect of material inequality by various processes including 'blaming' the individual and describing 'resistance' as abnormal or pathological (Williams and Watson 1988). This can lead to difficulties in relationships very rarely being seen as being directly related to gender inequality or to patriarchal discourse or beliefs. This in turn may lead to inappropriate if not actually inaccurate explanations of the problem and associated inappropriate attempted solutions to the problem. Couples may struggle to resolve their difficulties, fluctuate from one explanation to another, try different ways of attempting to change without being aware of the impact of inequality on their relationship. They may talk about their difficulties to others, read magazine articles or books, in an attempt to understand what might be going on and how to sort things out. The culmination of all this may be that pathological definitions are increasingly absorbed. This may lead to one partner entering therapy, in some cases becoming labelled as pathological. Alternatively, in some cases partners merely continue to accept a distressing state of affairs. Even when individual pathologizing is avoided, for example through interactional therapies, there can be a danger that in many cases the process effectively moves up a level so that the relationship is seen as faulty. This may lead to divorce or separation with all its attendant conflicts, disruptions and distress, not least for any children involved.

Pathological discourses are prevalent in Western societies. When individuals have difficulties or problems one of the main explanations they and others will give is that there is 'something wrong' with them. This may be constituted of different elements, different emphases, depending on the particular therapeutic perspective that is being used. Therapy and change necessarily involve a political process of active resistance to these dominant pathological discourses. In effect therapy cannot be neutral; simply going along with what partners are saying may implicitly be supportive of these discourses. This does not imply that therapy is about imposing a view on couples in some totalitarian manner. However, it does mean that we should find creative and interesting ways of introducing an exploration of power into the therapeutic process. It is no use trying to bludgeon couples into a discussion of power because we think it is 'good for them'. At the end of the day we must accept their wishes if they decide that this is not the most important issue they want to discuss. But we feel it is essential that they should at the very least be given this choice. All too often it is never even raised as a potentially salient issue.

On a more optimistic note one of the central conclusions we can draw is that financial independence is associated with more positive relationships. Specifically, women are less likely to lose interest in sexual intimacy and there appears to be less risk of pathology developing in either partner. This is perhaps a bold conclusion. We cannot claim to have shown that financial equality, and more general equality or a relative balance of power in relationships, is associated with greater happiness and satisfaction for both partners, but it does look that way. Increased general awareness of power and its centrality to relationships is important both generally, and more specifically in therapeutic contexts. Feminist writers have strongly advocated this and we hope that we have added a little to this by spelling out in more detail how inequality is the enemy of happy, satisfying sexuality. Even the most hardened anti-feminists might concede that this is worth knowing?

Appendix 1

RESEARCH QUESTIONNAIRE: POWER BASES AND INFLUENCE STRATEGIES (FOREMAN (1996))

INTRODUCTION

I am extremely grateful to you for agreeing to answer these questions. You may find some of them a little personal or embarrassing but please answer them. This is totally confidential and your names will *not* be disclosed or shown to anyone except my research supervisor.

Please be *totally honest*. I am not interested in being judgemental. The results from the research will be used to help people who are experiencing difficulties.

Please fill in the questionnaire and send it back to me *without* discussion with your partner. If you experience difficulties with the questionnaire please contact me at:

**QUESTIONNAIRE
Section 1: Power**

Name .... Age ....

Occupation ....

Children (ages and sex) ....

Previous marriages or long-term relationships ....

How long have you been married/cohabiting? ....

Please answer the following questions as honestly as you can. *Thank you.*

1 Are you financially dependent on your partner? ....

2 If you were on your own (e.g. split up) could you support yourself financially? ....

3 Who does the accommodation belong to? ....

4 If you split up could you afford reasonable accommodation? ....

5 Does your family live nearby? ....

6 Would your family help out in times of difficulty or if you split up with your partner? (how – money, accommodation, childcare, etc.?)

....

....

7 If you split up who would have custody of the children? ....

8 *Please* answer the following by placing a *tick* in whichever column is correct. ....

	SELF	PARTNER	SAME
A Who is closest to the children?	☐	☐	☐
B Who is physically stronger?	☐	☐	☐
C Which of you is more sexually jealous of the other?	☐	☐	☐
D Who is more secure?	☐	☐	☐
E Who is more confident?	☐	☐	☐
F Who is more emotionally dependent on the other?	☐	☐	☐
G Who is more interesting?	☐	☐	☐
H Who gets on better with people?	☐	☐	☐
I Who has more freedom?	☐	☐	☐
J Who would be the more upset if you split up?	☐	☐	☐
K Who gives in more?	☐	☐	☐
L Which of you is more in love with the other?	☐	☐	☐
M Which of you is more likely to complain that you don't have enough sex?	☐	☐	☐
N Which of you is more likely to go off sex if things are wrong between you?	☐	☐	☐
O Which of you has the most self-sufficiency (happy to be on their own)?	☐	☐	☐

9 How often do you disagree (tick the most appropriate)?

(Less than once a month) ☐	(About once a month) ☐
(About once a week) ☐	(More than once a week) ☐
(More than once a day) ☐	

10 What are the main things that you disagree about?

Children ☐	Money ☐	In-laws ☐
Friends ☐	Sex ☐	
Other ☐		

(Please specify) ....

11 Do you generally try to avoid raising issues that will cause disagreements? YES/NO
If YES what issues and why?

....

....

....

....

Section 2: Behaviour

If you are in disagreement with your partner, trying to make a decision or raising an issue which of the following do you do?

Put a *Y* for you. What behaviour does your partner use? Put a *P* for your partner's behaviour.

	Sometimes	*Often*	*Never*
1 Bargaining e.g. I will do A if you do B	☐ ☐	☐ ☐	☐ ☐
2 Bribing e.g. I will buy you a new dress if you do X	☐ ☐	☐ ☐	☐ ☐
3 Being especially nice	☐ ☐	☐ ☐	☐ ☐
4 Flattery	☐ ☐	☐ ☐	☐ ☐
5 Apologizing	☐ ☐	☐ ☐	☐ ☐
6 Say it is best for the family	☐ ☐	☐ ☐	☐ ☐
7 Complain about something else	☐ ☐	☐ ☐	☐ ☐
8 Say that you need to do it for your own fulfilment, etc.	☐ ☐	☐ ☐	☐ ☐

	Sometimes	Often	Never
9 Act helpless	☐ ☐	☐ ☐	☐ ☐
10 Verbal rational explanation	☐ ☐	☐ ☐	☐ ☐
11 Lying	☐ ☐	☐ ☐	☐ ☐
12 Say it is not fair	☐ ☐	☐ ☐	☐ ☐
13 Say it is your partner's duty	☐ ☐	☐ ☐	☐ ☐
14 Withhold information	☐ ☐	☐ ☐	☐ ☐
15 Accuse partner of being selfish	☐ ☐	☐ ☐	☐ ☐
16 Attack before your partner can accuse you	☐ ☐	☐ ☐	☐ ☐
17 Try to get your partner to forget complaint	☐ ☐	☐ ☐	☐ ☐
18 Use ultimatums – 'do it or else'	☐ ☐	☐ ☐	☐ ☐
19 Nagging	☐ ☐	☐ ☐	☐ ☐
20 Go silent	☐ ☐	☐ ☐	☐ ☐
21 Leave the room	☐ ☐	☐ ☐	☐ ☐
22 Shout	☐ ☐	☐ ☐	☐ ☐
23 Use violence	☐ ☐	☐ ☐	☐ ☐
24 Give in and feel OK	☐ ☐	☐ ☐	☐ ☐
25 Give in and feel resentful or not do what was agreed	☐ ☐	☐ ☐	☐ ☐
26 Make partner feel guilty	☐ ☐	☐ ☐	☐ ☐
27 Crying	☐ ☐	☐ ☐	☐ ☐
28 Put your partner down	☐ ☐	☐ ☐	☐ ☐
29 Withdraw affection	☐ ☐	☐ ☐	☐ ☐
30 Threaten to leave	☐ ☐	☐ ☐	☐ ☐
31 Go off sex	☐ ☐	☐ ☐	☐ ☐
32 Leave (temporarily)	☐ ☐	☐ ☐	☐ ☐
33 Threaten to withdraw money	☐ ☐	☐ ☐	☐ ☐
34 Draw the children in on your own side	☐ ☐	☐ ☐	☐ ☐
35 Use work as an excuse for not doing what your partner wants	☐ ☐	☐ ☐	☐ ☐

	Sometimes	Often	Never
36 Evoke jealousy	□ □	□ □	□ □
37 Complain about partner to others	□ □	□ □	□ □
38 Threaten to take the children	□ □	□ □	□ □
39 Wait until your spouse does something wrong then complain	□ □	□ □	□ □
40 Change the subject – evade, deny that the subject is worth talking about	□ □	□ □	□ □
41 Tell partner to shut up	□ □	□ □	□ □
42 Don't listen or stop listening – read a paper, etc.	□ □	□ □	□ □
43 Be assertive and stick to the issue	□ □	□ □	□ □

44 Other?   ....

....

Section 3: Effects on behaviour

For those who are, or have been *financially dependant* on their partner, do you think that this affected what you say or do in the relationship?

For instance you might feel that an issue needs to be resolved but you don't want to keep on about it because your partner might get angry and threaten to stop giving you any money.

OR

Your partner might want to move home for their job, you don't want to uproot but you agree because you are dependent on his/her job.

Please give brief details of how you feel your behaviour to be constrained:

....

....

....

....

....

Alternatively do you 'put up' with behaviour from your partner because you are financially dependent? For instance some people put up with aggressive or threatening behaviour because they feel they have nowhere else to go.

Please gives brief details if you feel you 'put up' with your partner's behaviour:

....

....

....

....

....

If you feel this is difficult perhaps you could think about what your relationship was like *before* you became dependent and whether it is different now.

Section 4: Interactional behaviour

Please try to think about one or more *typical* discussion or argument between you and your partner which has taken place recently. If you cannot think of a recent example give one from the past but specify how long ago these occurred.

I would like you to think about and note down the sequence of the argument in terms of the order of what each of you said and did in turn. The following is a simple illustration of what I mean:

Step 1   You ask your partner to help with the washing up

Step 2   Your partner says 'OK' but carries on sitting down

Step 3   You say 'Come on then'

Step 4   Partner gets up a bit reluctantly

Step 5   You say 'About time ...'   Steps 6, 7, 8, 9 etc.

Please give two examples of *typical* interactions between you and provide as much detail as possible:

EXAMPLE 1:

Step 1 ....

Step 2 ....

Step 3 ....

Step 4 ....

Step 5 ....

....

....

....

....

....

EXAMPLE 2:

Step 1 ....

Step 2 ....

Step 3 ....

Step 4 ....

Step 5 ....

....

....

....

....

....

Section 5: General information

	YES	NO
1 Have your arguments, disagreements generally been resolved amicably in the past?	☐	☐
2 In the example of the interactions you have given did you initially expect it to be amicable?	☐	☐
3 Do you generally feel that your views will be taken into account?	☐	☐

4 Do you feel that one of you is more likely to win? ☐ ☐

If *Yes*: Which of you is more likely to win? ....

How do you or your partner achieve this?

....

....

....

....

....

5 Please describe how you feel as the interaction between you proceeds: (Please tick the relevant adjectives)

	At the start	Middle	At the end or afterwards
Happy	☐	☐	☐
Hostile	☐	☐	☐
Anxious	☐	☐	☐
Tense	☐	☐	☐
Relaxed	☐	☐	☐
Resentful	☐	☐	☐
Determined	☐	☐	☐
Angry	☐	☐	☐
Affectionate	☐	☐	☐
Other	☐	☐	☐

6 In your view who in general places more emphasis on sex in a relationship?

Men ☐ Women ☐

7 In general who do you think are more interested in sex?

Men ☐ Women ☐

8 Do you think that you or your partner ever use your sexuality to get what you want? (Put a *Y* for *you* and a *P* for your *partner*)

	YES	NO
Flirt in public in front of the other?	☐ ☐	☐ ☐
Threaten to find another partner?	☐ ☐	☐ ☐

Other tactics please specify:

....

9 Do either of you avoid sexual contact with the
other directly by saying you don't feel like it?   ☐ ☐   ☐ ☐

10 Avoid sexual contact indirectly by saying you
have a headache or some other symptom, etc?   ☐ ☐   ☐ ☐

If *Yes* please describe what you or your partner does:

....

....

Appendix 2

1 BRIEF BIOGRAPHICAL DETAILS OF INTERVIEWEES

(People whose accounts are used in Chapters 5 and 6 to illustrate aspects of discourses on power and sexuality):

Jan was 50, married for 25 years, two daughters aged 16 and 18. Her husband was involved in the building trade and she had worked on and off in a bank for most of their married life. She described her marriage as 'very good'.

Mary was 43, married for 21 years, one daughter aged 18 and at university. She had trained as a librarian but had given up work to look after her daughter. She had returned to work six years previously and was currently engaged in the social services; her husband was a surveyor. She described her marriage as 'pretty awful'.

Felicity was 38, married for eight years, had one son aged 17 from a previous relationship and one daughter aged 6 from her current marriage. She had recently been on an 'access' course, was doing 'A' levels and aimed to go to university to do a degree. She worked as a playleader part-time; her husband worked full-time as a 'lighting' person in the local theatre. She described her marriage as 'good'.

May was 42, married for 16 years, three sons aged 15, 13 and 10. Her husband had been married previously and his children were now grown up; they did not seem to have much contact with these children. Her husband, aged 49, worked as a fireman. May had trained as a nurse, had stayed at home to look after the children and had recently gone back to work at a travel agency. She was far more highly educated and qualified than her husband and described her marriage as 'good'.

Wanda was 51, married for 30 years. She had worked as a hairdresser and had two daughters aged 16 and 19. Her husband worked in the building trade and they owned several houses that they let to students. She described her marriage as a 'bit sticky'.

Joyce was 37, no children, married for ten years, worked as a care assistant in a residential home. Her husband was currently unemployed and was trying to develop his own business: building conservatories. She described her marriage as 'very happy'.

Diedre was one of the clinical sample. She was 34, married for eight years, two children aged 4 and 7. She did not work outside the home but had an art degree and was a talented musician. She had recently given a concert and spent her time at home composing as well as looking after the children. Her husband was a full-time university lecturer. They both described their relationship as 'problematic'.

Josh was 50, divorced for seven years, not remarried and had a son aged 20 and a daughter aged 16 who lived with their mother but had plenty of contact with Josh. When he was married his wife did not work, though she had been trained as a nurse. Josh was a head of department in local government.

Howard was 52, divorced for two years, not remarried, one daughter of 17 whom he had very little contact with, was unemployed and had been for some time.

Bill was 54. His first wife had died three years previously; he had remarried recently. He had two sons and a daughter from his first marriage, aged 25, 23, 19. His new wife had a son of 18. Bill was an educational psychologist and his new wife was a teacher.

Ken was 38, divorced and now 'remarried'. He had one daughter aged 5 whom he had little contact with. His second wife had no children and they had decided not to have any. They both ran a shop though Ken had been her 'boss' when they first met. He described his second 'marriage' as 'fantastic'.

Jim was 37, married for 13 years, two daughter aged 8 and 12. He worked full-time as a nurse; his wife was also trained as a nurse and was thinking about going back to work in the near future. He described his marriage as very happy.

2   INTERVIEW GUIDE

(The interviews were semi-structured and broadly split into two sections: power and sexuality, each with a set of trigger questions intended to initiate a discussion of these issues in the person's current or previous relationship.)

(A) Power

1 Who do you think dominates in your relationship, yourself, your partner, or do you think you are equal?
2 What sorts of power do you each have?
3 Do either of you have a trump card?
4 Has the balance of power changed whilst you have been together?

(B) Sexuality

1 Do you think women and men are similar or dissimilar in terms of their sexuality?
2 (If yes) why do you think that might be?
3 What do you think the advantages are in initiating sex in terms of power?
4 What do you think are the disadvantages in initiating sex in terms of power?

Bibliography

Abbott, P. and Sapsford, R. (1988) The body politic. Health, family and society. Unit 11 of D211, *Social Problems and Social Welfare*. Milton Keynes: The Open University.

Abbott, P. and Wallace, C. (eds) (1991) *Gender, Power and Sexuality*. London: Macmillan.

Aristophanes (1973) *Lysistrata*, 421 BC. London: Penguin Books.

Arminstead, N. (ed.) (1974) *Reconstructing Social Psychology*. Harmondsworth: Penguin Education.

Armstrong, N. and Tennenhouse, L. (eds) (1987) *The Ideology of Conduct: Essays in literature and the history of sexuality*. New York: Methuen.

Armstrong, V. (1992) *Feminist Political Theory*. London: Macmillan.

Aronwitch, S. (1961) *The Ruling Class*. London: Lawrence and Wishart.

Averill, J.R. (1985) The social construction of emotion. With special reference to love, in K.J. Gergen and K.E. Davis (eds) *The Social Construction of the Person*. New York: Springer.

Bachrach, P. and Baratz, M.S. (1962) The two faces of power. *American Political Science Review*. 56: 947–52.

Bachrach, P. and Baratz, M.S. (1970) *Power and Poverty*. New York: Oxford University Press.

Baker Miller, J. (1977) *Toward a New Psychology of Women*. Boston: Beacon Press.

Bandura, A.L. (1965) Influence of model's reinforcement contingencies on the acquisition of imitative responses. *Journal of Personality and Social Psychology*, 1: 589–95.

Bandura, A.L. (1967) *Social Learning Theory*. Englewood Cliffs, NJ: Prentice-Hall.

Bandura, A.L., Ross, D. and Ross, S.A. (1961) Transmission of aggression through imitation and aggressive models. *International Journal of Abnormal Social Psychology*, 63: 375–82.

Bartholomew, K. and Horowitz, L.M. (1991) Attachment styles amongst young adults. A test of a four category model. *Journal of Personality and Social Psychology*, 61: 226–44.

Bell, D.C., Chafetz, J.S. and Horn, L.H. (1982) Marital conflict resolution. A study of strategies and outcomes. *Journal of Family Issues*, 3(1): 111–32.

Blood, R.V. and Wolfe, D.M. (1960) *Husbands and Wives: The dynamics of married living*. New York: Free Press.

Boccaccio, G. (1995) *Ten Tales from the Decameron*. Harmondsworth: Penguin Classics.

Bouce, P.G. (ed.) (1982) *Sexuality in 18th Century Britain*. Manchester: Manchester University Press.

Bradshaw, J. and Millar, J. (1991) *Lone Parent Families in the UK*. Department of Social Security research no. 6. London: HMSO.

Brown, G.W. and Harris, T. (1978) *The Social Origins of Depression*. London: Tavistock.

Cecchin, G. (1987) Hypothesising, circularity and neutrality revisited. An invitation to curiosity. *Family Process*, 26: 405–13.

Chafetz, J.S. (1980) Conflict resolution in marriage: towards a theory of spousal strategics and marital dissolution rates. *Journal of Family Issues*, 1(5): 397–421.

Chodorow, N. (1978) *The Reproduction of Mothering*. Berkeley, CA: University of California Press.

Comfort, A. (1994) *The Joy of Sex*. London: Quartet Books.

Cronen, U., Johnson, K.M. and Lannaman, J.N. (1982) Paradoxes and reflexive loops: An alternative theoretical perspective. *Family Process*, 21: 91–112.

Dallos, R. (1991) *Family Belief Systems: Therapy and change*. Milton Keynes: Open University Press.

Dallos, R. (1997) *Interacting Stories: Narratives, family beliefs and therapy*. London: Karnac Press.

Dawkins, R. (1978) *The Selfish Gene*. Oxford: Oxford University Press.

Devine, P.H. (1989) Stereotypes and prejudice. Their automatic and controlled components. *Journal of Personality and Social Psychology*, 56: 5–18.

Dicks, H.V. (1967) *Marital Tensions*. London and Henley: Routledge and Kegan Paul.

Dinnerstein, D. (1976) *The Mermaid and the Minotaur: Sexual arrangements and human malaise*. New York: Harper Row.

Dobash, R.E. and Dobash, R.P. (1980) *Violence Against Wives: A case study against patriarchy*. Shepton Mallet: Open Books Publishing.

Dobash, R.E. and Dobash, R.P. (1992) *Women, Violence and Social Change*. London and New York: Routledge.

Dollard, J. (1957) *Caste and Class in a Southern Town*. New York: Doubleday Anchor.

Donzelot, J. (1980) *The Policing of Families*. London: Hutchinson.

Doyle, J.A. (1989) *The Male Experience*. Dubuque, IO: Wm. C. Brown.

DSM (III-R) (1987) *Diagnostic and Statistical Manual of Mental Disorders* (3rd edn, revised). Washington, DC: American Psychiatric Association.

Edwards, S. (1981) *Female Sexuality and the Law*. Oxford: Martin Robertson.

Edwards, S. (1989) *Policing Domestic Violence*. London: Sage.

Ehrenreich, B. (1983) *The Hearts of Men*. London: Pluto Press.

Emerson, R.M. (1981) Social exchange theory, in M. Rosenberg and R. Turner (eds) *Social Psychology: Sociological perspectives*. New York: Basic Books.

Eron, J.B. and Lund, T.W. (1993) How problems evolve and dissolve. Integrating narrative and strategic concepts. *Family Process*, 32: 291–309.

Fairbairn, W.R.D. (1952) *Psychoanalytic Studies of the Personality*. London: Routledge and Kegan Paul.

Farrell, D. (1990) *Why Men Are The Way They Are*. Reading: Bantam.

Foreman, S.D. (1996) 'Inequalities of power, strategies of influence and sexual problems in couples', unpublished PhD thesis. Milton Keynes: Open University.

Foreman, S. and Dallos, R. (1992) Inequalities of power and sexual problems. *Journal of Family Therapy*, 14: 349–71.

Foucault, M. (1972) *The Archaeology of Knowledge*. London: Tavistock.

Foucault, M. (1979) *The History of Sexuality,* vol. 1. London: Allen Lane.

French, J.R.R. and Raven, B.H. (1959) The basis of social power, in D. Cartwright (ed.) *Studies in Social Power.* Ann Arbor, MI: University of Michigan Press.

Freud, S. (1905) Three essays on the theory of sexuality. *Standard Edition,* 7: 135–243.

Freud, S. (1915) Observations on transference love. *Standard Edition,* 12: 159–71.

Friedan, B. (1963) *The Feminine Mystique.* Harmondsworth: Penguin.

Friedan, B. (1981) *The Second Stage.* London: Abacus.

Gillespie, D.L. (1971) Who has the power? The marital struggle. *Journal of Marriage and the Family,* 33: 445–59.

Gilligan, C. (1982) *In a Different Voice.* Cambridge, MA: Harvard University Press.

Goffman, E. (1959) *The Presentation of Self in Everyday Life.* New York: Doubleday Anchor.

Goffman, E. (1972) *Interaction Ritual: Essays on face-to-face behaviour.* Harmondsworth: Penguin.

Goldberg, D. and Huxley, P. (1980) *Mental Illness in the Community: The pathway to psychiatric care.* London: Tavistock.

Goldberg, H. (1983) *The New Male–Female Relationship.* London: Coventure.

Goldner, V. (1985) Feminism and family therapy. *Family Process,* 24: 31–47.

Goldner, V. (1991) Sex power and gender. A feminist systemic analysis of the politics of passion. *Journal of Feminist Family Therapy,* 3: 63–83.

Goldner, V., Penn, P., Sheinberg, M. and Walker, G. (1990) Love and violence. Paradoxes of volatile attachments. *Family Process,* 29: 343–64.

Gordon, L. (1989) *Heroes of their Own Lives: The politics and history of family violence.* London: Virago.

Gottman, J.M. (1979) *Marital Interaction: Experimental investigations.* New York: Academic Press.

Gramsci, A. (1971) *Selections from Prison Notebooks.* London: Lawrence and Wishart.

Griffin, S. (1971) Rape. The all-American crime. *OZ magazine* (London), no. 41.

Gurley Brown, H. (1962) *Sex and the Single Girl.* New York: Geiss.

Haley, J. (1963) *Strategies of Psychotherapy.* New York: Grune and Stratton.

Haley, J. (1966) Toward a theory of pathological systems, in G.N. Zuk and I. Boszromenji-Nagy (eds) *Family Therapy and Disturbed Families.* Palo Alto, CA: Science and Behavior Books.

Haley, J. (1976) *Problem Solving Therapy.* San Francisco: Jossey-Bass.

Hall, A.D. and Fagan, R.E. (1956) Definitions of system, *General Systems,* vol. 1. 1: 18–28.

Hall, S. (1992) The West and the rest. Discourse and power, in S. Hall and B. Gieben, (eds) *Formations of Modernity.* Cambridge: Polity Press.

Hamblin, A. (1983) Is a feminist sexuality possible? in S. Cartledge and J. Ryan (eds) *Sex and Love: New thoughts and old contradictions.* London: The Women's Press.

Hare-Mustin, R.T. (1991) Sex lies and headaches. The problem is power. *Journal of Feminist Family Therapy,* 3: 39–61.

Harvey, J.H., Orbuch, T.L. and Weber, A.L. (1992) *Attributions, Accounts and Close Relationships.* London: Springer Verlag.

Hazan, C. and Shaver, P.R. (1987) Romantic love conceptualized as an attachment process. *Journal of Personality and Social Psychology,* 52: 511–24.

Henriques, J., Hollway, W., Unwin, C., Venn, C. and Walkerdine, V. (1984) *Changing the Subject.* London: Methuen.

Hite, S. (1981) *The Hite Report on Sexuality.* London: MacDonald.

Hoffman, L. (1972) Early childhood experience and women's achievement motive. *Journal of Socialization*, 28: 381–96.

Hoffman, L. (1985) Beyond power and control. Toward a second-order family systems therapy. *Family Systems Medicine*, 3(4): 381–96.

Hoffman, L. (1993) *Exchanging Voices*. London: Karnac Books.

Hollway, W. (1982) 'Identity and gender differences in adult social relations', unpublished PhD thesis, University of London.

Hollway, W. (1983) Heterosexual sex. Power and desire for the other, in S. Cartledge and J. Ryan (eds) *Sex and Love: New thoughts on old contradictions*. London: The Women's Press.

Hollway, W. (1989) *Subjectivity and Method in Psychology*. London: Sage.

Howard, J.A., Blumstein, P. and Schwartz, P. (1980) Sex, power and influence tactics in intimate relationships. *Journal of Personality and Social Psychology*, 51(1): 102–9.

Jackson, D. (1957) The question of family homeostasis. *Psychiatry Quarterly Supplement*, 31: 79–90.

Jackson, D. (1965) Family Rules. Marital quid pro quo. *Archives of General Psychiatry*, 12: 589–94.

James, K. and McIntyre, D. (1983) The reproduction of families. The social role of family therapy? *Journal of Marital and Family Therapy*, 9(2): 119–29.

Jeffreys, S. (1985) *The Spinster and her Enemies: Feminism and sexuality 1880–1930*. London: Pandora.

Jeffreys, S. (1990) *Anticlimax: A feminist perspective on the sexual revolution*. London: The Women's Press.

Johnson, P. (1976) Women and power. Towards a theory of effectiveness. *Journal of Social Issues*, 32: 99–110.

Jong, E. (1974) *Fear of Flying*. London: Paladin.

Jost, J.T. and Banaji, M.R. (1994) The role of stereotying in system-justification and the production of false-consciousness. *British Journal of Social Psychology*, 33(1): 1–29.

Kanter, R.M. (1977) *Men and Women of the Corporation*. New York: Basic Books.

Kaplan, H.S. (1974) *The New Sex Therapy*. London: Bailliere Tindall.

Kaplan, H.S. (1979) *Disorders of Sexual Desire*. London: Bailliere Tindall.

Kelley, H.H. and Thibaut, J.W. (1978) *Interpersonal Relations: A theory of interdependence*. New York: Wiley Interscience.

Kelly, G.A. (1955) *The Psychology of Personal Constructs*, vols 1 and 2. New York: Norton.

Kennedy-Taylor, J. (1994) Why aren't all women feminists?, in C. Quest (ed.) *Liberating Women for Modern Feminism*, Choice in Welfare Series no. 19. London: Institute of Economic Affairs Health and Welfare Unit.

Kinsey, A.C., Pomeroy, W.B. and Martin, C.E. (1948) *Sexual behavior in the Human Male*. Philadelphia, Sanders.

Kinsey, A.C., Pomeroy, W.B., Martin, C.E. and Gebhard, P.H. (1953) *Sexual Behavior in the Human Female*. Philadelphia: Sanders.

Kipnis, D. and Schmidt, S.M. (1980) 'Intra-organizational influence tactics. Explorations in getting one's way. *Journal of Applied Psychology*, 65: 440–52.

Klein, M. (1946) Notes on some schizoid mechanisms, in J. Riviere (ed.) *Developments in Psychoanalysis*. London: Hogarth.

Komter, A. (1989) Hidden power in marriage. *Gender and Society*, 3(7): 187–216.

Kopp, C.B. (ed.) (1979) *Becoming Female*. New York: Plenum.

Lawrence, D.H. (1928/1960) *Lady Chatterley's Lover*. Harmondsworth: Penguin Books.

Leites, E. (1986) *The Puritan Conscience and Modern Sexuality*. New Haven, CT: Yale University Press.

Lerner, H.E. (1983) Female dependency in context. Some theoretical and technical considerations. *American Journal of Orthopsychiatry*, 53(4): 697–705.

Lukes, S. (1984) *Power: A radical view*. London: Macmillan.

Madanes, C. (1981) *Strategic Family Therapy*. London: Jossey-Bass.

Marx, K. (1967) *The Communist Manifesto*. New York: Lasky.

Marx, K. and Engels, F. (1970) *The German Ideology* (ed. C.J. Arthur). New York: International Publishers.

Maslow, A.H. (1987) *Motivation and Personality*, 3rd edn. New York: Harper Row.

Maynard, M. (1985) The response of social workers to domestic violence, in J. Pahl, (ed.) *Private Violence and Public Policy*. London: Routledge and Kegan Paul.

McLennan, G. (1991) The power of ideology. Unit 17 of D103, *Society and the Social Sciences*. Milton Keynes: Open University.

Miller, J.B. (1976) *Toward a New Psychology of Women*. Boston, MA: Beacon Press.

Millett, K. (1977) *Sexual Politics*. London: Virago.

Minuchin, S. (1974) *Families and Family Therapy*. Cambridge, MA: Harvard University Press.

Nardi, P.M. and Sherrod, D. (1994) Friendship in the lives of gay men and lesbians. *Journal of Social and Personal Relationships*, 11: 185–99.

Noller, K.O. and Gallois, C. (1986) Sending emotional messages in marriage. Non-verbal behavior, sex and communication clarity. *British Journal of Social Psychology*, 25: 287–97.

O'Brien, M. (1990) The place of men in a gender sensitive therapy, in R.J. Perelberg, and A. Miller, *Gender and Power in Families*. London: Routledge.

Parton, N. (1991) *Governing the Family: Child Care, Child Protection and the State*. Hemel Hempstead: Harvester Wheatsheaf.

Penfold, P.S. and Walker, G.A. (1984) The psychiatric paradox of women. *Canadian Journal of Community Mental Health*, 5(2): 9–15.

Perelberg, R.J. and Miller, A. (1990) *Gender and Power in Families*. London: Routledge.

Perkins, H. (1969) *Origins of Modern English Society*. London: Routledge.

Perls, F.S. (1969) *Gestalt Theory Verbatim*. Moab, UT: Real People Press.

Plumb, J.H. (1950) *England in the 18th Century*. Harmondsworth: Penguin.

Poynton, C. (1989) *Language and Gender: Making the difference*, 2nd edn. Oxford: Oxford University Press.

Raven, B.H. (1965) Social influence and power, in I.D. Steiner and M. Fishbein (eds) *Current Issues in Social Psychology*. New York: Holt, Rinehart and Winston.

Raven, B.H., Centres, R. and Rodrigues, A. (1985) The bases of conjugal power, in R.G. Cromwell and D.H. Olsen (eds) *Power in Families*. London: Sage.

Ross, M., Amabile, T.M. and Steimetz, J.L. (1977) Social role, social control, and biases in social-perception processes. *Journal of Personality and Social Psychology*, 35: 485–94.

Rotter, J.D. (1966) Generalized expectations for internal vs external control of reinforcement. *Psychological Monographs*, 30(1): 1–26.

Rubin, J.Z. and Brown, B.R. (1975) *The Social Psychology of Bargaining and Negotiation*. New York: Academic Press.

Rubin, L. (1983) *Intimate Strangers*. New York: Harper and Row.

Safilios-Rothschild, C. (1970) Study of family power structure: 1960–1969. *Journal of Marriage and the Family*, 32: 539–52.

Safilios-Rothschild, C. (1976) A macro and micro-examination of family power and love. An exchange model. *Journal of Marriage and Family*, May: 355–62.

Sampson, R.V. (1965) *Equality and Power*. London: Heinemann.

Scanzoni, J. (1972) *Sexual Bargaining: Power politics in the American marriage*. Englewood Cliffs, NJ: Prentice-Hall.

Scanzoni, J. (1978) *Sex Roles, Women's Work and Marital Conflict*. Lexington, MA: Lexington Books.

Scanzoni, J. (1979a) Social exchange and behavioral independence, in R.L. Burgess and T.L. Huston (eds) *Social Exchange in Developing Relationships*. New York: Academic Press.

Scanzoni, J. (1979b) Social processes and power in families, in W.R. Burr, R. Hill, F.I. Nye and I.L. Reiss (eds) *Contemporary Theories about the Family*, vol. 1. London: Routledge and Kegan Paul.

Scanzoni, J. and Polonk, K. (1980) A conceptual approach to explicit marital negotiation. *Journal of Marriage and the Family*, Feb: 31–44.

Scarff, M. (1987) *Intimate Partners*. London: Century Paperbacks.

Scharff, D.E. (1982) *The Sexual Relationship: An object relations view of sex and the family*. Boston, MA: Routledge and Kegan Paul.

Seligman, M.E.P. (1973) *Helplessness: On depression, development and death*. San Francisco: Freeman.

Sillars, S., Pike, G.R., Jones, T.S. and Redmon, K. (1985) Communication and conflict in marriage, in R. Bostron (ed.) *Communication Yearbook 8*. Beverly Hills, CA: Sage.

Skynner, R. (1976) *One Flesh: Separate persons*. London: Constable.

Smart, C. and Smart, B. (eds) (1978) *Women, Sexuality and Social Control*. London: Routledge and Kegan Paul.

Spender, D. (1980) *Man Made Language*. London: Routledge and Kegan Paul.

Spiegel, J.P. (1968) The resolution of role conflict within the family, in N.W. Bell and F.T. Vogel (eds) *A Modern Introduction to the Family*. New York: The Free Press.

Stoltenberg, J. (1978) in K. Jay and A. Young (eds) *Lavender Culture*. New York: Harcourt Brace Jovanovich.

Stone, L. (1977) *The Family, Sex and Marriage in England, 1500–1800*. London: Weidenfeld and Nicolson.

Storr, A. (1970) *Human Aggression*. Harmondsworth: Penguin.

Strodtbeck, F.L. (1951) Husband–wife interaction over revealed differences. *American Sociological Review*, 16: 468–73.

Summers, I. (1991) Women and citizenship. The insane, the insolvent and the inanimate, in P. Abbott, and C. Wallace (eds) *Gender, Power and Sexuality*. London: Macmillan.

Swingle, P. (ed.) (1970) *The Structure of Conflict*. New York: Academic Press.

Tannahill, R. (1980) *Sex in History*. London: Hamish Hamilton.

Tannen, D. (1991) *You Just Don't Understand*. London: Virago Press.

Tawney, R.H. (1926) *Religion and the Rise of Capitalism*. Harmondsworth, Penguin, 1990.

Thibaut, J. and Kelley, H. (1959) *The Social Psychology of Groups*. New York: Wiley.

Vinacke, W.E. (1964) Variables in experimental games. Toward a field theory. *Psychological Bulletin*, 71: 293–318.

Von Bertalanffy, L. (1968) *General Systems Theory*. New York: George Braziller.

Walby, S. (1990) *Theorizing patriarchy*. Oxford: Blackwell.

Walster, E., Walster, G.W. and Berscheid, E. (1978) *Equity Theory in Intimate Relationships*. New York: Oxford University Press.

Watzlawick, P. (1964) *An Anthology of Human Communication*, Palo Alto, CA: Science and Behavior Books.

Watzlawick, P., Beavin, J. and Jackson, D. (1967) *Pragmatics of Human Communication*. New York: Norton.

Watzlawick, P., Weakland, J. and Fisch, R. (1974) *Change: Principles of problem formation and problem resolution*. New York: Norton.

Weakland, J., Fisch, R., Watzlawick, P. and Bodin, A.M. (1974) *Brief Therapy: Focused problem resolution*. Palo Alto, CA: Norton.

Weber, M. (1947) *Economy and Society*. New York: Charles Scribner's Sons.

Weeks, J. (1985) *Sexuality and its Discontents: Meanings, myths and modern sexualities*. London: Routledge and Kegan Paul.

Weeks, J. (1992) The body and sexuality, in R. Bocock and K. Thompson (eds) *Social and Cultural Forms of Modernity*. London: Polity Press.

White, M. (1995) *Re-authoring Lives: Interviews and essays*. Dulwich, Adelaide: Dulwich Centre Publications.

White, M. and Epston, D. (1990) *Narrative Means to Therapeutic Ends*. London: Norton.

Wiener, N. (1961) *Cybernetics*. Cambridge: MA: MIT Press.

Wilkinson, S. and Kitzinger, C. (1993) *Heterosexuality: A Feminism and Psychology reader*. London: Sage.

Williams, J. and Watson, G. (1988) Sexual inequality, family life and family therapy, in E. Street and W. Dryden (eds) *Family Therapy in Britain*. Milton Keynes: Open University Press.

Index

POWER IN STRUGGLE
FEMINISM, SEXUALITY AND THE STATE

Davina Cooper

What is power? And how are social change strategies shaped by the ways in which we conceptualize it? Drawing on feminist, poststructuralist, and marxist theory, Davina Cooper develops an innovative framework for understanding power relations within fields as diverse as queer activism, municipal politics, and the regulation of lesbian reproduction. *Power in Struggle* explores the relationship between power, sexuality, and the state and, in the process, provides a radical rethinking of these concepts and their interactions. The book concludes with an important and original discussion of how an ethics of empowerment can inform political strategy.

Special features:
- brings together central aspects of current radical, political theory in an innovative way
- offers a new way of conceptualizing the state, power and sexuality

Contents
Introduction – Beyond domination?: productive and relational power – The politics of sex: metaphorical strategies and the (re)construction of desire – Multiple identities: sexuality and the state in struggle – Penetration on the defensive: regulating lesbian reproduction – Access without power: gay activism and the boundaries of governance – Beyond resistance: political strategy and counter-hegemony – Afterword – Bibliography – Index.

192pp   0 335 19211 4 (paperback)   0 335 19212 2 (hardback)

COUPLES IN CONFLICT
INSIDE THE COUNSELLING ROOM

Dorothy Freeman

This is written in a unique way, in that it allows the reader to 'sit in' with the counsellor and see, hear and feel what is happening during the couples' therapy. The reader witnesses, on a case-by-case basis, a range of marital crises as they are unfolded, discussed and (with noted exceptions) resolved. At the heart of the book is the dialogue between Dorothy Freeman and one or both partners and between partners themselves; and a special feature is her running commentary on the therapy sessions in detailed notes in the margins of each page. These notes explain both the rationale and the timing of her therapeutic interventions, and record her occasional frustrations and failures.

> ... the accounts of the interviews themselves read rather like an engrossing collection of short stories by a very gifted author. Highly recommended for the beginning therapist as well as non-therapists who, as clergy, physicians and lawyers, are yet called upon to assist deeply troubled couples.
>
> (C.R. Fowler, Executive Director,
> American Association for Marriage and Family Therapy)

> ... well-written, candidly presented and amazingly clear in its explication of complicated processes. This casebook is bound to be of great value for beginning and experienced practitioners in social work, mental health and marriage counselling.
>
> (Milton Wittman, former Chief Social Work Education Branch,
> National Institute of Mental Health)

> ... One feels clearly in the presence of an eminently experienced, skilled, sensitive, solid and resourceful therapist ...
>
> (Kitty LaPerriere, 'Contemporary Psychology,'
> *Journal of the American Psychological Association*)

Contents

288pp   0 335 09422 8 (Paperback)

FAMILY BELIEF SYSTEMS, THERAPY AND CHANGE
A CONSTRUCTIONAL APPROACH
Rudi Dallos

Rudi Dallos discusses the understandings, beliefs, explanations, the *constructs* that people use in order to manage their relationships in families. 'Family' here is a shorthand term for a group of people who are intimately involved over an extended period – and includes one-parent families, step-families, couples without children, homosexual relationships, and communal structures. Dallos considers how families construct shared systems of beliefs which serve to guide their perceived options. His argument is well illustrated by material drawn from both clinical practice and research into families, and employs theories originally formulated in terms of individuals – especially personal construct theory. His aim is to explore intimate relationships in families from the standpoint of people *inside* them; and to link this exploration to the substantial body of literature which examines families from the *outside*. In short, this book bridges the gap between systems theory (as applied to families) and Kelly's personal construct theory and, in so doing, aims to encourage new ways of seeing and doing therapy. It reveals how a family's problems are related to its shared beliefs, and how we can use therapy to challenge those beliefs, and help with those problems.

> This book is a valuable contribution for family therapy ... it is successful in broadening the theoretical base of 'constructivist' family therapy. The author gives us a fascinating glimpse at how other disciplines view the proposition that families construct and share a social reality. It could be a primer in theory integration.
>
> *(Journal of Family Psychotherapy)*

> ... Dallos makes a valuable contribution to the understanding and treatment of families. The use of direct language with plenty of examples makes the book easily understandable even for newcomers. The theory sections of the book are clear, concise and operative.
>
> *(Contemporary Psychology)*

> This is a useful addition to the family therapy literature ...
>
> *(Journal of Family Therapy)*

Contents

208pp   0 335 09492 9 (Paperback)   0 335 09493 7 (Hardback)